Mont Blanc Massif   Volume I

SELECTED CLIMBS
by Lindsay Griffin

General Editor: Les Swindin

Published (two volumes) in Great Britain by the
Alpine Club, South Audley Road, London.

This edition first published. Copyright 1990
This edition (with additions). Copyright © 1990 by the Alpine Club

First edition (Français, Comic 1987).
Second Edition (Italian). (W. Crack Guides) 1972 in three volumes

British Library cataloguing in Publication Data

ISBN 0-900523-57-3

ALPINE CLUB · LONDON
1990

Mont Blanc Massif, Volume I *Selected Climbs*

Published *(with Addendum)* in Great Britain by the
Alpine Club, 55/56 Charlotte Road, London EC2A 3QT

This edition first published, Copyright © 1990 by the Alpine Club
This edition *(with Addendum)* Copyright © 1996 by the Alpine Club

First Edition *(Collomb, Crew)* 1967 in two volumes
Second Edition *(Collomb, O'Connor, Griffin)* 1978 in three volumes

Produced by the Alpine Club

Designed by John Bowler ARCA

Topo diagrams drawn by Rod Powis

Mont Blanc Massif in 2 volumes:
  I   Col de la Bérangère to Col de Talèfre
  II Col de Talèfre to Swiss Val Ferret, Chamonix Aiguilles
      and Aiguilles Rouges.

Cover photographs
Front: Mont Blanc from the Cosmiques Arête *(Roger Payne)*
Back: Rochefort Arête from the Dent du Géant *(Les Swindin)*

Typeset in Plantin from the author's word processor
by Factel Limited, Cheltenham

Produced by The Ernest Press, Glasgow

Printed in Hong Kong by Colorcraft Ltd.

British Library cataloguing in Publication Data

  Griffin, Lindsay
  Mont Blanc Massif. – 3rd ed. Vol.I, *Selected Climbs*
  1. Europe. Mont Blanc range. Mountaineering
  I. Title II. Collomb, Robin G. Mont Blanc range III.
  796.522094449

  ISBN 0-900523-57-3

Contents

List of topo diagrams and photographs

Text Photographs:
Alpine Club Collection AC, Gino Buscaini GB, John Cleare JC,
Rob Collister RC, David Cuthbertson DC, Rob Durran RD,
Lindsay Griffin LG, Stephen Hartland SH, Joyce Hodgson JH,
Will Hurford WH, Pat Littlejohn PL, Douglas Milner DM,
Efusio Noussan EN, Bill O'Connor BOC, Roger Payne RP,
Andy Perkins AP, Simon Richardson SR, Les Swindin LS

General Editor's Preface

This edition and its companion volume form the third in the new series of guidebooks to the major European alpine regions being prepared by the Alpine Club. These two volumes replace the three volume edition published in 1978. Although the number of volumes has been reduced the number of routes that are described has been more than doubled. The features introduced in the two guidebooks already published in this new series, Ecrins Massif and Dolomites, have been retained whilst a new feature in these volumes is the inclusion of topo diagrams for the first time in Alpine Club guidebooks.

These two volumes between them provide the reader with a very wide selection of routes in all grades that will suit everyone from the novice to the experienced alpinist and the dedicated rock climber who may have little or no interest in actually reaching summits. The policy adopted has been to maximise choice, so that whilst some routes have been described in considerable detail, others have only brief descriptions. Thus, in the latter case, experienced alpinists will know whether or not a route is suitable for their ability and degree of commitment but will be left on their own to judge the exact details of routes. At the very least this should enable them to select routes that are much less frequented and uncrowded. The former will almost certainly include the sort of route that a novice alpinist or first time visitor to the region might undertake. Those who wish to climb the magnificent rock in the massif either at high or low altitude, should find plenty here to suit them. Most of the rock climbs are described with topo diagrams whilst the selection made in general allows the climb to be used as a means of ascent to a summit.

Lindsay Griffin, the author, is a well known name among mountaineers. He is a member of the Alpine Climbing Group with a wealth of experience of climbing in the Alps in both summer and winter and was co-author of the previous guidebooks to the Mont Blanc Range. Whilst working with him in the preparation of these volumes I have been greatly impressed by his attention to detail and to the sheer volume of work that he has put into the task. Lindsay has many friends and as you will see from the acknowlegements he has called on many of them to help with the detail. My personal thanks go to them all.

As with all our guidebooks the Alpine Club welcomes helpful

comments about the climbs described and any worthwhile ones that we have omitted that might be included in future editions. We also welcome offers of good quality photographs that might be used in the preparation of photo-diagrams. All comments or offers should be addressed to the general editor at the Alpine Club.

My thanks too go to those people who have helped me in the work and are not mentioned elswhere, particularly Jeremy Whitehead, Marian Elmes and Ted Maden for their proof reading of text.

Les Swindin

Author's preface

There is no doubt that the Mont Blanc Range provides the alpinist with some of the finest quality routes in Europe, whether it be along the delicate snow crests, on rough red granite or steep ice.

For such a relatively compact range, a staggeringly large number of climbs have been recorded, approximately 4000. This guide covers the whole area in two volumes and although recording only one quarter of that number and therefore in no way definitive, does indicate most of the worth-while projects available to the visitor.

Inevitably, for this is the Mecca to which most alpinists aspire, over-crowding can now be a serious problem during the summer months in certain parts of the range and on high quality classic routes. Lovers of tranquillity may now have to seek the more esoteric corners or climb outside the main season; information is provided to help them on their way.

I hope that this guide will not only allow the reader to make the best use of weather and mountain conditions when visiting the area, but will also stimulate inspiration during the preceding months of planning. Throughout the text you will be treading in the footsteps of the great pioneers – Whymper, Mummery, Ravanel, Charlet and Contamine – and frequently following Bonatti, Desmaison, Rébuffat, Seigneur and in more recent years Gabarrou, Grassi and Piola. Whatever your ambitions, from mountain walking in spectacular scenery through to the most demanding alpine climbs in the world, there is plenty to go at.

Special thanks must go to the series editor Les Swindin for contributing a tremendous amount of work to the project and making allowances for my interim expeditions to other regions over the last two years. Simon Richardson and Jon Silvester provoked argumentative discussion and helped enormously with the text. Sheila Harrison took on the mammoth job of word-processing.

Other people who helped with the text are Gino Buscaini, Chris Dale, Rob Durran, Roger Everett, Andy Perkins, Roger Payne, Godefrey Perroux, Christine Richardson, W.L. Robinson and Mike Woolridge. Monique Faussurier, Pietro Giglio, Jerry Gore, Mark Miller, Martin Moran, Efusio Noussan, Tony Penning and D 'Smiler' Cuthbertson. Credits for photographs are given with the list of photographs elsewhere in the book but my thanks must be extended to Bob Lawford, Frank Solari and Paul Kent for all they did in preparing photographs and to John Bowler for all the art work on them. I must also thank Rod Powis for all his efforts in interpreting and drawing topo diagrams from my originals.

Lindsay Griffin, North Wales 1989

General information

RECENT DEVELOPMENTS

Whereas the seventies saw a concentration in and development of the ice/mixed climbing potential due to the introduction of curved tools, this has been superceded in the eighties by the enormous development of climbing on the granite faces throughout the range.

The style in which these ascents have been made has undergone several changes and it is important to differentiate between 'mountaineering' with its associated level of commitment and what could now be termed a climbing exercise.

These days, climbs are quite often terminated at the natural finish to the route, be this a mountain ridge, the top of a pillar or simply a ledge at the end of the difficulties. Descent is then effected by rappeling the route of ascent or one close at hand. By leaving boots and rucksacks at the foot of the climb, together with any ice gear required on the approach, a fast ascent in rock shoes can be made of a route that traditionally might have necessitated the carrying of bivouac equipment.

Short routes completed in this fashion are very much in vogue as relatively unsettled weather can still allow a good deal of climbing to be achieved in a limited holiday period. Many modern rock routes are now created and climbed in this style, though it must be emphasised that some of these entail long and badly-protected runouts that require a high degree of boldness and commitment. Popular routes now have well-equipped fixed rappel points allowing a rapid retreat at the first sign of inclement weather and give an overall impression of non-seriousness. However a lightweight approach can produce dire consequences at higher altitudes when indecision prevents parties from making this retreat in good time. The popularity of certain rock faces has created its own problems. Serious danger areas for rock fall, attributed to parties above, are now considered to lie beneath the W faces of Dru, Blaitière and the L side of the Grand Capucin. The importance of experience, route-finding skills and sound mountaineering judgment have in no way lessened in recent years!

Advances in ice climbing have taken alpinists into the narrow gullies that often face S or E and are rarely in good condition during the summer. Spring or autumn ascents are preferred, when the nights are longer and colder and the routes well plastered in snow and ice. As yet, few parties appear to indulge in this facet of the sport.

MAPS

The guide is designed to be used in conjunction with the French I G N Series 1:25,000 which covers the entire range in two sheets – the 1986 3531 Est, St Gervais-le-Bans Mont Blanc and the 1984 3630 Ouest, Chamonix-Mont Blanc. All heights and nomenclature are taken from these maps. Approaches to huts and various peaks/cols are often well-marked, obviating the need for comprehensive guidebook description.

USING HUTS

HUTS allow a night to be spent high in the range and close to the proposed ascent, without the burden of a heavy rucksack. Fees can be reduced on production of a reciprocal rights card (an Alpine Club or UIAA reciprocal rights card, etc). However with more and more overcrowding in high season, many parties are finding it preferable to camp/bivouac a suitable distance away from the hut. In August a veritable 'village' can appear in the Vallée Blanche.

In all CAF wardened huts it is necessary for all groups to pre-book and is generally advisable for individuals to pre-book in order to reserve bedspace. In the case of the Grands Mulets and Gouter Huts it is necessary for individuals to pre-book.

   In CAF huts there is usually provision for self-catering, but not at the Grands Mulets or at the Goûter Huts. If you do self-cater then it is advisable to take stove, cooking and eating implements with you. If you borrow these from the guardian you will be charged. The same applies to Italian huts. Please take all your refuse back to the valley with you. The CAF provide polythene bags for the purpose. In Swiss huts there are no self-catering facilities and stoves are not allowed in the huts. The guardian will cook food you provide but don't make his task difficult. Food which can be quickly cooked in a single pan is best. No charge is made for this service but expect to pay for hot water during the day. It should be free at breakfast and in the evening.

   Bivouac huts generally have blankets but do not rely on there being fuel for stoves or any cooking and eating implements.

USING THIS GUIDE

ROUTE DESCRIPTIONS vary from one or two line explanations through to very detailed accounts. A number of modern climbs together with several older ascents have seen few, or in some cases no, repeats and descriptions should thus be treated with a degree of

13

caution. Undoubtedly these routes will appeal to those of a more exploratory nature. Some older climbs described with short sections of aid have almost certainly been climbed free but details have been unforthcoming.

Common British usage in naming routes and features has been maintained despite apparent inconsistencies, e.g. 'Fissure Brown' as opposed to 'Mummery Crack'. Modern route names have not been translated.

The terms L and R or L and R side are always used with reference to the direction of movement of the climber. For mountain features such as glaciers or couloirs etc. the orographical reference to L or R banks is applied when viewed in the direction of flow or looking downwards.

Information on certain routes appears in the form of a topo diagram and the appropriate reference number is given in the margin in an open rectangle.

FIRST ASCENT details have been included to supplement information on the climb. Thus it was felt important to include the date and duration of first winter ascents, where known and thought reevant. The UIAA ruling that the period designated for alpine winter ascents should run from 21 December to 20 March inclusive has been adhered to implicitly. Some ascents in this guide are described under winter conditions only and the first ascent is credited accordingly.

GRADING OF CLIMBS as indicated in the margin is determined not only by the general level of technical difficulty but also by the seriousness of the enterprise as reflected by the associated objective danger, length, altitude and commitment.

Shorter rock climbs that are often termined below the summit of the peak, where a quick and efficient rappel descent can be made back down the route, are given an overall numerical grading in an attempt to distinguish them from longer undertakings in a more committing situation. This grading is generally that of the hardest section encountered and the route description or topo will indicate whether or not the climb is sustained at that level.

Other routes and all mixed or snow/ice climbs are given an adjectival grading which should not be confused with British rock climbing grades.

In order of rising difficulty: F Facile (Easy) PD Peu difficile (not very hard) AD Assez difficile (fairly hard) D Difficile (hard) TD

Tres difficile (very hard) ED Extremement difficile (extremely hard)

FURTHER REFINEMENT is possible by adding plus or minus signs to the grades TD and below, but the ED grade has been made open-ended to cater for rising standards, e.g. ED1, ED2 etc. On traditional rock climbs, unless otherwise stated, the overall grading reflects a free ascent even though there may be a wealth of in situ protection (aid?) on various pitches. Certain climbs, graded from AD to TD, although not technically demanding under good conditions, are extremely serious for their grade and this has been noted in the introduction to the route in question.

UIAA NUMERICAL GRADING has been used for all rock sections and will avoid the confusion that sometimes occurs with French gradings below 6a. A table of international grading comparisons has been included but should only be used as a general indication, especially at higher levels. Problems often arise when first ascent parties have given a 'blanket' VI or VI+ grade to all the hard sections.

ARTIFICIAL CLIMBING is graded from A1 to A4. On A2 and above, slings and/or etriers will generally be necessary but short sections of A1 with in situ aid points can be overcome by most strong climbers wearing rock shoes simply by pulling on the gear.

SNOW AND ICE. With climbs involving technical difficulty on snow/ice, grading is less precise due to the variable conditions throughout the season and from year to year. Areas of glacier travel can, at certain times, become almost impracticable. Indeed, routes that involve hanging glaciers and ice slopes with serac formations are undergoing constant change. The difficulty and objective danger on these climbs will vary enormously and it would be wise to seek up-to-date information before making an attempt (eg Triolet and Plan N faces). From time to time the Scottish ice grading of 1 to 6 has been used in the text to indicate the difficulty of certain sections. This grading approximates the technical difficulties that are typically encountered on a reasonably protected Scottish climb of that standard. This is not to suggest that a leader who is competent at that grade is fully qualified to attempt the alpine route in question. The latter, in reality, will almost certainly feel considerably more demanding than the Scottish grade would imply.

THE OFFICE DE LA HAUTE MONTAGNE in the Place de

l'Eglise in Chamonix Tel 50 53 00 88 provides an excellent service offering information on routes, mountain conditions and detailed weather forecasts. They encourage climbers to leave details (forms are available) of their proposed itinerary with them before setting out on an excursion so that in the event of non-return, search and rescue facilities will be alerted. Do remember to tell them when you do return if you use this service. The office also keep details of new routes climbed in the region and has reference copies of guidebooks to this and other alpine areas.

PHOTOGRAPH NUMBERS are shown in the margin in black rectangles below the route grade. On the photographs the route numbers are marked and the lines of ascent indicated. Some routes or parts of routes may be visible on more than one photographs, and where this occurs, these additional photo numbers appear at the end of the introduction to the route. A dashed line signifies that this section of the route is not visible. Not all routes described in the text have necessarily been marked on the photographs in order to avoid overcrowding. In such cases reference is only made to the photograph in the introductory text to the route.

HEIGHTS quoted for the whole climb refer to the vertical interval from the base of the route to its top and not to the amount of climbing involved, which may be much longer. The final TIME gives a good indication for a rope of two climbers, competent at that standard and experiencing no delays due to other parties, weather etc. It may also aid the decision as to whether bivouac equipment should be carried on longer routes.

ABBREVIATIONS are used for points of the compass and for left and right. Others frequently used are Aig (Aiguille), Mt (Mont) and Pt (Point where this refers to a spot height or Pointe used in a name).

EQUIPMENT

With so many manuals now available on the craft of alpinism, there is little point in dwelling on the subject here. When it comes to equipment, most parties tend to use a single 11mm rope on middle-grade climbs where long rappels are not involved. They will carry a few hexentrics, wires, slings for spikes and plenty of karabiners for the in situ pegs. On modern rock routes 50m ropes and a full rack of hexentrics, wires, Friends etc are considered de rigueur. On the less frequented climbs, difficult pitches may require blade pegs, RPs or a very bold approach!

OTHER GUIDEBOOKS TO THE AREA

At the time of writing there are no longer any definitive guidebooks to the range. The French Guide Vallot series 'La chaine du Mt Blanc' in 4 volumes is more than ten years old and is out of print. It has been replaced by a selected climbing guide in two volumes (Francois Labande, 1987). Similar comments apply to the Italian guides, though a recent Swiss Alpine Club publication covers the Swiss end of the range including parts of France.

There are a number of large hardback publications, in several languages, with a 'Selected Climbs' format. These generally contain a superb photographic coverage. Perhaps the most well-known is Gaston Rébuffat's The Mont Blanc Massif – The 100 Finest Routes. Unfortunately the English edition is presently unavailable. For pure rock climbing, the excellent topo guides by Michel Piola cover many of the modern creations. There is also a valley crags guidebook available using topo diagrams – Grandes Ecoles d'Escalade de la Vallée de Chamonix by François Burnier and Dominique Potard.

VALLEY BASES

CHAMONIX VALLEY. Although pleasant and often much quieter bases can be found in the small villages from Les Houches to Le Tour, convenience ensures that most parties will stay close to either Chamonix or Argentière.

CHAMONIX is situated on the main road and railway line between Le Fayet and the Franco-Swiss border with numerous shops, hotels, 'bunkhouses' and camp sites of all standards. The Montenvers rack railway lies across a bridge just beyond the main station and téléphériques are clearly marked on the map. Recorded weather forecasts can be heard by dialling (50) 53 01 31 40 or Geneva (022) 98 24 24. See the note about the Office de la Haute Montagne.

The main tourist information centre opposite the office provides details on trains, buses and téléphériques. The Mont Blanc tunnel connects Chamonix to Courmayeur in Italy and is a toll road. There is a bus service and officially passports are necessary although alpinists having descended on the Italian side of the range can normally get back with some other form of identification.

ARGENTIERE is served by a very regular bus and train service from Chamonix. This small village 8km up the valley from

17

Chamonix has a good selection of shops, hotels and camp sites. The guides' bureau and the Tourist Office, both near the centre of the village, provide detailed weather forecasts etc.

VAL MONTJOIE is a picturesque and somewhat quieter valley on the W side of the massif and has several small resorts. Le Fayet at the entrance to to the valley is reached easily by regular train or bus service from Chamonix. Onward bus connections reach St Gervais-les-Bains and Les Contamines where shops and accommodation are available. The roadhead is at Notre-Dame de la Gorge and a large car park and camp site are situated 2km before this point.

COURMAYEUR is quickly reached from Chamonix by road through the Mont Blanc tunnel. A popular resort with a wide selection of shops, accommodation etc. The Office du Val Veny in the rue du Mont Blanc Tel (0165) 84 10 21 offers information on routes, weather forecasts etc. A weather forecast is also posted in Toni Gobbi's sports shop in the main street. Most parties use the various camp sites in either the Val Veni or Val Ferret. Roadheads in these valleys are reached from Courmayeur by a very regular bus service during the summer months. Unfortunately the incidence of theft from unattended vehicles in these valleys has risen alarmingly in recent years.

SWISS VAL FERRET. A tarmac road runs from Orsières as far as Ferret at 1700m. The main village at Praz de Fort can be reached throughout the year by bus from Orsières and has a good selection of shops etc. The bus continues to the simple villages of La Fouly (large camp site) and Ferret during the summer months only. A side road reaches the picturesque resort of lakeside Champex at the entrance to the Arpette valley (bus service from Orsières in the summer).

GRADING COMPARISONS

UIAA	UK	France		USA	DDR	Australia
III	V Diff	III		5.4	III	
IV−	V Diff	IV−			III	
IV	M Severe	IV		5.5	IV	
IV+	M Severe	IV+			IV	12
V−	4a	V−		5.6	V	13
V	4a	V			V	
V+	4b	V	5a	5.7	VI	14
VI−	4c	V+	5b	5.8	VIIa	15
VI	5a	V+	5c		VIIb	16
VI+	5b	6a		5.9	VIIc	17
						18
						19
VII−	5b	6a		5.10a / 5.10b	VIIIa	20
VII	5c	6b		5.10c / 5.10d	VIIIb	21
					VIIIc	22
VII+	6a	6c		5.11a / 5.11b	IXa	23
VIII−	6a	6c		5.11c	IXb	24
VIII	6a	7a		5.11d	IXc	25
VIII+	6b	7b		5.12a / 5.12b	Xa	26
IX−	6b	7b		5.12c	Xb	
IX	6c	7c		5.12d	Xb	27
	6c	7c		5.13a / 5.13b	Xc	28
IX+	6c				Xc	29

19

Huts

H1   **Conscrits Hut** 2730m. An old and rather inadequate building belonging to the CAF. Situated on the R bank of the Tré la Tête glacier. Warden mid-June to mid-September. Unlocked the rest of the year. Officially room for 40 but often has to cope with twice this number.

First reach the Tré la Tête Hotel (1970m, a privately-owned edifice with room for 80, open all summer, Whitsun and Easter), from Les Contamines either by road to Le Cugnon and then by mule track via Les Plans (1534m) (2½hr) or by road to Notre-Dame de la Gorge and then a track up through the Combe Noire (3hr).
    From the hotel follow the footpath E taking the L branch to the terminal moraines and follow these until a shelf leads down to the glacier (¾hr). Continue up the central moraine and then the glacier itself until below the Tré la Grande seracs. Cross to the L side of the glacier and reach the start of a well-cairned path that, after the initial rocky climb, contours the hillside to the hut (1¾hr). 5–6hr from Val Montjoie.

In winter or spring, continue up the glacier working more towards the centre in order to pass through the seracs of Tré la Grande. When level with the hut at approx 2600m move L onto the moraine and reach it by an ascending traverse.

H2   **Robert Blanc Hut** 2750m. Privately owned. Situated at the foot of the central spur of the Pointe des Lanchettes. Conveniently placed for routes on the S side of Mt Tondu and the Aig des Glaciers. Warden in summer. Room for 40. Reservations can be made at Arc 2000. Tel 79 07 24 22

From La Ville des Glaciers (reached via Bourg Saint Maurice and Les Chapieux) follow the unmade road to the Lanchettes chalets (1970m). Continue on a good track towards the Lanchettes glacier then climb up R to the hut 3hr.

H3   **Elisabetta Soldini Hut** c2280m. CAI property. Situated just
above the lower chalets of Lée Blanche at the end of the unmade motor road in the Val Veni. Buses to La Visaille (1659m) and the road is tarmaced to this point. Room for 60. Restaurant service.

Warden July 10–September 10, otherwise locked though key available in Courmayeur. 1½hr from La Visaille. ½–¾hr from the car park at Lac de Combal.

The Val Veni can be threatened by large avalanches after heavy winter snowfall.

H4 **Estelette Bivouac Hut** 2958m. Bivacco Adolfo Hess. Owned by
33 the CAAI. Situated just above the Col d'Estelette. Room for 4 and in poor condition.

From the Elisabetta hut follow a good path N of the Pyramides Calcaires, ignoring 2 L forks, then traverse R below the tongue of the Estelette glacier. Climb up the R side of the glacier (traces of a path) to below the col and reach it by a steep rocky couloir. Follow the broken rocky ridge W for 50m to where the hut is situated a little below the crest on the R(N). 2½hr

H5 **Petit Mont Blanc Bivouac Hut** 3047m. Biv Giovane Montagna
33 and owned by the same group. Situated immediately below the snowy section of the SE ridge of Petit Mont Blanc. Room for 10.

Start from the Lac de Combal in the Val Veni, turning R off the unmade road just before the bridge over the Doire (c1960m) to reach a car park after a few minutes. Down to the L a path continues NW along the edge of the 'flats' to the base of Mt Suc where it makes a rising traverse L(W) across the flanks to a narrow cwm/valley coming down from between the Aig de Combal (2839m) on the L and Mt Suc above R. The path actually continues its traverse line. Ignore this and ascend the narrow valley on a vague path that improves with height. Reach the saddle behind the Aig de Combal then continue at first on the L then more directly up the ridge to the hut 3hr.

In winter, good conditions will be necessary to render a safe approach.

H6 **Durier Hut** 3367m. Situated towards the N end of the true Col de
32 Miage, the northmost of two saddles which has a prominent rock spike (3358m), somewhat below the crest on the French side at the top of the central rock buttress rising from the Miage glacier. Room for 8 people. No guardian. Water source just below the hut.

From the Conscrits Hut follow Route 14 to the Col Infranchissable then take Route 5 to Pt 3672m of the Dômes de Miage. Descend the

21

steep and narrow rock and snow crest of the NE ridge to the true Col de Miage. The hut is 30m past this on the L side. 5hr. PD+

Italian side: start from the Lac de Combal in the Val Veni. Leave the road at a bridge over the Doire (c1960m) following a much rougher road for a few minutes to a car park. The continuation track leads NW under the large lateral moraine of the Lac du Miage, crosses R and reaches the Miage glacier. Gradually working towards the middle, go up the glacier to below the Aigs Grises where it becomes more crevassed (2½hr) and finally reach the foot of the fairly steep snow slope descending from the col, near Pt 2925m (1½hr). Climb easy rock and snow on the L towards a small snow cap (3390m) L of the col. Just below this summit slant up R to the col (1½hr). 5½hr from the car park. PD

From Tresse (1016m) in the Val Montjoie, follow the lane and the continuing large track via the Maison Neuve pasture (1290m) to the Miage chalets (1589m, 1¾hr). Follow a small track across the alluvial plain keeping L of the main stream and cross a rock barrier near Pt 1710m, just R of a waterfall. Go up the moraine and a slabby rock barrier finally moving L into a small valley below and S of Pt 2092m (falling ice possible). Go up this, move onto the grassy lateral moraine to the R and follow it to reach Plan Glacier at c2550m (2¼hr). Cross the glacier to the SE either above or below the crevassed steepness in the slope and so reach the base of the big broken buttress (2760m) under the Col de Miage. Climb the buttress on progressively steeper and looser rock to the top, where the hut is found. Under good snow conditions the couloirs on either side of the buttress can prove quicker (2½hr). 6hr from Tresse. PD

H7 **Tête Rousse Hut** 3167m. Situated on the L bank of the small Tête Rousse glacier below the Aig du Goûter. CAF property. Warden and simple restaurant service in summer. Room for 30. Telephone 50 58 24 97

From St Gervais take the Mont Blanc tramway to the Nid d'Aigle 2372m. From the Chamonix valley take the téléphérique from Les Houches to the Bellevue station (c1800m) and either catch the tram or walk up a good track to the Nid d'Aigle. Now follow the well-marked path that zigzags up under a rocky escarpment to reach a small hunters' cabin (2768m, 1hr). Turn sharply R (SE) and zigzag up the ridge of the Aig du Goûter on a good path till it flattens out just above 3100m (cairn). Cross the glacier to the hut (1–1¼hr). 2½–3hr from Bellevue.

In descent it is often quicker to go down to the SW and reach the Bionnassay glacier. Descend close to the R bank and climb onto the moraine at c2600m where tracks lead down to the Nid d'Aigle.
¾–1hr

H8
36

Goûter Hut 3817m. CAF property. Situated just N of the summit of the Aig du Goûter (3863m). Room for 76 with hotel service. Warden in summer, otherwise generally locked. Bedspace must be reserved in advance otherwise you will be turned away. Telephone 50 54 40 93. An extension was being built in 1989 on the site of the old hut.

A long rocky rib descends from near the summit of the Aig du Goûter and lower down divides the Tête Rousse and Bionnassay glaciers. Reach a low and broad depression in this ridge at the top R hand (SE) corner of the Tête Rousse glacier either from the hut or directly from the top of the path coming up the ridge from the hunters cabin. See Route H7. The easiest and normal route crosses the big couloir to the R which is exposed to stonefall and has fixed cables to assist the passage. An early crossing is advised: it is the scene of regular and sometimes fatal accidents. On the far side a broad broken rib of rock (traces of a path) leads to the hut. 2–3hr from the Tête Rousse hut. PD–/PD

VARIANT–The Payot Ridge. Follow Route H7 towards the Tête Rousse hut. Instead of crossing the glacier, continue up the easy ridge, steepening for the last 200m, to the summit crest. Follow this S for 100m to the hut. This route is quite difficult, more time consuming but safer than the normal route. Loose rock dislodged near the top could endanger parties crossing the couloir on the normal route. PD/PD+

In winter, ascent and descent from Mt Blanc is generally made via the Grands Mulets on ski. Winter winds will prevent any snow accumulation on the upper ridges.

36

Vallot Hut 4362m. CAF property. A large unguarded duralumin bivouac shelter with room for 24 situated near the foot of the Bosses Ridge on Mont Blanc and just above the old observatory building. It is only to be used in emergencies and not as a base to ascend Mt Blanc. See also Photo 37

H9
37

Grands Mulets Hut 3051m. CAF property. Situated on the rocks above the junction of the Taconnaz and Bossons glaciers. Room for 70. Hotel service. Warden in summer and part of the spring. Closed in winter but one dormitory for 20 people is left permanently open. It is advisable to pre-book places. Telephone 50 53 16 98.

Although the hut can be reached directly from the valley in 6–7hr, it is usual to begin from the Plan de l'Aiguille téléphérique station (2310m). See also Photo 36

Follow a good path to the Pélerins glacier, crossing it almost horizontally to reach another good path leading to the derelict téléphérique station 'Gare des Glaciers' (2414m). The path makes a rising traverse to the Bossons glacier under several couloirs emanating from the Aig du Midi (possible stonefall). Go up the L side of Plan Glacier a short distance and cross it SW to La Jonction. Work up to below and R of the Grands Mulets rocks (very crevassed ground with seracs) until at their S end one can move L to a path with an iron handrail going up to the hut. 3hr. A popular spring ascent on ski. PD–

H10 **Col du Midi Hut (Abri Simond)** 3600m. A disused and derelict wooden structure with one usable room giving an adequate though often very crowded bivouac shelter. Reached in 15–20min from the Midi téléphérique station by descending the NE ridge for 100m or so until steep snow slopes (several crevasses) lead back underneath the S face of the Aig du Midi to the upper section of the Vallée Blanche. F

Care must be exercised in this region, indeed in the whole summit area of the Midi, as fatal accidents have occurred due to contact with 'disused' electrical cables. In 1989 one room had been refurbished but was being used by workmen reconstructing the Cosmiques Hut. It is rumoured that the Abri Simond will be removed when this work is completed.

Cosmiques Hut 3613m. This was the Alpine Glaciology Laboratory situated close to the Abri Simond and which provided accomodation until it was destroyed by fire. In 1989 work was in progress to rebuild a large hut for alpinists. Completion date is set for summer 1990.

Aiguille du Midi Téléphérique Station 3795m. Situated on the N summit of the Aig du Midi, this is a popular starting and finishing point for many expeditions. A rock tunnel and gallery lead to the start of the NE ridge which in turn gives access to the Vallée Blanche. Difficulty can be experienced in winter if the snow tunnel leading onto the NE ridge has not been excavated. Entry and exit is then made via a small metal door in the wall on the S side of the ridge. Officially, climbers are not allowed to stay here but in emergencies it is often possible to bivouac in the tunnel.

H11 **Gonella Hut** 3071m. Also called the Dôme hut. CAI property. Situated above the R bank of the Dôme glacier on a spur descending SE from the Aig Grises ridge. Room for 50. Warden in summer, otherwise locked. However the old wooden hut with room for 30 is always left open.

From the Lac de Combal in the Val Veni follow Route H6b up the Miage glacier until below the Aigs Grises ridge at c2600m (2½hr). Cross the glacier and take a small path well L of the lowest point on the ridge at the entrance to a scree couloir. Follow this steeply up to the R, cross a shoulder and continue the rising traverse NE on the Dôme glacier side of the ridge, crossing snowfields and couloirs, to the rocky spur where the hut is situated (1½–2hr). 4–4½hr, F

H12 **Quintino Sella Hut** 3396m. CAI property. Situated on the SW slopes of the Rocher du Mont Blanc. No warden. Always open. Room for 15.

From the Lac de Combal in the Val Veni follow Route H6b up the Miage glacier until below the Mt Blanc glacier (2hr). Go up the L side of the latter close to the buttress of the Rocher du Mt Blanc and take the first grassy couloir on the L at c2600m. This area is often very crevassed and access to the couloir can be difficult. In this case a slanting chimney on the L side of the couloir may give an easier alternative. Leave the couloir at one-third height, slanting R up steep grassy slopes (faint path). After crossing a rock wall take a vague couloir to the Rocher ridge and follow this generally on the R side, passing an old hut at c3100m and turning the last rock buttress on the R to arrive, rather abruptly, at the new hut (4–4½hr). 6–6½hr from Val Veni bridge. F+

From the Gonella Hut: This useful connection between the huts is slightly exposed to stonefall in the couloir, but is probably the most reliable way.

Reach the Dôme glacier and cross it to the foot of the Y-shaped couloir almost 400m high which descends from the SW spur of the Rocher du Mont Blanc. Climb the rocks on the R side to avoid stonefall in the couloir, then take the R branch to the crest of the spur near the Quintino Sella Hut. 2½hr, F+

H13 **Franco Monzino Hut** 2590m. Property of the Courmayeur Guides
Association. Situated on the N spur of the Aig du Châtelet between
the lower reaches of the Brouillard and Frêney glaciers. Room for
50. Hotel service and warden in summer. Locked the rest of the
year although a winter room for 6 is always open. Service
téléphérique from near La Visaille which can be used to send up
rucksacks to the hut. There are no self-catering facilities or reduced
fees but there are hot showers.

From the téléphérique station in La Visaille continue along the road
crossing the Doire and immediately turn R onto a path, well-
marked with orange flashes. Follow this, crossing the Miage glacier
stream via a footbridge and continue W along the main path
towards the Miage glacier. At c1760m another well-marked path on
the R climbs up grass and scree slopes to a steep barrier of slabs
which are ascended with the aid of fixed cables. Above, the path
continues to the crest of the spur and, shortly afterwards, the hut.
2½–3hr

H14 **Eccles Bivouac Huts** c3850m (top hut). Formerly the Guiseppe
Lampugnani Bivouac Hut. Property of the CAAI. Situated on the
SW ridge of Pic Eccles. The top hut is a tiny wooden structure with
room for 6, protected by an overhanging block. About 30m below is
a new metal hut with room for 9. A long and serious approach on
snow and ice.

Under good snow conditions and especially in descent it is much
quicker to follow the E side of the Brouillard glacier from the
moraine above the Monzino Hut. In some years this can be very
crevassed and in such a state is too time-consuming to be
recommended. In this case take a faint track from the Monzino Hut
leading N to the tiny Châtelet glacier. Go up the R side and traverse
L at the top, crossing a short barrier of smooth wet rock to reach
easy scree slopes and snow fields on the S side of the Punta
Innominata. Trending L reach the shoulder (3281m) below the first
gendarme on the S ridge of the Innominata and make a short
diagonal descent on the other side to reach the Brouillard glacier.

Go up the glacier and cross the rimaye to the L of the foot of a
rock buttress (3376m). Slant up and around the slope above to Col
Frêney (3680m) (4–5hr). Climb a steep icy slope towards Pic Eccles
and reach the huts by slanting up L on snow and finally loose mixed
ground (1–2hr). 5–7hr from Monzino Hut. PD/PD+

In winter, routes climbed from the Eccles Hut will generally be approached via the Trident Hut and Col Peuterey.

42

Dames Anglaises Bivouac 3490m. Bivouac Piero Craveri. CAAI property. Situated on the Brèche Nord des Dames Anglaises. Room for 5 but little used except by parties doing the Peuterey Integral. Approached from the Monzino Hut in 5–hr following the 300m couloir above the Frêney glacier. AD/AD+. Frequent stonefall. See Route 85 and Photos 45 and 47

H15

Noire Hut 2316m. The Borelli-Pivano Bivouac Hut. CAAI property. Situated beneath the rocks of Mt Noir de Peuterey on the R side of the Fauteuil des Allemands. Room for 35. Warden much of the summer. Always open.

From the Peuterey chalets and campsite in the Val Veni (1501m), follow the path SW alongside the Doire taking the R fork shortly before crossing the main stream coming down from the Fauteuil. Reach the steep scree cone by parties descends from the entrance to the Fauteuil and zigzag up this by a fairly indistinct path at first over rocky terrain then more distinct as the ground more scree-like (1hr). From the top of the cone the going becomes much steeper but the route is obvious and easily followed, being well endowed with chains, ladders and metal spikes wherever there is any technical difficulty. As the angle eases follow the grassy rib near the main stream into the cwm and continue Rwards on the path to the hut (½–1½hr). 1½–2½hr, PD

H16

Brenva Bivouac 3140m. CAAI property. Situated halfway up the Rognon on the L bank of the Brenva glacier and wrongly marked on the map, the true location being just below the 0 in spot height 3140m. An old and very seldom used shelter with room for 4. Always open.

From Entrèves reach the Brenva chalets. Continue W in a small valley round the base of the Rochers de la Brenva and climb the moraine on the L of a small stream to the top. Cross the glacier at a flattish section to the NW and reach the couloir just L of 2807m. Climb this on scree for 100m then trend up R to the hut which is near the edge of the glacier. 5½hr, PD–

H17

62

Trident Hut 3690m. Lucia e Piero Ghiglione Hut. CAI property. Situated close to the Col du Trident (3679m) on the Brenva side.
        Considerably more popular than the Col de la Fourche Hut as it is larger and more easily reached from the glacier bays on either

side of the frontier ridge. For a time this hut was closed because it was thought to be slipping off the mountain. It has now officially re-opened.

From the Midi téléphérique station traverse the Vallée Blanche to the Col du Gros Rognon (3415m). Descend under Mt Blanc du Tacul and go round into the Maudit-Tacul glacier bay. Reach the foot of the Col du Trident to the R of the prominent Trident Pinnacle (3720m). Gain the NW spur of the Trident and climb up its R side (fixed ropes) to the col. The hut is up to the L. 3hr, PD+. See also Photo 52

From the Torino Hut cross the Col des Flambeaux (3407m) and continue beneath the Tour Ronde to join the previous route. 2½hr

Although an unlikely means of approach, the hut can be reached from the Brenva Bivouac by continuing up the narrow snowy ridge S to a flat section S of the Col de la Tour Ronde, cross the narrow glacier to the L and reach the upper Brenva glacier plateau. A wide snowy ice couloir climbed on the L side leads to the Col du Trident. 2½hr. Easily reached on ski in winter from the Midi or the Torino Hut.

H18   **Col de la Fourche Bivouac Hut**   3680m. Alberico e Borgna
[50]   Bivouac Hut. CAAI property. Room for 10. This is situated further along the frontier ridge towards Mont Maudit than the Trident Hut. Both N and S side approach couloirs involve steep snow and ice climbing which makes the hut less preferable than the Trident for parties attempting routes other than the Frontier Ridge. It is located a little to the SE of the col on the Brenva side. See also Photo 62. 3½hr from Midi or Torino. AD

H19   **Torino Hut**   3375m. CAI property. Room for 180. Hotel service. Situated a few minutes above the Col du Géant (3365m). The only available water is bottled mineral water which is quite expensive. Tel:0165 84 22 47

The hut is generally reached by téléphérique from La Palud (Courmayeur) or via the Midi téléphérique station and a crossing of the Vallée Blanche by the télécabine to Pt Helbronner or by following Route H17 to beneath Mt Blanc du Tacul, then continuing in the same line to cross the Col des Flambeaux (3hr). F

From La Palud, a path, well-marked on the map, reaches Le Pavillon half-way station (2174m, 1¾hr). It then continues in a series of steep and laborious zigzags to a broken rocky ridge. Pass through La Porte (2726m) and follow the broken crest, or scree/snow fields on the R, to the hut (the old hut and téléphérique station—the new hut is reached via a tunnel or zig-zag path, 3½hr). About 5–6hr from La Palud, 3½hr in descent.

Le Pavillon can also be reached by a newer path which starts just W of the Mt Blanc tunnel entrance and zigzags steeply up the hillside past avalanche barriers.

H20
69

Grandes Jorasses Hut 2804m. Boccalatte-Piolti Hut. CAI property. Room for 30. Situated on the rocky rognon alongside the L bank of the Planpincieux glacier. Restaurant service and warden at times in summer.

From Planpincieux in the Val Ferret, take the path up through the woods and the open slopes beyond to the rock barrier below the Planpincieux glacier. Cross the stream and go up its R side to a chimney (ladder). Above this reach the moraine on the R side of the glacier and follow it to the top. Slant L across snow to the rock barrier supporting the hut and climb it with the help of fixed chains. 5hr. See also Photo 11

In winter, good conditions are necessary as most of the route can be subject to avalanche. After heavy snowfalls giant avalanches originating in the region of Aig de Rochefort can obliterate the forests and roads in the Val Ferret.

Canzio Bivouac Hut 3825m. Owned by the Turin Section of the CAI and situated at the E end of the Col des Grandes Jorasses near to the rocks of Pt Young. Room for 10. Always open.

The approach from France is long and serious, over badly crevassed glacier terrain. However it is by far the safest and most frequented approach, that from the Italian side being exposed to stonefall.

H21
72

French side: From the Leschaux Hut follow Route H31 past the Périades Bivouac until roughly below the Col du Mt Mallet. Make a wide arc below the Calotte de Rochefort and reach the steep snow/ice slope descending from the Col des Grandes Jorasses. The rimaye can often be difficult to cross. 6hr to the hut. AD serious. See also Photo 67

Can be approached on ski in winter from the Midi station by first descending the Vallée Blanche and Glacier du Tacul.

H22 Italian side: c350m serious: From the Grandes Jorasses Hut go up
69 the Planpinceux glacier to the Rocher de Reposoir then work L to
the foot of the col. Climb the R side of the snowy couloir to the
point where it is blocked by a high wall cut by two gullies. Climb
slabs on the R for 40m to the crest of a ridge just below the point
where it steepens. Work up R over ledges and short steps to a large
smooth buttress with overhangs on the R. Cross a slab at the base of
the buttress to its LH end and climb short cracks passing two
detached flakes to a dièdre. Climb this turning the final overhang on
the R (IV+, 25m from foot of slab) and continue more easily on
good rock to the E end of the col. 5hr. D−

   Fixed anchors allow a rappel descent if necessary. 3 rappels
directly from the hut lead to the base of the smooth buttress.
Scramble down R and rappel the L side of the couloir.

H23 **Jacchia Bivouac Hut** c3250m. Property of the Courmayeur
Guides. Situated on the Tronchey (SE) ridge of the Grandes
Jorasses just N of the Aig.de l'Evêque (3258m). Always open. Room
for 6.

From the Pra Sec chalets in the Val Ferret follow the path NNW
from the road taking the L fork after about 400m. This zigzags up
through open ground to the Pra Sec Torrent. Continue on the R
side to a grassy hump where a vague path leads up to the smooth
vertical walls that form the base of the S ridge of L'Evêque (2hr).

   At c2350m trend up to the R and climb across these walls by a
steep grassy ramp (pegs and cables) to reach a scree shoulder after
100m. Climb up on easy ground moving L to a shoulder on the S
ridge (c2800m cairn) (1½hr). Move down L onto the W face then
traverse horizontally on easy slabs to a large couloir descending
from the ridge between the Aigs de Tronchey and de l'Evêque
(stonefall). Climb the R side of this couloir trending L towards the
top and finishing directly to a shoulder on the ridge where the hut
stands (2½hr). 6hr from Pra Sec. PD−/II

H24 **Gervasutti Hut** 2833m. CAI property. Situated on a small rock
73 island in the Frébouze glacier. Room for 12. No warden. Cooking
equipment and wood burning stove. Always open.

From the chalets of La Vachey (1642m) in the Val Ferret, follow the
road NW for 400m to the sharp bend. Cross a bridge on the L and
slant NNE through the woods leaving a well-marked path which
runs below and to the R. Continue up the moraine slopes (cairns) to
where the glacier confluents merge into one stream. A little higher,

cross the streams and continue N up the moraine to a large cairn (1½hr).

Go up a little grassy valley to a steep rocky escarpment on the R side of the most easterly stream coming from the narrow E branch of the glacier. Cross the stream and climb a V-shaped rocky gully for 50m then work L up grassy slopes on a faint track, continuing over rock and snowfields to pass below the foot of the SSE spur of Pt 3654m. Go up the glacier to the NW and reach the rock island on which the hut stands (2½hr). 4hr from the road. F

Sections of this route can be threatened by avalanche in winter though less so than the ascent to the Grandes Jorasses Hut. It is best to follow the R side of the Frebouze Torrent all the way from the road to maximise shelter from large avalanches originating higher up.

H25 Gianni Comino Bivouac Hut 2430m. This recently constructed building with room for 9 is well placed for routes on the SE side of Mt Gruetta and the rock walls flanking the Gruetta cirque. Property of the Mondivo section of the CAI and always open. There is no cooking equipment.

From the car park near the Arnuva restaurant (1769m) in the Val Ferret, continue along the track towards the Col Ferret for a few minutes where a L fork, signposted to the Gianna Comino bivouac, leads to a bridge across the river. The path, though often indistinct, is well marked by cairns and red paint flashes. Continue through a small wood (larch, rhododendrons and alpine rosemary), then climb steeply up the crest of the moraine to reach a little valley that is often snow covered until late summer. Go easily L, up ledges and short walls, to reach the crest of the SE shoulder of Mt Gruetta. Bear up L over bands of rock and small grassy ledges to reach the hut. 2–2½hr

H26 Triolet Hut 2590m. Dalmazzi Hut. Situated on the L bank of the Triolet glacier under a rock wall at the base of Pt 3228m of Mts Rouges de Triolet. CAI property. Room for 18–20. Always open. Warden resident much of the summer. Good cooking equipment, gaz stove etc.

From the Arnuva Restaurant in the Val Ferret (1769m) continue along the unmade road for about 20min to a sharp bend level with the moraine on the R side of the Triolet glacier opening. Follow a well-marked path across the river and up the moraine till just past 2267m a large grassy gully appears on the R. The path goes up the

L side of the gully then crosses it to zigzag up the R side until the upper terraces lead horizontally back L across the top of the gully to the hut. The gully can be climbed direct, large blocks with an easy finishing chimney. 2–2½hr

In winter the slope between the hut and the upper plateau of the Triolet glacier can be avalanche-prone. It is often possible to ascend the L side of the glacier quite easily, between the ice-fall and the rocks of Monte Rouge de Gruetta (stonefall). This gives an avalanche-free and rapid means of access to the upper plateau and is worth considering as a summer possibility for routes on Mt Gruetta, Aig de Leschaux etc.

H27   **Requin Hut** 2516m. Property of CAF. Situated below the Dent du Requin on the L bank of the Tacul glacier. Warden in late winter, spring and summer. Room for 118. Restaurant service. Tel:50 53 16 96.

From the Aig du Midi téléphérique station descend the NE ridge for 100m or so until steep slopes (several crevasses) lead down into the Vallée Blanche. Traverse this to the Col du Gros Rognon (3415m) and continue under Mt Blanc du Tacul until level with the Pyramide du Tacul. Continue round in a wide arc to the N and go down the glacier to just above the Petit Rognon. Descend the Géant icefall (the route and difficulty varying from year to year with some danger of serac fall) and just below the base traverse horizontally L to the hut. A good track is usually to be found in summer. 2hr, F

H28   Because of a land slip the start from Montenvers has changed. Walk S on a good path above the glacier following signs to 'Les Refuges'. Descend ladders to the Mer de Glace. At the point at which the glacier is reached there are cairns indicating the route on the glacier. However, it is usually better to ignore these and instead follow the edge of the glacier over moraine, ice and bolders (there is usually a track with some waymarks) as far as l'Angle. From there it is fairly easy to work out into the middle of the glacier. (If the cairns are followed, work out towards the centre through the very crevassed region of the glacier then go up the middle to easier ground). Trend R below the Trélaporte promontory (c2000m). (In reverse keep to the middle until level with a conspicuous white square painted on a large slab at the point where the path from Montenvers meets the glacier. Then head directly for the square and so reach the ladders, or before reaching the very crevassed region of the glacier move over to the L bank at about level with l'Angle and follow the edge of the glacier to the ladders). Melt steams on the glacier can be difficult to cross.

Keep on the R side and reach a steeper more crevassed section followed by a longer easier-angled section leading to the Géant icefall. The correct route along the Mer de Glace from Montenvers is usually well-marked with painted stones and oil drums. Reach the moraine on the L side of the Envers de Blatière glacier. The path zig-zags up this then slants L across the broken hillside to the hut; or continue along the R side of the Tacul glacier and up its steep section below the Géant icefall until a path leads horizontally back R to the hut. 3hr

H29 **Couvercle Hut** 2687m. A large hut and excellent viewpoint situated below the SE ridge of the Moine. Room for 137. Warden in summer. Tel:50 53 16 94. Locked in winter but the old hut, situated under a large tilted slab of granite 100m to the NE, remains open. Room for 30.

From Montenvers (1909m) follow Route H28 to below the Trélaporte promontory then cross the glacier and moraine crests (faint track, cairns, painted boulders etc) towards the foot of the Egralets cliffs. Keep going up the moraine and ice parallel to the cliffs until directly opposite a series of ladders (2230m, 1½–2hr).
A steep but easy path, well-adorned with ladders and cables, reaches the top of these cliffs. Follow the path over grass and moraine to the L side of the Talèfre glacier. Directly below the hut the path forks. Take the L branch which zigzags up to the hut in a few minutes (1–1½hr). 2½–3½hr from Montenvers.

In winter the slopes above the Egralets cliffs can be threatened by avalanche. A safer approach uses the old path ascending the rib of the Pierre à Bérenger (2466m) on the R side of the Talèfre seracs. A rope is in place to ascend the moraine. At the top traverse L onto the flat section of the glacier, head N towards the rocky Jardin de Talèfre, then cross the glacier to the SW in order to reach the hut.

H30 **Leschaux Hut** 2431m. CAF property. Situated on the R bank of the Leschaux glacier opposite the Aig du Tacul. Room for 12–15. Warden in summer.

Follow Route H29 to the moraine below the Egralets cliffs. Continue along more complex moraine (cairns) to the Leschaux glacier and go up the centre, finally working L to cross the lateral moraine NW of the hut. Climb a large gully until a fixed chain leads up and across the R wall. A good track ascends gradually to the hut. 2½–3hr from Montenvers.

In winter this is most easily reached on ski by descending the Vallée Blanche from the Midi téléphérique station.

H31 **Périades Bivouac Hut** 3450m. CAF property. Situated on the
66 Périades ridge just S of Pt Sisyphe (3460m). Room for 4. Always open but in poor repair (the roof leaks). A badly crevassed approach. PD

From the Leschaux Hut cross the glacier due S and go up the Mt Mallet glacier keeping as near to the rocks on the R side as possible. The angle eases below the Périades pinnacles. The lowest depression on the ridge is the Brèche des Périades (3401m). On the L climb a snow slope directly below Pt Sisyphe then a short couloir on the L to the ridge. The hut is just up to the R. 3½hr

Aiguille de la Bérangère 3122m

Dôme de Miage 3670m

Col de la Bérangère 3348m

Between the Dôme de Miage 3670m and the Aig de la Bérangère. The NW side is long and unpleasant. The short couloir on the SE side is subject to stonefall.

1
F

SOUTH-EAST SIDE
E Coleman with F Mollard and J Jacquemont, 2 Sept 1858

From the Conscrits Hut follow the R bank of the Tré la Tête glacier, ascending to a small glacial bay below the col. Climb the snowy couloir leading to the ridge R of the col. 2hr

Aiguille de la Bérangère 3425m

T Hare with D Fournereaux, Aug 1858

This very popular summit and marvellous viewpoint is often combined with a traverse of the Dômes de Miage.

2
F

SOUTH-WEST FLANK NORMAL ROUTE
First ascent party

From the Conscrits Hut reach the crest of the moraine to the NW and continue towards Pt 2931m. Go up steeper snow slopes on the L to reach the Bérangère glacier. Ascend the glacier, finishing up easy rocks leading to the summit. 2½hr

3
PD

NORTH-EAST RIDGE
E Coleman with F Mollard and J Jacquemont, 2 Sept 1858

From the Col de la Bérangère (Route 1). Follow the narrow corniced ridge finishing up steep rocks to the summit. ¾hr

Dômes de Miage 3673m

First ascent of the highest point: E Coleman with F Mollard and J Jacquemont, 2 Sept 1858

An attractive snow ridge capped by five summits. The complete traverse is a classic undertaking and relatively easy. The NW face boasts a good selection of long snow and ice routes that are seldom climbed.

4
PD

TRAVERSE OF MAIN RIDGE WEST TO EAST

First traverse not recorded. Winter traverse with a continuation over the Aig du Bionnassay: M Berruex with P Curral and Galinier, Jan 1977

A complete traverse is often made in this direction by first climbing the Aig de la Bérangère and continuing to the Durier Hut on the Col de Miage. This aesthetic excursion can be rounded off the next day by a descent of the Miage glacier or by a lengthy continuation along the ridges of the Bionnassay to Mt Blanc.

From the Conscrits Hut, traverse the Aig de la Bérangère by Routes 2 and 3. Continue NE along the ridge at first on shattered rock then snow to the summit 3670m (3½hr). Continue along the crest which can often present small cornices to the Col des Dômes, then up the narrow snow ridge to the highest point (2hr). A rocky ridge leads to the last dôme (3672m). Continue down the crest all the way to the Col de Miage (2hr). 8hr to the Durier Hut.

5
PD

TRAVERSE OF MAIN RIDGE EAST TO WEST

First traverse not recorded

It is in this direction that the traverse is usually taken. The Tré la Tête glacier can be ascended early in the morning when it is firm and the descent over the Aig de la Bérangère is straightforward. This highly recommended excursion is a good introduction to long alpine ridges.

From the Conscrits Hut reach the Col Infranchissable by Route 14 (2hr). Just before the col slant L up fairly steep snow slopes then return R, avoiding a very crevassed zone, to reach the rocky frontier ridge. Ascend this to Pt 3672m (2hr). Follow the main ridge easily to the highest point (3673m) then descend a narrow and sometimes corniced crest to the Col des Dômes (½hr). This col can also be reached directly from the Tré la Tête glacier by the wide and easy-angled SE couloir (2½–3hr from the Conscrits Hut – a popular alternative with some crevassed areas).

    Continue along the crest in a splendid position but with due regard for cornices, over all the dômes. Descend a broader snowy ridge then broken rocks to the Col de la Bérangère (2½hr). It is less complicated and, in effect, hardly any longer in time to traverse the Aig de la Bérangère to the Conscrit Hut (Routes 3 and 2, 2hr) than to descend directly to the hut by Route 1. About 8–9hr for the round trip.

Dômes de Miage: North West Face

This vast and remotely situated glacier face has numerous snow and ice routes of medium difficulty.

6
D
`32`

POINT 3670m NORTH-NORTH-WEST FACE

B Grillon and J Denis, 3 Aug 1957. Winter: J Bessat, P Chappelland and P Curral, 17 Jan 1976

A fine line, which on the first ascent forced an overhanging serac barrier using artificial aid.

Approach from Les Contamines via the Lac d'Armancette and the Pt de Covagnet, where it is possible to bivouac (4–4½hr). The upper part of the glacier can be reached by descending the Armancettes glacier from the Col de la Bérangère. 900–1000m from the Covagnet glacier; 500m from the rimaye below the final steep ice slope.

7
D/D+
`32`

POINT 3666m NORTH-WEST FACE

M and Mme D Colin with P Gabarrou, 12 Sept 1974

This follows the fine ice slope and steep mixed pillar directly below the summit of Pt 3666m and just L of Route 6. 900–1000m from the Covagnet glacier.

8
AD
`32`

POINT 3633m NORTH-WEST RIDGE

C Bosviel and A Estivin, 19 Sept 1895. Winter: P Lachenal and Novel, 6–7 Feb 1971

Probably the easiest route on the face. This takes the line of the big rocky spur descending directly from the summit and reached by traversing the upper Covagnet glacier plateau to its top L corner. The spur gives steep and easy climbing on poor rock. 900–1000m from the Covagnet glacier.

9
D
`32`

POINT 3633m NORTH-NORTH-WEST FACE

P Blanc and P Dujon, June 1950. Winter: M Berruex and P Curral, 5 Jan 1974

Approach this via Route H6 from Tresse. Climb the L flank of the spur via a depression and then a wide sloping rock terrace to the final ice slope. This gives good climbing (50°–55°) in a fine, safe situation. About 1400m.

10   **DELACHAT-IMBERT ROUTE**
D+   C Delachat and G Imbert, 10–11 Jan 1984

`32`

A more direct route from the Miage valley was made to the summit of Pt 3633m cutting through Route 9.

11   **POINT 3630m NORTH-WEST FACE**
D/D+   P Gabarrou and P Lagrange, 24–25 Sept 1978

`32`

This varied ice climb takes the upper slope L of the previous route. About 1400m.

12   **POINT 3673m NORTH-WEST RIDGE**
AD/AD+   H Mettrier with F Carley and J Cayetto, 26 Aug 1902. Winter: F & P Curral, B Favray, A Fisseau and M Morand, 19 Jan 1964

`32`

The classic and most frequently accomplished climb on the face. Highly recommended early in the season before the upper section becomes too icy.

Follow Route H6 from Tresse to Plan Glacier where it is possible to bivouac. Reach the crest of the lower rocky ridge by a couloir coming down from a depression on the ridge and climb it easily over Pt 2944m to the upper snow crest. The rocky spur can be avoided completely in good snow conditions by climbing the couloir to the L, but this is exposed to stone and serac fall. The upper crest is 50° and may end in a cornice. 1000m, 6hr

13   **POINTS 3672m/3673m NORTH-NORTH-WEST FACE**
D   M Bozon, H Leblanc, M Lenoir and P Revilliod, 1 July 1960

`32`

This route weaves its way through the serac barriers that characterise this part of the face. The line will vary from year to year. 1000m

Col Infranchissable 3349m

First traverse J Eccles with M Payot and M Bellin, 1870

The Italian side of this col is steep, exposed to stonefall and rarely climbed (AD).
     The French side is important as an approach to climbs on the Dômes de Miage and Tré la Tête.

14 **FRENCH SIDE**

F *A long glacier trudge.*

From the Conscrits Hut go up the centre of the Tré la Tête glacier to the broad snowy saddle of the col. This is a very crevassed journey and in a snowy season many are concealed. 2hr

Aiguilles de Tré la Tête 3930m

A Reilly and E Whymper with M Croz, M Payot and H Charlet, 12 July 1864

This mountain comprises 4 distinct summits on a kilometre-long ridge, the highest point adorned with the local radio station aerial. The normal routes, while not difficult, give excellent mixed climbs of their class and the views towards Mt Blanc amply justify the effort. The NE side of the mountain above the Miage glacier has a wealth of dangerous rock routes and couloirs and is not described.

15 **NORTH RIDGE OF NORTH PEAK**

PD L Kraul, W Martin, E Mayer and R Weitzenbock, 17 Aug 1912

A fine climb which is possibly the best of the normal routes on these Aigs.

From the Conscrits Hut follow Route 14 towards the Col Infranchissable (1¾hr). Then take a snowy rock rib on the R coming down from the frontier ridge about 100m R of the Tête Carée (1hr). Continue up the main ridge, often corniced, to the N summit (¾hr). In good snow conditions it is often possible to follow the glacier face to the R of the snowy rock rib. 3½hr from the hut.

16 **CENTRAL AND S PEAKS VIA COL DE TRE LA TETE**

PD+/AD Upper section: M Baretti with J Maquignaz, A and V Sibille, 8 Aug

31 1878. Lower section: M Averton, G Bullock, H Hopworth and R Irving, Aug 1923

A very varied excursion which is also the easiest route to the highest summit from the Tré la Tête glacier. See also Photo 33

From the Conscrits Hut follow Route 14 to below Pt 3569m on the SW ridge of the Aig de Tré la Tête. Climb the slopes to the L of Pt 2968m, then the easy rocky crest on the R towards Pt3569m. Finish up a snow crest on the L. Follow the rocky main ridge to the Col de Tré la Tête (3hr).

Climb the SW ridge to the central peak (snow crests with a couple of rock buttresses. 2hr). The most delicate part of the climb, a narrow snow crest with awkward cornices, leads to the S summit. 5½hr from the Conscrits Hut.

17 SOUTH RIDGE OF EAST PEAK

PD/PD+   F Gonella with A Berthod and J Petigax, 28 July 1887

33

A crevassed glacier approach leads to an easy rocky ridge.

From the Estelette Bivouac follow Route 29 to the snowy saddle at the foot of the steep part of the SE ridge of the Aig des Glaciers. A snow slope leads to the upper Lée Blanche glacier. Cross the glacier to the rock barrier forming the E ridge of the Aig de la Léc Blanche and climb it easily just R of Pt 3300m (possible stonefall). Cross the upper glacier to the S ridge and climb a line of weakness just L of a couloir to reach the ridge slightly R of Pt 3459m. Follow the rocky crest easily to just below the E summit, then climb the final step directly (III) to the top. 6hr

18 SOUTH COULOIR

AD   J Buzio and R Gréloz, 20 July 1952

33

The couloir immediately L of the preceding route gives a direct and satisfying route to the main summit but should only be attempted in cold snowy conditions. 6hr from the Estelette Bivouac Hut.

19 SOUTH-EAST RIDGE OF EAST PEAK

PD   First ascent party

22

The easiest and most popular of all the routes offering excellent panoramic views.

From the Petit Mt Blanc Bivouac climb the snowy ridge to the summit of the Petit Mt Blanc (3424m) (1½hr). Descend a rocky couloir to the Petit Mt Blanc glacier and go up the L side to the rimaye below a couloir/slope close to Pt 3644m. Climb this and follow the fine snow ridge to the E peak (2½hr). 4hr from the hut.

20 TRAVERSE OF THE AIGUILLES FROM FRANCE

AD   First traverse is not recorded but possibly B Arsandeaux and E Labour, 25 July 1929. Winter traverse: F Braize with O Bégain, J Demarque and F Mollard, 17 Jan 1974

A classic excursion in this relatively unfrequented part of the range where both length and altitude add to the seriousness. The very fit may continue

via the Aig and Col des Glaciers to the Tré la Tête Hotel (AD/AD+)

From the Conscrits Hut reach the N summit by Route 15. Follow the ridge towards the central summit climbing over the first gendarme (poor rock) and the second, after turning the first section on the R (equally poor rock). Climb past two blades of rock on their L side and follow the ridge to the summit rocks which are climbed directly on sound rock or by-passed by a couloir on the R (1¾hr).

Continue along the narrow corniced crest to the S summit 20–30min. It is possible to make a return trip to the E summit in 1½hr by keeping L on the slope below the large cornice. From the E summit it is obviously possible to descend to the Petit Mt Blanc Bivouac by Route 19 in 2½hr. Otherwise return to the central summit and descend Route 16 to the Conscrits Hut (3–4hr). 9–10hr for the round trip; about 14hr to the Tré la Tête Hotel via the Aig des Glaciers.

21   **TRAVERSE OF THE AIGUILLES FROM ITALY**
AD–/AD *This is rarely done and the N summit is generally omitted. In adopting the direction described below, the safest descent can be utilised at the end of the day.*

From the Estelette Bivouac follow Route 17 to the upper glacier and reach the Col de Tré la Tête easily in 3½hr. Continue up Route 16 to the S peak (2½hr) and reach the E summit by keeping L on the slope below the large cornice (¾–1hr). Descend Route 19 to the Petit Mt Blanc Bivouac Hut (2½hr). 9½hr from the hut.

Aiguille de la Lée Blanche 3697m

V Attinger and L Kurz with J Croz and J Simond, 25 July 1889

Although only a secondary summit this peak offers interesting and worthwhile snow and ice possibilities in the lower grades.

22   **SOUTH RIDGE FROM COL DES GLACIERS**
F+ Unknown

31 *The easiest route to the summit and the normal descent route to the Tré la Tête glacier. See also Photo 33*

From the Tré la Tête Hotel, Conscrits or the Robert Blanc Huts, reach the Col des Glaciers by Routes 39 or 40. Follow Route 25 to the Aig des Glaciers as far as the Dôme de Neige (3592m) then continue along the snowy crest to the Col de la Scie (3626m). The ridge leading up to the Aig is generally corniced but straightforward. 2½hr from the col; 1½hr in descent.

23 **NORTH RIDGE**

PD/PD+ First ascent party

31

The upper section of this ridge is a narrow corniced crest. See also Photo 33

From the Conscrits Hut follow Route 16 to the main ridge near Pt 3569m and continue via the Col de la Lée Blanche to the summit. 4hr

24 **NORTH-WEST FACE**

AD+ R Gaché, P Gayet, Tancrède and R Jonquière, 31 July 1931. Winter:

31 M Bozon, C Mattal, F and G Mollard, 16 Jan 1971

A glacier face, steepening near the top and varying in form from year to year.

From the Conscrits Hut reach the foot of the glacier bay in ½hr. The rock band at half height is generally taken on the L side and the most aesthetic finish is directly up the 50° headwall to the summit. Easier variants can be made R onto the W ridge or L on a glacial shelf to join the N ridge. About 700m and about 5hr from the hut.

The W ridge bounding the face on the R can be followed in its entirety. AD, poor rock.

Aiguille des Glaciers 3816m

E del Carretto and F Gonella with L Proment and G and A Henry, 2 Aug 1878. Winter: A Adami, 14–15 March 1948

A complex mountain with a snowy fore-summit on the W side christened the Dôme de Neige. Largely snowy to the W, the Aig presents a fine rocky eastern aspect overlooking the Lée Blanche glacier.

25   **WEST RIDGE FROM COL DES GLACIERS**

PD   A Archinard, E Dunand, C Fontannaz, F Geny, S Miney and C
Montandon, 18 July 1900

`31`

The easiest route from France but nonetheless a fine excursion.

From the Tré la Tête Hotel, Conscrits or Robert Blanc Huts,
follows Routes 39 or 40 to the Col des Glaciers. Follow the ridge
NE, rocky at first then broad and snowy to the Dôme de Neige.
Shortly before reaching the Dôme contour to the R around a snowy
cwm and reach the base of a poorly-defined rock rib descending
from the main summit (2¼hr). Climb it for 100m on steep loose yet
easy rock to a snow crest leading to the summit (1hr). 3¼hr from the
col.

From the Robert Blanc Hut one can go directly up the L side of the
Glaciers glacier joining the previous route just before the Dôme de
Neige. Obviously quicker but much less interesting.

26   **NORTH-WEST RIDGE**

AD   J Lasneret with C Blanc, 14 Aug 1926

`31`

*This provides a direct ascent from the Tré la Tête glacier. Steep loose rock
followed by a fine snow crest.*

From the Conscrits Hut reach the second rock spur descending
from the W ridge N of the Col des Glaciers. Start on the R side of
the ridge in a small snow bay and climb smooth slabs to the crest.
After joining the W ridge follow Route 25 to the summit. About
1100m, 4hr from the hut.

27   **NORTH-WEST FACE**

D   R Gréloz, H Martin and A Roch, 15 Aug 1929

`31`

This takes the steep glacier slope to the L of the previous route and
may be very dangerous in its lower section where large unstable
serac formations can develop in the narrows. Finish via the Dôme
de Neige. About 1000m, 6hr

28   **SOUTH RIDGE**

PD   M Baretti with S Henry, J Maquignaz and A Sibille, 7 July 1880

`33`

The simplest and most popular route from the Elisabetta Hut goes
via the Col de la Seigne. Above the col, the ridge can be followed
directly (slightly on the L side) on scree and snow to the Petite Aig

des Glaciers. It is also possible to reach the latter by leaving the ridge above Pt 2747m and reaching the edge of the Glacier des Glaciers between Pts 3000m and 3102m (3-3½hr). (This point is easily reached from the Robert Blanc Hut). Go up the R side to rejoin the S ridge above the Petite Aig. Follow the S ridge directly to the main summit. Care is needed with the rock and there are pitches of III.8–9hr from the Elisabetta Hut.

29   **SOUTH-EAST RIDGE**

AD/AD+   M Von Kuffner with A Burgener and J Furrer, 29 July 1887.The

33   direct ascent described below and normally followed today was climbed by L Bergera and I Brosio, 25 Aug 1925

A long and classic route with a certain element of danger from stonefall. Snowy conditions can make it very time-consuming.

From the Estellette Bivouac follow the snowy ridge keeping to the L side. After turning a large gendarme cross to the R and traverse steep slabs and small gendarmes to reach the snowy shoulder at the foot of the main ridge. Climb the ridge passing a loose and narrow serrated section until higher up it levels out. Above is a steep section climbed on good rock (III), followed by a delicate traverse L across the head of a couloir 100m below the summit. Above on the ridge is a huge red gendarme with an overhanging base. Starting a few metres to the L of this, climb steep exposed walls (IV) to the summit blocks. 6–7hr from the hut.

Aiguille des Glaciers: East Face

This 500m high face overlooks the upper Lée Blanche glacier and can be reached easily in about 2hr via the snowy shoulder of Route 29. Certain sections are exposed to stonefall but the rock is fairly reasonable and the routes are of good quality.

30   **EAST-NORTH-EAST SPUR**

D   G Machetto and M Rava, 24 July 1972

33   The prominent spur on the R side of the face is sheltered from stonefall and is climbed directly up the crest. 5hr

31 DIRECT

D G Boccalatte, P Ghiglione and M Piolti, 4 Sept 1933

`33` *An excellent rock climb needing dry conditions.*

Start directly below the summit by climbing an ice slope (stonefall). At the top traverse L and climb a steep icy couloir. Now move R and climb the easier but interesting central rock pillar. After a difficult smoother section higher up, more pleasant climbing leads to the N ridge 5min from the summit. 4½hr

32 NORTH-EAST COULOIR

D/TD D Brocherer and M Mochet, 19 April 1982

`33` This excellent route takes the line of the great couloir on the L side of the face. Cold and snowy conditions are needed to render this climb at all practicable and safe.

33 EAST FACE AND SOUTH-EAST RIDGE

AD/AD+ A Ferrari with J Proment and F Melica, 19 Aug 1901

`33` This climbs the rock on the L side of the couloir taken by Route 32. On reaching the SE ridge slant up R (IV) and join Route 29 about 100m below the summit. The climbing appears to be relatively stonefall-free, but less satisfactory than the other routes on the face.

Petit Mont Blanc 3424m

G Bobba with C Thérisod and M Bognier, 4 Aug 1897

This superb viewpoint which commands an excellent panorama of the SW side of Mt Blanc is easily reached in 1½hr from the Petit Mt Blanc Bivouac Hut. Route 19.

34 EAST-NORTH-EAST COULOIR

D/D+ G Grassi, M Marone and C Stratta, 11 March 1983

This narrow ephemeral couloir gives a worthwhile climb when well iced. 700m

The first pitch is 75° hard water ice and the second narrower pitch only slightly easier (70°). Thereafter the gully gives more straightforward snow/ice work (45°–50°). Finish L of the summit about 100m down the SE ridge.

35   **NORTH-EAST COULOIR**
C Stratta, winter of 1985

The obvious wide couloir to the R of the previous route. 900m

Aiguille de l'Aigle 3517m

Easily reached from the Petit Mt Blanc glacier. See Route 19.

36   **NORTH-EAST COULOIR**
AD/AD+   B Domenech and J Janel during the night 12–13 July 1977

Only cold and snowy conditions render this couloir, which rises 1100m above the Miage glacier, a practical proposition. 40°, 4–5hr

Pyramides Calcaires

These impressive little limestone spikes lie just NE of the Col de la Seigne and give good training climbs on dolomitic rock. The climbs described are on the SE summit (2696m).

37   **SOUTH RIDGE**
III   P Nava and G Sena, 14 Aug 1961

A pleasant rock climb following the crest throughout. 1½hr

The flanks of this ridge give good short hard routes.

38   **SOUTH-SOUTH-EAST FACE**
IV   G Barelli, C Quario Rondo and G Vignolo, 7 Sept 1964

Climbs up the centre of this wall starting with a wide crack above some old military dugouts situated directly below the summit. There is one pitch of V. 350m, 4–5hr

Col des Glaciers 3063m

First traverse: W Mathews with D Balleys and Mattex, 24 Aug 1866

Although an easy way of crossing this part of the range, it is rarely done.

39 **FROM FRANCE**
F+
From the Tré la Tête Hotel follow Route H1 to the small glacier
below the col at c2500m (2hr). Generally it is best to go up the R
side to avoid various crevasses, returning to the middle of the slope
where it gets much narrower and steeper. The final rimaye can
sometimes be turned on the L close to the rocks (2hr). 4hr from the
Hotel.

From the Conscrits Hut descend S then SW across the Tré la
Tête glacier to join the route above. ¾hr

40 **FROM ITALY**
F+
From the Robert Blanc Hut, walk down and around Pt 2562m at
the base of the S ridge of the Pt des Lanchettes and go up an easy
couloir to the col (½hr).

From the Col de la Seigne, go up the frontier ridge for about
10min then work L crossing a slabby ridge to reach the Glaciers
glacier a little above its base. Cross it to the foot of the easy couloir
descending from the col. 2–2½hr to the col.

Aiguille des Lanchettes 3073m

F Tuckett with J Bennen, P Perron and Mollard, 8 July 1861

41 **WEST RIDGE**
F
First ascent party
34
A minor summit giving a short excursion from the Robert Blanc Hut.

From the hut reach the Lanchettes glacier and go up to the steep
headwall. Climb it to arrive on the ridge at a rounded rocky hump a
little to the R of the Col du Mont Tondu. Follow the W ridge over
large loose blocks to the summit. 1½hr

Mont Tondu 3196m

First recorded ascent: M Bauday and P Puiseux, 21 Aug 1889, but
ascended before this date. Winter: Mme V Bally Leirens with J and
C Ravanel, Jan 1925

A popular ascent and fine viewpoint. Snowy slopes to the N
converge on a fore summit called the Pain de Sucre (3133m,

wrongly marked on IGN) from where a narrow rock ridge extends south to the highest point.

The classic excursion is a traverse by Routes 42 and 43.

42   **NORTH-WEST RIDGE**
PD–
     First ascent party

`34`

Interesting scrambling with some narrow snow ridges and a final summit crest that is pleasantly exposed.

From the Tré la Tête Hotel follow Route H1 to above the Seracs de Tré la Grande (2hr). Cross to the R side of the glacier and climb the large open snowy couloir, or rocks on the R side, to the Col des Chasseurs. Climb up the W ridge (rock steps and snow crests leading to the Pain de Sucre) and continue S on good rock along the serrated, almost horizontal, crest to the main summit (the sharpest teeth can be turned on the R, 2½hr). 4½hr from the hut.

43   **NORTH-EAST RIDGE IN DESCENT**
F+
     A Hutter and Captain X with A Magnin and N Allantaz, 19 Aug 1894

`34`

The most practical descent route on the mountain and easiest route to the summit.

From the Pain de Sucre descend the NE slopes L of the ridge and continue down the Mont Tondu glacier to the Tré la Tête glacier (2½hr from summit). It is also possible to cross the Col du Mont Tondu and reach the Robert Blanc Hut by Route 41 (1½hr from the summit).

This route is very popular in ascent. Parties generally follow the rocky crest from the Col du Mt Tondu, which offers a superb scramble on good rock. 4–4½hr from the Tré la Tête hotel.

EAST FACE

There are now a number of rock routes on this face from AD+ to TD, climbed in the years 1983–1985. Several short 100m routes were also discovered on the walls to the E of the Col du Mont Tondu.

44   **SOUTH-EAST RIDGE**
PD
     M Picard and Decker with Delachat, 11 Sept 1923

`34`

A pleasant route once the Brèche de Bellaval is reached. The climbing below the brèche is rotten and exposed to stonefall. There is one section of III.

From the Robert Blanc Hut reach the Lanchettes glacier and climb the snowy couloir leading to the Brèche de Bellaval (3035m). In the upper section it is best to use the rocks on the L side. Climb the SE ridge pleasantly on slabs of good rock to the notch between the S and main summits of Mont Tondu. Reach the latter by a steep pitch. 3hr

Têtes de Bellaval 2892m and 2885m

These unfrequented summits offer some short rock climbs. There are two fine routes which offer good climbing on rock that is soundthough lacking in friction.

45   **EAST FACE OF NORTH SUMMIT**
IV/IV+   G Loyer with G Mollard, Aug 1973

Reached from Les Mottets via the chalets and Combe de Bellavalin 2 – 2½hr.

Take the line of the Rward slanting dièdre above the lowest point on the face. Slabs lead to the summit. 300m, about 5hr

46   **EAST FACE (BONNARD-MOLLARD ROUTE)**
IV/V   H Bonnard with G Mollard, Sept 1973

Further R is a couloir. Start 20m to the R of some reddish overhangs and climb dièdres and chimneys. The crux pitch turns a large overhang on the L just below the summit ridge. 300m, about 5hr

Descent can be made down the R flanks of the face. (PD)

47   **SOUTH-SOUTH-WEST RIDGE OF SOUTH SUMMIT**
PD   First ascent unknown

`32`

The normal route.

From Plan Jovet the ridge is reached at the brèche N of theCol des Tufs. Follow the crest, climbing over several gendarmes or turning them on the R (4hr from Plan Jovet).

     It is possible to traverse the summits, descending to the Brèche des Têtes on the L side of the ridge at AD standard.

Col de Miage 3342m

It was probably first traversed as early as the late eighteenth century.

Rarely used as a pass but often climbed to reach the Durier Hut just below the saddle near its N end. See Huts Section.

Aiguille de Bionnassay 4052m

E Buxton, F Grove and R MacDonald with J Cachet and M Payot, 28 July 1865. Winter: A Charlet and R Frison Rochc; H Hoerlin, E Schneider and H Schroeder, 20 March 1929

One of the most attractive satellite peaks of Mt Blanc. The summit is a classic knife edge of snow. All routes are splendid and serious snow and ice climbs.

48   **SOUTH RIDGE**
PD+   G Gruber with K Maurer and A Jaun, 13 July 1888

Although the easiest route to the summit, it is seldom climbed and tends either to be used as a descent route when conditions make it inadvisable to descend the E ridge, or as a means of traversing the mountain in conjunction with the Dômes de Miage.

From the Durier Hut move delicately up the ridge climbing over two snowy shoulders to the final rock step. Climb this just R of the crest by a series of chimneys. (It is possible to turn the rock step on the L or, by climbing much lower down on the R flank, to reach a plain snow band leading back to the crest. These alternatives are generally harder (AD)). Continue up a fine snow crest to the summit ridge. 4hr

49   **EAST RIDGE**
AD−   The ridge itself was first done by K Richardson with E Rey and J
`35`   Bich, 13 Aug 1888 as part of a traverse from the Col de Miage to the Dôme du Goûter.

A superb snow crest which is often precarious and delicate due to large cornices. The easier approach, from the Gonella Hut, has few crevasse problems.

Follow Route 63 from the Gonella Hut to the Col des Aigs Grises

(4hr). Traverse horizontally L across steep slopes to reach the Col de Bionnassay or follow the ridge to the Piton des Italiens (a shoulder, 4002m) and descend the steep and narrow ridge to the col. Go delicately up the very sharp E ridge paying careful attention to cornices. 5–6hr from the hut.

AD   *The route is generally taken in the reverse sense as part of a grand traverse of Mont Blanc.*

From the summit descend the E ridge to the Col de Bionnassay then continue up the frontier ridge, steep and narrow, to a shoulder – the Piton des Italiens. Follow Route 63 to the Dôme du Goûter and Mont Blanc. 6½hr

Aiguille de Bionnassay: North-West Face

Four routes have now been established on this face.

50 **ORIGINAL ROUTE**
AD/AD+ First true ascent of the face: R Lloyd with A and J Pollinger, 18 July
35 1926. Winter: R Simond, 29 Jan 1964

The finest route on the mountain and indeed one of the best snow/ice routes of its class in the Alps. A glacier face on which the line taken will vary from year to year according to changing serac formations. It is advisable to start very early in order to find the descent routes in reasonable condition.

From the Tête Rousse Hut go up towards the Aig du Goûter for 100m or so then descend a scree couloir to the Bionnassay glacier. Cross the glacier to the S passing under some seracs then head towards the base of the glacier ribbon just L of Pt 3181m. Climb the ribbon and at half height slant up L to the summit. It is also possible to escape R to the Tricot ridge and follow it to the summit. 1050m, average angle 40°–45°, 4–6hr

51 **CENTRAL ROUTE**
D+ B Kempf and C Laurendeau, 30–31 Aug 1953
35 Rarely climbed. There is a good deal of poor rock with little protection and considerable objective danger from the upper serac barriers. 1000m

52

D+

35

DIRECT ROUTE

J Afanassief and B Domenech, July 1975. Winter: C Jond, B Dolliguez and P Thevenard, Jan 1986

Entirely on ice, this route crosses a large serac barrier at its weakest point. The stability of these seracs will determine whether the climb is unjustifiably dangerous or not. 1000m

53

D+

35

LEFT-HAND ROUTE

M Parmentier and J Vaudelle, 17 Sept 1977

This is considerably safer than the previous two. It has a difficult mixed section of 250m at half height with several pitches of V. The upper slopes average 50°. 1000m, 9hr

Aiguille du Tricot 3665m

This minor summit on the NW ridge of the Bionnassay has a fine N face which is steeper and harder than the original route (Route 50) on the Bionnassay.

54

D

35

NORTH FACE

P Blanc, P Dujon and R Conseth, 30 June 1950. Winter: J Ménégoz and J Tripard, 23 Dec 1975

Fine climbing, though often very icy. The approach traverse is threatened by large serac barriers on the L side of the face.

From the Tête Rousse Hut follow Route 50 onto the NW face of the Bionnassay and immediately after the first slope cross an easy rotten rock ridge on the R. Traverse horizontally until below the summit and climb directly up the steep face to the top. About 600m, 5hr

It is easiest to descend on to the Miage glacier but more practical either to traverse the Bionnassay or climb across to its NW face and descend Route 50 in about 3hr.

Pyramide des Aiguilles Grises 3237m

This rock pyramid dominating the Gonella Hut and wrongly marked on the map as 3227m gives some fine little routes on sound rock. Perhaps the best of these is the E spur (IV).

Aiguille du Goûter 3863m

F Cuidet and F Gervais, before 1784

This summit lies a little to the S of the Goûter Hut and is crossed on the normal Route 57 to Mt Blanc. The N face has a number of routes with very different approaches. Two are described below.

55
AD
36

NORTH FACE
This triangular face rises out of the much reduced Bourgeat glacier. The first route by E Livacic and F Martinetti on 1 July 1941 climbed the face directly from Les Houches via the Chavanne Vieille and the Bourgeat glacier. On 7 July 1957 P Labrunie, M Vaucher, A Contamine, P Julien and Y Pollet-Villard climbed the centre of the face using a much shorter approach from the Tête Rousse Hut.
Cold snowy conditions will help to minimise stonefall danger.

From the hut descend the path a little way then go down the Griaz glacier until it is possible to cross the NW ridge of the mountain just above Pt 2912m. Traverse steeply into the centre of the face and climb it, finishing up delicate mixed ground. 800m, 4hr in good conditions.

56
AD
36

NORTH-NORTH-EAST (TACONNAZ) RIDGE
R Baumont and G Decorps, 9–10 Oct 1976

This excellent route gives a long yet safe climb to the summit of the mountain from Taconnaz via the Gros Bechar ridge, and a bivouac in the vicinity of Pt 3154m.

Mont Blanc 4807m

J Balmat and M Paccard, 8 Aug 1786. Winter: I Straton with J Charlet and S Couttet, 31 Jan 1876

The highest summit in the Alps. This complex and beautiful mountain is often compared favourably with many of the great Himalayan peaks; an ascent from the Plan de l'Aiguille for example involving over 2400m of glacier work. There are well over 100 different routes to the summit offering a wide variety of climbing and these give more than 2000 people each year the opportunity of reaching the top. However in bad weather ferocious winds and extremely low temperatures can make escape a nightmare especially as route-finding can become unusually difficult due to the complex nature of the terrain. The safest descent route is down to the Grands Mulets. It is more sheltered and the track may remain visible for a longer period of time than that to the Goûter Hut.

57 GOUTER RIDGE (NORMAL ROUTE)
PD–

36

First complete ascent L Stephen and F Tuckett with M Anderegg, J Bennen and P Perren, 18 July 1861

The most frequented ascent route which sometimes sees more than 100 people reach the summit on the same day. It has the advantage of little technical difficulty in good conditions, marvellous views and the summit day is shorter than other approaches. Despite this, the descent from the Aig du Goûter is exposed to stonefall and is the scene of a considerable number of accidents. In bad weather route-finding between the Bosses and the Dôme is very tricky and the whole route is very exposed to wind. Above the Goûter Hut these constitute the main difficulties that might be encountered. See also Photo 37

From the Goûter Hut follow the snow ridge and a slope broken with seracs towards the flat and indistinct summit of the Dôme du Goûter: pass underneath it, usually on the L (NE) side (2hr). Descend to the broad saddle of the Col du Dôme and continue up in the same direction to the Vallot Hut (1hr). The slope narrows, steepens and merges into the Bosses ridge. Follow this over the two prominent snow humps or Bosses and higher keep L of the Rochers de la Tournette to reach a well-defined snow ridge leading to the summit. 5hr from the hut.

58 GRANDS MULETS ROUTE
PD–

37

First complete ascent: E Headland, G Hodgkinson, C Hodson and G Joad with F Couttet and two other guides, 29 July 1859

The normal route for spring skiers and the most reliable descent route in bad weather. The ascent to the Col du Dôme is long, tedious and, in one section, exposed to seracfall, though in descent this is quickly passed. The route to the hut (H9) is often technically harder than anything above. See also Photo 36

From the Grands Mulets Hut go up the glacier towards Pt 3330m on the rocks of the N ridge of the Dôme, then work back L up a steepish snow slope to gain the Petit Plateau. Cross this shelf on the L, away from the seracs of the Dôme du Goûter and go up another slope to the Grand Plateau (3hr). (The ascent to here from the hut is badly crevassed and needs constant attention). Cross the plateau to the SW and go up the long slope to the Col du Dôme (1½hr). Follow Route 57 to the summit. 6½–7hr from the hut.

59 NORTH RIDGE OF DOME DU GOUTER

PD+

J Balmat, J Carrier, F Paccard and J Tournier, 8 June 1786, as far as the Col du Dôme

37

Although little frequented, this provides an elegant and thoroughly recommendable means of ascent from the Grands Mulets Hut. It is safe, easy to follow and climbs slopes of up to 45° in the central section. See also Photo 36

From the Grands Mulets Hut go up the glacier and get onto the ridge below the rocks of Pt 3330m. Follow the ridge to the summit of the Dôme or just before, traverse L to the Col du Dôme and follow Route 57 to the top of Mt Blanc. 7–8hr from the hut.

60 CORRIDOR ROUTE

PD

C Fellows and W Hawes with M and M Balmat, J and P Couttet, S Dévouassoud, M Favret, D Folliguet, J Payot and P Simond, 25 July 1827

37

Although as easy as any of the classic routes on Mt Blanc in good conditions, it is ascended much less frequently. In bad weather it should be avoided as the correct line is difficult to locate.

Follow Route 58 from the Grands Mulets Hut to the Grand Plateau then cross this to the foot of the Corridor, a snowy valley between the lower Rochers Rouges and Mt Maudit.

Either climb the slope between the lower Rochers Rouge and a small rocky rognon (3928m) below (this is quicker, easier to find but more prone to avalanche and has a certain danger from serac fall), or climb between the rognon and Mt Maudit (difficult route-finding through crevassed terrain).

Climb the steep narrow snow slope L of the lower Rochers Rouges – the Mur de la Côte – and continue across a small plateau to the broad snowy ridge leading to the summit. 6–8hr from the hut.

61 ROCHERS ROUGE DIRECT

AD/D

J Asseline, H Bouvard and P Gabarrou, 8 Aug 1986

37

This variant was climbed on the bicentenary of the first ascent of Mt Blanc.

Follows the crest of the upper Rochers Rouges ridge above the Grand Plateau. Over 300m of interesting mixed climbing leads to the easy upper slopes. 4½hr

62
PD
37

VIA MONT MAUDIT AND COL DU MIDI

R Head with J Grange, A Orset and J Perrod, 13 Aug 1863

*With the increasing difficulty in guaranteeing accomodation at the the
Goûter Hut and the great risk of stonefall below this, many parties are
using the Col du Midi as the starting point for the ascent of Mt Blanc.
This fine ascent is only slightly longer than that from the Goûter Hut and
is often combined with the Grands Mulets route to give a classic and safe
traverse of the mountain. With the opening of the new Cosmique Hut it
may well become the normal route. It has also been combined with a
traverse of the Bionassey or even the Dômes de Miage. In normal
conditions the climbing is neither difficult nor dangerous but at certain
times Mt Maudit and Mt Blanc du Tacul can develop slopes with serious
avalanche danger.*

From the Cosmique Hut follow Route 189 to the shoulder of the W
ridge of Mt Blanc du Tacul (the summit can be easily reached from
here in ½hr). Cross the snowy cwm below Col Maudit and climb the
steep snow slope to the Col du Mt Maudit (4345m). There is usually
a huge rimaye here that is best turned on the L. Above, snow stakes
will often be found in place. From the col either traverse S across
easy slopes to reach the Col de la Brenva or climb the NW ridge to
the summit of Mt Maudit and descend the SW ridge to the same
point. Climb the steep slopes of the Mur de la Cote and follow the
broad ridge to the summit of Mt Blanc. 6–7hr

In descent from the summit of Mt Maudit either descend the NE
ridge to the Col Maudit (much longer) or the NW ridge to Col du
Mt Maudit. The slopes on the W side of Mt Maudit, leading
directly to Col du Mt Maudit from Col de la Brenva, can deteriorate
badly in the afternoon sun. The huge rimaye is often rappelled from
snow stakes in place near the lip. 4–6hr from the summit to the
Cosmique Hut.

Mont Blanc: Italian side

63
PD–

AIGUILLES GRISES ROUTE

Original route first descended by L and J Bonin and A Ratti with J
Gadin and A Proment, 1 Aug 1890. Aiguilles Grises ridge first
ascent as far as the Dôme du Goûter by R Irving, 7 Aug 1919

*The normal route from Italy and certainly the shortest and most reliable
route of descent on this side of the mountain. There are two distinct*

alternatives above the Gonella Hut. The original route follows the Dôme glacier which is complicated by badly crevassed areas. Slightly longer but more interesting and a better bet towards the end of the season is the Aigs Grises ridge which avoids the crevassed section.

Original route: From the Gonella Hut work up seracs near the L side of the Dôme glacier then move into the centre. Higher up the glacier divides. Follow the branch to the L of the long rocky spur coming down from Pt 4051m. Reach the Col des Aigs Grises and continue up the snowy ridge to the Piton des Italians (3½hr). Follow the steep narrow and often corniced ridge to the Dôme du Goûter and continue to the summit via Route 57. 6–7hr

In descent the hut is invisible. Stay on the glacier to a small plateau opposite the foot of a narrow couloir to the E which descends from the col containing the Quintino Sella Hut. From here slant R to broken rocks leading up to the Gonella Hut. 3–4hr

Aiguilles Grises Ridge: From the Gonella Hut climb easily up to the NW and reach the ridge at c3350m. Follow it easily to the Calotte des Aigs Grises turning gendarme 3671m on the L side. Descend a broad snow crest to the Col des Aigs Grises (4hr) and continue on the original route. 8hr to the summit.

64 **ROCHER DU MONT BLANC**
PD
[38] T Kennedy with J Carrel and J Fischer, 2 July 1872. Winter: 3 Sella brothers and 6 guides, 5 Jan 1888

Often called the Tournette Spur. A direct and elegant line that gives pleasant and interesting climbing. It is somewhat exposed to stonefall so an early start is essential and the route is not recommended as a means of descent.

From the Quintino Sella Hut there are two possibilities:
(a) Climb the small crevassed glacier to the NE and reach a snow saddle at the SE foot of the Rocher du Mt Blanc (1½hr).
(b) If the glacier is too crevassed, traverse E level with the hut and scramble up the rocky crest on the R of a narrow couloir, to the saddle (1¾hr).
Descend to the upper plateau of the Mt Blanc glacier and cross it Nwards to reach the base of the spur coming down from La Tournette (¾hr). Pass the rocky rognon 3620m on the L side and above, cross a rimaye on the R (sometimes tricky). Climb a little snowy couloir or the rocks bordering it and reach the crest of the ridge that marks the R side of the large wall at the base of the spur. Follow the steep crest turning any obstacles on the R and continue

up the snow ridge, crossing several rocky outcrops, until the last can be avoided by a diagonal ascent Rwards to the Bosses Ridge. Continue to the summit. 1100m, 6½–8½hr from the hut.

65 LES BOSSES SOUTH-WEST SIDE
AD · H von Hertling and H Pfann, 29 July 1909

38

A nice route which can be reached from the Quintino Sella or Gonella Huts in 3hr. Less exposed to stonefall than the Rocher du Mt Blanc but infrequently climbed. Recommended.

It is probably easier to approach from the Quintino Sella Hut. Follow Route 64 and continue up the glacier to the foot of Pt Pfann. It is possible to reach this point directly from the Gonella Hut by climbing the glacier situated to the SW of the Rocher du Mt Blanc and a snowy couloir at its head.

Climb the flanks of the ridge to the col above and to the N of Pt Pfann. Follow the narrow ridge, rock then snowy crests, to the Bosses Ridge and continue to the summit. 8–10hr

66 GASTON REBUFFAT
TD– · W Colonna, P Gabarrou and C Stratta, 2 June 1985

38

Fine, mostly mixed, climbing in the central couloir of the Tournette spur, L of the crest. It is especially recommended in the spring season with good snow cover and a hard frost to prevent an otherwise considerable stonefall risk.

From the Quintino Sella or Gonella Hut follow Route 65 to the upper Mt Blanc glacier. Climb the snowy couloir and above take rocky spurs (III and IV) plus mixed ground to the upper slopes. Continue along Route 64 to the summit. 850m, 8–10hr

Mont Blanc: Miage Face

This vast semi-circular face overlooking the Mont Blanc glacier remains for lovers of solitude. The mountain's most remote and hidden facet, offers, to the R of the Tournette spur, a number of climbs in the same mode and with the same ambiance as those on the Brenva face.

This side of the mountain remains in the shade until later in the day and thus stonefall is delayed. However, an early start is recommended to find good conditions on the upper slopes.

67 **LEFT-HAND SPUR**

D   D de Frouville and J Perrodgau with B Domenech and C Jaccoux,
38   22 Aug 1976

*A magnificent route that is comparable with the Red Sentinel. The
approach to the spur is exposed to serac fall.*

Climb directly up the crest of the spur crossing the main serac
barrier above (60–80m high) to reach the summit slopes. 1100m,
8–10hr from the Quintino Sella Hut.

68 **CENTRAL SPUR**

AD   T Kesteven and A Marshall with E and J Gentinetta and R
38   Kaufmann, 16 Aug 1893

Not as interesting as the previous route but easier. The rib is fairly
well sheltered from stone and serac fall. The main difficulty arises
in crossing the serac barrier above this to reach the summit slopes.
1100m

Pointe Louis Amédée 4460m

A rocky prominence on the Brouillard ridge, above the Col Emile
Rey. The rock around the summit area is very poor but lower down,
on the flanks of the ridge, it appears as good sound granite.

In the centre of the NW face is a prominent red pillar flanked on
each side by deep narrow couloirs.

69 **LUNE DE MIAGE**

TD–/TD   P Gabarrou, T Pastore and D Radique, 21 June 1986

38   A series of curving couloirs on the L side of the face. c600m, 12½hr

70 **FANTA COULOIR**

TD–   G Grassi and E Tessera, 22 April 1984

38   This climb takes the couloir immediately L of the red pillar.Cold
and snowy conditions, that generally prevail early in the year, are
necessary to make this very fine ice climb a practical proposition.
On the first ascent stonefall was experienced even in perfect
conditions. 600m

71 **RED PILLAR**
D+   G Grassi and J Roche, 29 July 1983

38

The monolithic red pillar is 350m high and clearly visible from the Quintino Sella Hut. The pillar itself is composed of excellent granite in complete contrast to the upper 200m wall which gives easy climbing on black, rotten rock.

Start at the centre of the pillar about 50m R of the Fanta Couloir and climb the red slab via a grey dièdre (IV+) to a good ledge. On the R climb a dièdre then move L into a parallel one and follow it, or the L wall (V−), to more slabs on the crest of the pillar. Climb these (IV) passing a subsidary spur on its R side and continue more or less on the crest of the pillar via cracks (IV+) until a long pitch in a dièdre-gully just L of the crest leads to a slab on the R (III and IV). Climb the slab (IV) then continue up and R of an overhang to a splendid dièdre (IV+). Reach a prominent shoulder below the final buttress of the pillar (IV) then work up R on a ledge and climb a 40m crack (V−, strenuous). Climb the wall on the L of the obvious loose ground via cracks and flakes to the summit of the pillar (IV and V−).

Continue along the shattered crest and over two steps (III) until the final 100m leads easily to Pt Louis Amédée. 550m, 5½hr

72 **SOUTH-WEST RIDGE**
D/TD− T Gilberti and G Rivetti with E Croux and A Ottoz, 17−18 Aug
38   1940

Remotely situated above the Mt Blanc glacier, this route follows the crest of the ridge throughout. The climbing in the first two thirds, on good granite, is considered extremely fine. The rock above is, however, very friable. Over 1000m to the junction with the Brouillard Ridge.

Mont Blanc: Brenva Face

Together with the E face of Monte Rosa this is the largest sweep of snow and ice in the Alps. The height of the face is 1400m and the routes become steeper, more difficult and more serious as one progresses towards the Grand Pilier d'Angle. There are more than a dozen routes and variations which all exhibit, to a lesser or greater degree, serious objective danger. Climbs face E and it is essential to be well established on the routes before dawn. As some of the routes, together with those on the Grand Pilier d'Angle, have complex approaches in the dark, it may be wise to bivouac at Col Moore the previous evening to enable a visual inspection of the lower face in daylight.

73 **BRENVA SPUR**

AD/D   G Mathews, A Moore, F and H Walker with J and M Anderegg, 15 July 1865. Winter: J Couzy and A Vialatte, 26 Feb 1956

39

A tremendous classic and the easiest route on the face taking the ridge above Col Moore. Difficulty varies from year to year but the upper seracs are generally stable and objective danger minimal. While the technical difficulty is not high, fitness and good acclimatisation are important.

Reach the upper plateau of the Brenva glacier from either the Trident (easier) or Col de la Fourche Huts, and cross this crevassed ground to reach Col Moore (c3500m, 1hr)
    The lower section of the ridge is climbed on the L flank and there are many variations as the ground is fairly vague. The most common mistake when zig zagging up easy terrain on the flank is to work too far L, away from the crest.
    From Col Moore climb the first little rock step on the L side by a small chimney. Make a descending traverse L (awkward and exposed) and then head towards the crest on broken rock. Below a large buttress follow a ledge on the L and at its end climb up steep yet easy rock to the top of the buttress and follow the crest to a narrow horizontal ridge (2hr). This famous ice ridge is normally snowy and is followed to the upper slopes. Starting these can be quite steep in some years but above, a uniform slope (possibly crevassed) leads to the highest rocks. Turn these on the L and so reach the vicinity of the serac barrier. According to conditions, either move delicately up L and climb a steep snow/ice slope directly through the barrier, or traverse R, to find a gully that normally leads up between the seracs. As a last resort, traverse below the seracs on the L to reach a big snow slope that runs up through the final barrier. (4–6hr)
    Join Route 60 and continue to the summit of Mt Blanc. 900m to the exit, 1300m to the summit, 9–11hr from the hut.

74 **RED SENTINEL**

D+   T Graham Brown and F Smythe, 1–2 Sept 1927. Winter: W Bonatti and G Panei, 9 March 1961

39

This splendid route, the first of the Brenva triptych is a masterpiece of route finding which leads directly to the summit. Though the difficulties are not great, the objective dangers are potentially very high. The route is threatened by serac fall throughout most of the first half and it is essential to reach the Great Couloir or preferably the base of the Twisting Rib before dawn. Though not very difficult it is a serious undertaking.

Follow Route 73 to Col Moore (1hr). Make a rising traverse L for 250m on snow and rock, crossing four vague couloir lines to a larger ice slope (stone and icefall danger on most of this section). Climb the slope to the base of a high rock tower – the Red Sentinel (c3800m, 1½hr). Climb up L to the crest of a long rocky ridge that forms the R side of the Great Couloir. Climb the R side of the couloir then make a long ascending traverse L across it to reach the 'Twisting Rib' (danger from avalanche and serac fall). Climb the R side of the rib then the crest, turning a steep high step on the R, to reach an icy crest. The rock wall above is split by a diagonal chimney leading to the upper slopes. Slant R up the slopes on snow and rock, then climb more directly avoiding serac barriers to reach easy slopes leading to the summit (7–9hr). 1300m;8½–10½hr from the hut.

75   ROUTE MAJOR

TD–   T Graham Brown and F Smythe, 6–7 Aug 1928. First calendar
39   winter ascent: M Shigi, Feb 1976

The finest route on the Brenva face and one of great character. More sustained than the Red Sentinel with strenuous climbing at 4400m on the final rock buttress. It is essential to have crossed the Great Couloir before dawn but once established on the spur, the route is sheltered from avalanche and seracfall. Very occasionally the top seracs become unstable and it would be wise to try and check on this before departure. Another serious route.

Follow Route 74 to the Red Sentinel (2½hr). (A commmon mistake on this section is to end up too low where the Sentinel can be difficult to identify in the dark). Climb up L to the crest on the R of the Great Couloir. Cross the couloir above its lower and steeper narrow section (60–80m, 45°) to reach the base of a large rock buttress on the L side (about 1hr). Gaining the crest can be quite difficult so it is easier to turn this whole buttress on the R using the steep snowy flank of the Great Couloir. Alternatively climb the crest and turn a steep step with a thin gendarme, on the R. Continue up a series of snow crests separated by small rock buttresses in a magnificent position. The final buttress now looms above. A short wall climbed by a 5m icy chimney leads to a snow-covered shelf. It is possible to climb directly up the buttress from here but it is steep, strenuous and icy (V). The best solution traverses up and R under the buttress to a short leaning corner whose R wall is a rib projecting finger-like down the slope. Climb the short crack to the crest (IV). One can also traverse down and around the toe of the rib reaching this point from the far side. Climb a snow couloir on the R and a steep icy chimney above (100m, III/IV) to the top of the buttress. Above lies the final serac barrier which can often be the crux of the climb. Cross it to the final slopes (6–8hr). These are easy (30°) but can be prone to wind slab, and lead via Col Major to the summit (1–2hr). 1300m, 10½–13½hr from the hut.

76 THE PEAR BUTTRESS

TD

39

T Graham Brown with A Graven and A Aufdenblatten, 5 Aug 1933.
Winter: A and A Ollier and F Salluard, 8–9 Feb 1965

The third of the Brenva triptych and a magnificent route. The climbing is harder and more sustained than the Major and considerably more dangerous. There are very few sections of the route that are not exposed to avalanche and stone/ice fall and for this reason the climb still sees few ascents. It is essential to reach the base of the 'Pear' before dawn. A serious route. See also Photo 40

From Col Moore traverse almost horizontally across rock ribs and couloirs to the large ice slopes below the Great Couloir. Slant L up these (30°) to the ridge line rising towards the Pear Buttress (2hr). Follow the crest and climb the initial steep lower slabs of the Pear. Climb the L side for 4 pitches then trend R climbing increasingly difficult rock (III and IV) to the top of the buttress – the last 40m being quite exposed to serac fall from the L. Continue up the crest, passing to the L of the little Aig de la Belle Etoile (4349m) and climb up some rocks over a hump. There is a steep snow/ice couloir on the R. Either cross it and climb to the top of the rock rognon, then continue up snow slopes to the summit ridge generally turning the final serac barrier on the R, or slant L to a rock buttress coming down from the Peuterey Ridge and climb steep snow and ice to the R of this finishing up the ridge to Mt Blanc de Courmayeur. 1300m, 11–14hr from the hut to the summit of Mt Blanc de Courmayeur.

Mont Blanc: Grand Pilier d'Angle 4243m

This shoulder of the Peuterey Ridge has two distinct faces rising above the Brenva glacier. The NE face, which contains a considerable number of routes in close proximity, offers some of the finest mixed climbing in the range. The large serac barrier on the upper part of the face is often fairly stable especially towards its L end, and the main danger lies on the approach which is seriously threatened by the large seracs on the L of the Pear. The E face is a huge rock wall and contains areas of both good and bad granite, subjecting the routes to stonefall. An ascent of the Grand Pilier d'Angle is a serious proposition as the only logical way off is to continue over the summit of Mt Blanc by following the Peuterey Ridge, which adds another 4–8hr to the ascent.

77 **NORTH-EAST FACE (BONATTI-ZAPPELLI ROUTE)**

ED1 W Bonatti and C Zappelli, 22–23 June 1962. Winter: R Chéré and D Monaci, 22–24 Dec 1975

40

The original route on the face and although the technical difficulties are not great, the climbing in the lower section is quite dangerous and speed is important. It is essential to reach the rocks of the 'sinuous rib' before dawn, and to undertake the climb only in cold and snowy conditions. See also Photo 39

Follow Route 73 to Col Moore and descend to the upper plateau of the Brenva glacier. Cross it in a wide arc to the L, so minimising the avalanche danger from the Great Couloir, and reach the vicinity of the lower point of the Grand Pilier d'Angle (about 1hr). Cross a rimaye that can often prove problematical, and climb steep slopes close to the rock wall of the Grand Pilier d'Angle on the L. Slant up R on a big snow slope to reach the foot of the sinuous rock rib. Climb this to a steep icy rock wall. Traverse R 30m then climb icy grooves for 120m (crux) to reach, on the R, the base of the large ice couloir running up to the R of the hanging glacier. Traverse across and climb the R side of this, slanting back L near the top above the large serac barrier (stonefall possible). Continue directly up the ice slope to the Peuterey Ridge where several small bivouac sites are available. 750m, 11–14hr from Col Moore.

78 **DUFOUR-FREHEL ROUTE BY DIRECT FINISH**

TD+/ED1 G Dufour and J Fréhel, 11 Aug 1973. Direct Finish: J Boivin and P Vallençant, 23 July 1975

40

This combination of routes has become the most popular means of ascent of this section of the face, and is probably the quickest and technically the easiest line. Although observation has shown that the upper serac barrier invariably avalanches into the gully on the R of the face, any debris from the L side of the barrier, however minimal, will be channelled down the direct finish.As always on this face, a hard frost is essential. See also Photo 39

Follow Route 77 and continue up the ice slope to the L of the sinuous rock rib for 200–300m (45°–50°) until the central rock wall is reached. Trend L up steep mixed ground to a gully line and climb it for 4 or 5 pitches (70°, 5m wide and about Scottish 4). Pass the 50m high serac barrier on the L (45°–50°) and climb the snow/ice slopes above for 200m to the Peuterey Ridge. 750m, 9hr from Col Moore.

79 **DIRECT START**
ED1 J Bouchard (who finished to the L of the couloir via a difficult rock
39 buttress), 14 July 1975. Winter: R Ghilini and B Muller, 3–5 March 1976

The Boivin-Vallençant couloir of the previous route can be reached directly by a steeper and more difficult line on the L side of the lower ice slope. This crosses several icy rock bands and a good covering of snow is preferable. Excellent mixed climbing – probably safer than the Dufour-Fréhel start. 750m. See also Photo 40

80 **GABARROU-LONG ROUTE**
TD+ P Gabarrou and A Long, 15 July 1983
40

This takes the rock buttress, starting at its lowest point, to the R of the Cecchinel-Nominé route. The rock needs to be dry but the granite is magnificent and the difficulties not too high (IV to V+). Either finish up Route 81 or climb the ice couloir on the R. 750m, 8–10hr. See also Photo 39

81 **CECCHINEL-NOMINE ROUTE**
TD+/ED1 W Cecchinel and G Nominé, 16–17 Sept 1971. Winter: I Ganahl, T
40 Holdener, R Homberger and H Kasper, 22–23 Dec 1974

This modern classic provides the best and safest route on the face, giving fine steep climbing with equal interest on rock and ice. Once established on the route the risks are minimal, the fall line of the hanging glacier above being well to the R. See also Photo 39

Follow Route 77, climbing the steep slopes above the initial rimaye to cross a second rimaye, finally slanting up to the first main gully on the L. This gully is more of a steeply inclined ramp which rises diagonally to the L and bounded on the R by an almost vertical rock wall. Climb the gully (55°) to its end under a steep rock wall. Climb the overhanging and icy crack on the R (15m, V and A1) and continue up a very narrow runnel (70°, Scottish 3/4) which eases and broadens (50°–60°) to an icefield. Go up this for several pitches until a diagonal ramp leads out R onto the rock spur. Follow the ramp on mixed ground to a small icefield then work up L to a small tower 15m high. Climb the tower on the L by a crack that opens into a chimney (V+, icy). Trend R to the crest and climb it for 50m (V). A 10m diagonal rappel is then made to reach a block on the R from where a diagonal traverse is made further R on a large flake line (40m) leading to the top of the spur. Climb mixed ground and the ice slope above to a sharp col just R of the highest point. 750m, 10–12hr from Col Moore.

82 NORTH-EAST PILLAR

TD+/ED1

40

Lower section: L Cherenka, V Launer, P Mizicko, F Piacek, M Svec and P Tarabeck, 1–6 March 1976. Upper section: D Caise, C Grandmont and E Munting, 20–21 July 1977

The best line on this pillar, which maximises the ice climbing, is a logical combination of Czech and Belgian routes. Although some stonefall is possible on the lower section, the substance of the route is objectively safe and probably easier than the Cecchinel-Nominé. See also Photo 39

An initial steep couloir on the L of the pillar leads to a snowfield. Slant R up this and climb steep difficult rock into a long narrow couloir on the L of the crux section of Route 81. Follow this to its junction with Route 83 and continue to the summit of the Grand Pilier d'Angle. 800m, 8–10hr from Col Moore.

83 EAST FACE

TD+/ED1

40

W Bonatti and T Gobbi, 1–3 Aug 1957. Winter: A Dvorak, J Kurczak, A Mroz and T Pietrowsky, 5–9 March 1971

This was the first route to be completed on the Brenva face of the Grand Pilier d'Angle and although considered of classic status, it is still infrequently climbed. Though the difficulties lie primarily on rock, this is often quite loose on the first half of the route and there is always danger from stonefall. The icy transition onto the N face can often provide very delicate mixed climbing. There are numerous good bivouac sites, though a fast party should be able to complete the route in a day. See also Photo 39

The route follows a huge diagonal chimney line beginning up and L of the lowest rock on the E face. One can follow this from the start but it is better to climb a steep dièdre, at the lowest point on the face, which slants up L for 200m. From its end climb up for 4 pitches and gain the chimney line. Follow this in its entirety, a succession of wide cracks, chimneys and overhangs. Often the back walls are full of loose blocks and the ribs or walls on either side provide the best means of ascent (sustained IV and V with several pitches of V+). At the top of the chimneys a narrow snowy terrace line leads Rwards to another series of chimneys. Climb these and the grooves above (IV and IV+) to the crest of the NE spur. In dry conditions it is possible to climb the crest directly but generally it is necessary to traverse R over difficult mixed ground for 50m to a vague couloir line and climb this for 150m to reach the crest on the L. Continue up the ridge on good rock (III and IV) to the summit. 900m

Other routes on the face appear to be seriously threatened by stonefall except for:

84
ED3/4
39

DIVINE PROVIDENCE
P Gabarrou and F Marsigny, 5–8 Aug 1984

A hard direttissima which climbs the red tower situated high on the face above the Bonatti-Gobbi chimneys. The substance of the route, the 350m tower, was compared to the S face of the Fou. It is probably the hardest climb to date leading to the summit of Mt Blanc. Good bivouac sites are rare. See also Photo 40

To the R of the start of Route 83 is another rock spur coming down just as low on the glacier. On the R side of this a huge ramp line slants up L for 400m to join the Bonatti-Gobbi chimneys (IV and V with a few harder pitches). On the L climb straight up in wide cracks and continue fairly directly up the steep red walls above (sustained V to VII/VII+ and A2/A3) to join Route 83. Follow this for another 150m to the summit. 900m

This tremendous ridge rises from the Col de Peuterey but the name is often applied to include its lower continuation over the Aigs Blanche and Noire. It is one of the best and certainly the longest ridge route of its class in the Alps. Although in good conditions difficulties are not that great and are mainly on snow/ice, the level of commitment is very high and a good standard of fitness is essential. Escape from the Col de Peuterey is a lengthy and serious undertaking. The upper ridge, first climbed by J Eccles with M Clémont and A Payot, 30–31 July 1877, was a remarkable exploit for its time.

85   **DAMES ANGLAISES RIDGE**
D+   L Obersteiner and K Schreiner, 30–31 July 1927

39

This is the normal approach and the classic method of climbing the Peuterey Ridge. Only a very fast party will complete the route from the Monzino Hut in a day and it is better to bivouac in the Dames Anglaises Hut or, as is more popular nowadays, on good sites before the Schneider Couloir which provides quicker and safer access to the ridge. See also Photos 42, 45 and 44

From the Monzino Hut go N to the Châtelet glacier. Go up the R side and climb the couloir descending from the Col de l'Innominata on rotten rock (2½hr). Descend or rappel down equally rotten rock to the Frêney glacier and cross this very crevassed area, with some danger of serac fall from above, to the rimaye below the couloir leading to the Brèche N des Dames Anglaises (1½hr).

Either climb the couloir taking the L branch, which is narrow and enclosed, to the brèche (300m, stonefall, 1–2hr). Now traverse horizontally L on the Frêney side to a short chimney. Climb this and traverse L for c40m to a notch between two gendarmes (½hr). Or go up the glacier passing to the R of a rocky rognon close to the rocks below the Gugliermina. Just above, go horizontally R on an overhung gangway (the Schneider Ledges, good bivouac sites) and reach the Schneider Couloir by a chimney (III). Climb the couloir to the notch (1hr or more).

Continue up the secondary ridge above on easy rock to join the main SE ridge of the Aig Blanche above a steep buttress. Go up the ridge for a minute then traverse R across the Brenva flank crossing a couple of rocky crests until the third can be taken back to the main ridge at approximately ⅓ of the distance between the Gugliermina and the Aig Blanche. Follow the ridge, crossing a gap on the Brenva side, and continue up the long rocky crest (pitches of II) to the SE summit (3hr).

Continue along the sharp crest to the highest point of the Aig Blanche (or pass it on the Brenva flank). Follow the ridge to the NW summit which can be turned on the Frêney side to reach the ridge going down to the Col de Peuterey (1–2hr). Descend this on the Frêney side and then the ice slope below to the col (1hr, can be completed in 3–4 rappels if conditions are difficult).

There are now two alternatives to reach the top of the Grand Pilier d'Angle.

(a) Slant up L on snow or ice below the rocks of the Grand Pilier for about 60m. The angle above appears to ease so climb up rocks to the crest and follow it steeply to the shoulder. Continue along this on a fine snow crest turning a large gendarme on the R (2½–4½hr).

(b) Quicker in good snow conditions but more exposed to stonefall. Slant up L for 150m until directly below the large gendarme and reach it via a steep ice/mixed slope (2–4hr). There is an excellent bivouac site below the gendarme.

Continue up the ridge climbing a buttress on the R side and higher, fine snow or ice crests. A final ice slope and often a cornice leads to the summit of Mt Blanc de Courmayeur (4–8hr). Follow the ridge to the main summit (1hr). 17–21hr from the Monzino Hut.

86 PEUTEREY RIDGE INTEGRAL

TD+/ED1 R Hechtel and G Kittelmann, 24–26 July 1953. Winter: L Audoubert, M Feuillarade, M Galy, Y Seigneur, A and O Squinobal, 22–26 Dec 1972

This is the longest and probably the most difficult traverse of its kind in the Alps. There is more than 4500m of ascent over all types of terrain and in magnificent situations. Perhaps the most feared and sensational section of the route is the long series of free rappels from the summit of the Aig Noire which are badly exposed to stonefall in the lower reaches. Two bivouacs are normally necessary: in the vicinity of the summit of the Noire and on the Aig Blanche. The length and commitment of the climb make the overall grading higher than the sum of its individual parts and it is still rarely completed.

Starting from the Noire Hut climb the S ridge of the Noire by Route 142. Descend the N ridge by Route 143 to the Brèche S des Dames Anglaises and reach the Brèche N by Route 135. En route, it is possible also to include traverses of the Pt Casati and l'Isolée (both IV, 2 rappels on the descents). Continue up Route 85 to the summit of Mt Blanc.

For an escape from the Col de Peuterey in the event of bad weather, see Routes 124 and 125.

Mont Blanc: Frêney Face

Facing SE above the narrow upper plateau of the Frêney glacier, this face is characterised by four huge granite pillars which give some of the best and hardest rock climbing on Mt Blanc. The approach is long and serious and a retreat in the event of bad weather can be a very arduous and somewhat dangerous expedition.

The steep couloirs separating the pillars can offer difficult and relatively safe climbing but only at certain times of year and under the correct snow/ice conditions. At all times objective danger, in terms of falling rock and ice fragments, must be considered a risk.

The shortest and most popular approach to the face starts from the Trident Hut and involves climbing the NE side of the Col de Peuterey.

87	**DIRECT**
TD	W Bonatti and C Zappelli, 21 Sept 1961. Winter: T Hakuno, K Miyake and H Tsuda, 19–21 Jan 1976

This route rapidly comes into condition, giving varied climbing in exhilarating surroundings. After the initial section in the Great Couloir, which is best climbed at night, the route is objectively safe and offers a worthwhile if more remote alternative to the climbs on the Brenva face.

From the upper plateau of the Frêney glacier go up the R side of the Great Couloir for c200m then climb up R in a series of icy grooves (Scottish 3) to reach the crest of a broken rock buttress above. This buttress slants down L into the Great Couloir and it is possible to continue further up the couloir and climb the buttress in its entirety. Trend R across snowfields to another rocky crest and climb this and the mixed ground above (IV, icy) to the summit of Mt Blanc de Courmayeur. 800m, 9–11hr.

88
TD+
41

GREAT FRENEY COULOIR

M Bernardi, G Grassi and R Luzi, 2–3 Sept 1980. Winter: P Gabarrou and F Marsigny, 14 March 1984

The direct ascent of this involves climbing the only vertical ice-fall above 4500m in Europe! Although only 80m high, it is rarely in good condition and should be reached before sunrise. Above and below, the couloir is a straightforward 55° slope and the ice-fall can be avoided by climbing the rock barrier on the side (IV+, and a lower overall grading). 700m, 10–12 hr

89
TD+
41
1

RIGHT-HAND PILLAR

P Bollini and G Gervasutti, 13 Aug 1940. Winter: (direct finish) J Coudray, C Daubas and R Renaud, 24–28 Jan 1974

This is an exceptionally fine high altitude mountain route on generally excellent rock. It has unfortunately been overshadowed by its more famous neighbour and is still infrequently climbed. The climbing is not sustained having several sections of easier mixed ground that may in very dry conditions be subject to stonefall. Normally, once on the pillar the route is considered to be objectively safe. 700m

90
ED2
41

FRENEYSIE PASCALE

P Gabarrou and F Marsigny, 20–21 April 1984

The discontinuous couloir between the R-hand and central pillars gives a series of snow/ice slopes cut by difficult rocky/mixed pitches. The top section contains a series of 4 ice-falls that give steep and difficult climbing on a thin ice covering. 700m, 20hr

91
ED1
41
1

CENTRAL PILLAR

C Bonington, I Clough, J Djuglosz and D Whillans, 27–29 Aug 1961, followed immediately by R Desmaison, P Julien, I Piussi and Y Pollet-Villard, 28–29 Aug 1961. Winter: R Desmaison and R Flematti, 1–6 Feb 1967

An outstanding route that in its day was considered the hardest to the summit of Mt Blanc. The difficulties are nowadays not considered that great and are concentrated on the Chandelle. After many ascents the route has assumed classic status and it is possible to climb the hard sections almost entirely on the in situ aid. A fast party will reach the summit of Mt Blanc in a day, but there are good bivouac sites below and above the Chandelle. 500m for the pillar, 700m to the summit ridge.

92   **JORI BARDILL ROUTE**

ED2/3   J Bardill, M Piola and P Steiner, 10–12 Aug 1982

41

1

Although not considered in the same class as the original line, this route (originally V+ and A2) climbs directly up the L flank of the pillar. It was climbed completely free (VII+) in a day on the second ascent to qualify it as perhaps the most difficult high altitude rock climb in the Alps. Good rock and numerous bivouac sites throughout its length.

There are fixed rappel anchors all the way down the side of the steep chimney separating the Central and Hidden Pillars, but being very exposed to falling debris this descent can hardly be recommended.

93   **HIDDEN PILLAR**

ED2   T Frost and J Harlin, 1–2 Aug 1963. Winter: E Escoffier, A Estève and P Royer, 23–24 Jan 1983

41

1

Originally climbed largely by artificial means, this short but serious rock route nowadays gives fine free climbing on excellent granite (VII/VII+). Unfortunately there seems to be considerable objective danger even on the pillar itself due to rock and ice falling from large ledges at the top of the route. It is essential to climb the initial couloir at night to minimise the considerable stonefall risk from the gullies on either side of the pillar. 300m on the pillar.

94   **FANTOMASTIC**

ED2   P Gabarrou and F Marsigny, 4–5 April 1985

41

The steep gully on the L of the Hidden Pillar gives six difficult pitches on ice, mixed ground and finally rock, with bolt belays at every stance. Above, two steep mixed pitches lead to the easy summit snow slopes. 700m to the ridge.

95   **SOUTH PILLAR**

TD–   L Dubost and Y Seigneur, 25–26 July 1972. Winter: G Decorps, G Gaby and R Mizrahi, Jan 1976

41

More of a mountaineering route but still offering good climbing of a mixed nature. The upper section was first done as a variation finish to the Innominata by T Graham Brown with A Graven and A Aufdenblatten, 9 Aug 1933. Infrequently climbed.

Start up the couloir leading to the Hidden Pillar and almost immediately slant up L to the crest. This is fairly easy and broken

(III and IV) until a narrow snow ridge is reached below steep smooth walls. Climb down steeply on the R, then ascend cracks and an overhanging dièdre (V+ and A1) followed by an easier series of cracks (IV) to regain the crest below a monolithic gendarme. Turn the gendarme on the L side (IV, icy) then slant R up a ramp line (IV) on the upper pillar. Chimney lines (IV and V) followed by cracks on the crest of the pillar (IV) lead to a fine snow crest. Follow this to the summit ridge. 700m to summit ridge, 8–10hr

96   **ABOMINETTE**
TD–   P Gabarrou, C Profit and S Tavernier, 25 April 1984

41

This is the easiest of the new ice routes on the S face but is still a very fine climb with several quite steep sections offering good belays and protection. As always a good snow covering and a hard frost are essential to minimise stone and ice fall in the upper section.

Climb the couloir to the L of the S Pillar finishing with a steep ice-fall (50m, 70°). Go up the central snow slope and reach the gully on the L of the upper S Pillar either directly or via the rock on the R (IV and V). Climb the gully (50m, 65°–80°) to the upper slopes and follow these to the Brouillard Ridge. 700m, 6–7hr

97   **INNOMINATA DIRECT ROUTE**
TD–   J Galmiche and F Leduc with H Agresti, 18 Aug 1973

41

An interesting mountaineering route with the technical difficulties primarily on excellent rock. The climb finishes directly up the final steep tower avoided by the Innominata route, and is rarely repeated.

The initial climbing takes place on the spur just R of the lower Innominata Ridge and is most conveniently reached from the Eccles Hut. On the L side of the first 200m red pyramid climb a snowy couloir and when almost at the top, traverse out R to the crest of the pyramid (V). Climb up the crest (IV+) crossing Abominette and continue on snow to the ridge above the second tower of the Innominata. Climb the ridge avoiding a tower by traversing R into the Abominette gully and traversing back L to the crest below the top ice-fall. Climb the final steep tower just L of the crest by cracks and chimneys (V+ and A1, then IV) and continue up the fine snow ridge. 700m, 11hr

98   **INNOMINETTE**
TD+/ED1 P Gabarrou and A Long, 9 July 1985

To the L of the Innominata lower ridge is a large concave face which is climbed in its centre via three steep ice-falls easily visible from a distance (ice up to 90°). After crossing the large central snow slope, climb the gully L of the final tower on Route 97 (mixed, IV and V) to reach the long snow crest leading to the Brouillard Ridge. 800m, 12–14hr

99   **INNOMINATA RIDGE**
D/D+   S Courtaud and E Oliver with A Aufdenblatten, A and H Rey, 19–20 Aug 1909. First calendar winter ascent: H Boisier, J Choffat, N Poutel and Y Seigneur, 30–31 Jan 1981

41

A classic excursion at high altitude with difficulties on snow, ice and rock. It is shorter, and harder and less committing, than the Peuterey and perhaps as good. The crossing of the huge central basin is exposed to stonefall though the rock climbing, a trifle strenuous at times, is on excellent granite. See also Photo 42

From the Eccles Bivouac Huts traverse L and climb a snow slope to the Col Eccles (c4000m). A snow crest leads to the first step. Climb it directly up the L side on good steep rock (III) to below 2 red towers. A 40m chimney leads to a ledge R of the first tower (IV). Climb a short wall (IV) then turn the tower on the R and go through a hole to reach the col behind it. Climb the crest to the R of the second tower (III). A snow crest leads to the second step which is turned on the L (mixed ground) to reach the base of the central snow basin. Cross it and slant up snowy rocks on the L for about 140m to reach a narrow icy couloir at the foot of a vertical red tower. The couloir slants up to the L and is followed to the crest of the buttress. Follow this long buttress over rock steps and short ice slopes to a steep snow crest merging at mid-height with the true line of the Innominata Ridge on the R. Follow this to the Brouillard Ridge at c4650m (800m. 5–8hr from the huts). Continue over Mt Blanc de Courmayeur to the summit of Mt Blanc (3hr). 8–11hr from the Eccles Bivouac Huts.

100   **INNOMINATA RIDGE INTEGRAL**
First ascent in this manner by V Etis and F Lorenzi, Aug 1972. Winter, finishing up the final tower on Route 97: L Audobert and M Batard, 21–22 Feb 1981

The continuation of the ridge below the Eccles Huts can be followed in its entirety beginning with either the S ridge, or classic route on the SE face of the Aig Croux. Continue over the Punta Innominata to descend the N ridge on loose mixed ground to the Col Frêney. See Routes 119, 118 and 116

101   **BROUILLARD SPUR**
TD–   B Bougé, R Ducournau, J Franchon and R Mizrahi, 13–14 July 1975

The lower section of the long rock buttress on Route 99 takes the form of a wide rounded spur falling to the upper plateau of the Brouillard glacier. The first buttress, lying on the L of a vertical pillar, is climbed slightly R of the crest (V and V+). Slant L up the snow slopes above then climb a rock buttress on the L (IV+) to the crest of the upper spur. After a snow ridge, climb the R flank of the buttress above to join Route 99 (IV and V) and continue up this to the summit. 800m, 12hr

Mont Blanc: Brouillard Face

Rising 600m above the upper plateau of the Brouillard glacier, this face is split in its lower half by four vertical pillars separated by narrow couloirs containing numerous vertical ice-falls and is reached from the Eccles huts via Route 114. The pillars themselves are only 350m high, giving way to easy loose mixed ground above. They can be rappelled. A complete ascent to the Brouillard Ridge and finally the summit of Mt Blanc is a long, serious and sustained enterprise which is subject to all the vagaries of weather for which this side of the mountain is well known. The climbs are graded accordingly.

As with the Frêney Pillars, approaches are long though perhaps not as serious due to the haven afforded by the Eccles Huts. However retreat in bad weather can still be an arduous and dangerous undertaking due to avalanche-prone slopes and a badly crevassed glacier. For those leaving the valley late in the day it is worth bearing in mind that the foot of the pillars can be reached in 3–4hr from the shoulder 3281m on the approach to the Eccles Huts.

102 GABARROU-LONG ROUTE

ED1

43

P Gabarrou and A Long, 20–21 July 1983

This climbs the rock immediately to the R of the Hypercouloir and is characterised in its upper section by a spur comprising a succession of four rock buttresses. Whilst the line in the upper half is escapable, doing so would expose one to stonefall.

Start just R of the couloir and climb a huge dièdre/chimney to the top of the buttress (V+). Continue in the same line (IV to VII−) before crossing a large couloir on the L to gain the upper spur. Climb the buttresses directly, the fourth being the hardest (VII). 800m, 15hr.

103 HYPERCOULOIR

ED2

43

P Gabarrou and P Steiner, 13–14 May 1982. Winter: E Escoffier, C Profit and R Royer, 11–12 Jan 1983

Immediately R of the R-hand pillar of Brouillard is a steep and narrow couloir which gives a succession of 5 vertical ice-falls with a number of overhanging bulges in its first 400m. It has received several ascents and is considered one of the finest and most difficult ice climbs in the range. 600m, 16–19hr from the Eccles Hut to Mt Blanc.

104 RIGHT-HAND PILLAR OF BROUILLARD

TD+/ED1

43

2

C Bonington and J Harlin; R Baillie and B Robertson, 21 Aug 1965 to just below the Brouillard Ridge. Rappel descent. It was repeated in the same fashion before completion to the summit of Mt Blanc by a Polish team in 1974.

A magnificent climb, especially in the upper section of the pillar which has still received relatively few ascents. At present it is essentially free with a few short sections of artificial climbing. After bad weather snow on the lower section clears surprisingly slowly. 600m, 10–14hr to the ridge.

105 ETICA BISBETICA

ED1

43

G Grassi, I Meneghin and M Rossi, 28–29 July 1986

This climbs the prodigious red dièdre that cleaves the L side of the R-hand pillar and was the scene of the original attempts on the upper wall by Bonington and Baillie. A tremendous free climb on excellent granite and highly recommended by the first ascent party. A selection of blade pegs could prove useful.

From the start of the original route traverse L across the snow slope and reach an area of good granite lying to the L of an intrusion of steep shattered rock. Climb up cracks to some ledges then reach the base of a dièdre where the solid wall meets the shattered rock on the R (50m, IV). Climb a deep chimney in the L wall of the dièdre for one pitch (VI) then continue up less difficult slabs (V) to a dièdre-crack. Climb it (VI) to some ledges then continue up slabs to a good terrace beneath the zone of overhangs (V−). Climb up a few m then traverse L round a corner and climb a big slab (V). Continue up a dièdre-crack (V+) then traverse L and and take a second dièdre (V+) finally reaching the extensive terraces (which are clearly visible from afar) via easier ground (V−).

Reach a system of cracks on the L and climb them to the base of the huge red dièdre (V+ and VI). Climb up on the R at first but pretty soon there is no alternative but to follow the single layback crack in the back of the dièdre – an excellent pitch (VI+). Follow the line of the dièdre for three more pitches, at first climbing round a roof on the L side and continuing up cracks and flakes, then the dièdre itself. Finish up a wide crack in the back onto a terrace with big blocks (V and VI).

Climb an overhang on the R (V) and continue up easier slabs (IV+) to exit into a broken gully. One more pitch on easy slabs leads to the top of the pillar where the original route is joined. 11 pitches, 350m.

106 **HYPERGOULOTTE**
ED2/3 B Grison and L Mailly, 20 April 1984. Winter: E Escoffier and D
43 Lacroix, 25 Feb 1985

This thin runnel between the R-hand and Central Pillars is probably the hardest of the S facing ice gullies. It rarely forms. 600m

107/8 **CENTRAL PILLAR**
TD+ British Route: E Jones, 15–16 July 1971, to the Brouillard Ridge.
43 Polish Route: A Dvorak, M Grochowski and W Jedlinski, 16–17
2 Aug 1971. Winter: P Berhault and J Boivin, 13 Feb 1982

This lies in the depression between the R-hand and Red Pillars and does not stand proud of the face. Consequently there is stonefall danger throughout its length and no protected bivouac sites. Two routes have been completed which both share a common start, the British Route perhaps giving the better climbing on the R edge of the pillar. Neither route has received many ascents. 650m

109   **CASCADE DE NOTRE DAME**

ED2   P Gabarrou and F Marsigny, 14–15 Oct 1984. Winter: B Grison, 24

43   Feb 1985

Considered to be equally as good as the Hypercouloir it has already seen several ascents. The substance of the route lies in the upper gully, although the initial ice-fall is very steep. The top of the gully is reached via a succession of 3 ice-falls all having vertical sections and supplied with good belays. The second is the longest (80m) and most sustained. c700m, 10–12hr for the difficulties.

The L branch, named The Devil's Ice-fall, was climbed by E Escoffier and D Lacroix on 24 Feb 1985 in 5hr.

Mont Blanc: Brouillard Face continued below

Mont Blanc: Brouillard Face, Red Pillar

The well-defined tower of superb red rock is the most obvious attraction in this remote amphitheatre and consequently the original route has received enough ascents to be considered of classic status.

110   **ORIGINAL ROUTE**

EDI   W Bonatti and A Oggioni, 5–6 July 1959. Winter: R Ito and N

43   Ogawa, 21–23 Jan 1972

2

This has become relatively popular in recent years though the climbing, of a strenuous nature up a series of chimneys (V+/VI and A1) on the L side of the pillar, is somewhat overrated. The first ascent party approached these chimneys from the gully on the L but this is very exposed to stonefall and on the second ascent a direct start was added which makes the route both safer and more homogeneous. Nowadays this is the preferred method of ascent. The chimneys are often icy and will require sections of aid climbing. However when dry the route has been climbed completely free when it is a grade harder (VII). 700m (350m for the pillar). 6–8hr for the pillar, 10–12hr to Pt Louis Amédée.

111 **DIRECTISSIMA**

ED3 P Gabarrou and A Long, 28–29 July 1984. Winter: T Cesen, 4 Feb

43 1989

2

This brilliant route has understandably seen few ascents. It offers extremely difficult free climbing at high altitude and is considered one of the harder rock climbs on Mt Blanc. A good bivouac can be made on the ledges below the crux pitch. 350–400m on the pillar. 700m to Pt Louis Amédée.

Mont Blanc: Brouillard Face continued

112 **BROUILLARD GIVRANT**

ED1 E Bellin and J Boivin, 24 Feb 1985

43

The short couloir to the L of the Red Pillar leading to the gap behind the S Pillar. 400m, 7hr

113 **SOUTH PILLAR**

TD+ R Kowalewski, J Maczka and W Wroz, 13–14 Aug 1971

43

A short route with sections of poor rock. It has not gained popularity. 600m to Pt Louis Amédée, 10hr

114 **BROUILLARD RIDGE**

AD+ K Blodig, H Jones, G Young with J Knubel, 9 Aug 1911. Winter: J

38 Clémenson, B and G Dufour, 14–15 Jan 1976

A long and tiring ascent at high altitude. The upper ridge is a fine high level snow crest but below Pt Louis Amédée the ground is loose, dangerous and the approaches to Col Emile Rey exposed to stonefall. Cold and snowy conditions would render the ascent much safer and give more enjoyable though more difficult climbing. It is essential to be above the Col Emile Rey at dawn. Though not often done in its entirety, the upper ridge is often followed after an ascent of the Frêney or Brouillard faces. A serious route.

Scramble down the ridge directly below the Eccles Huts to the Brouillard glacier and traverse underneath a serac barrier to reach the plateau beneath the pillars. Alternatively it is possible to traverse horizontally NW for 100m and then descend to the plateau, but this can involve a difficult crossing of a huge rimaye. Cross the plateau and climb the couloir to the Col Emile Rey (4030m, 1½hr). It is also possible to reach the Col Emile Rey via the 45° snow couloir on the W side. From the Quintino Sella Hut traverse horizontally across the little glacier and continue in the same line, crossing three rounded buttresses separated by couloirs, to the Mt Blanc glacier (1½hr). Cross the crevassed glacier to the couloir (3½–5hr from the hut to the col).

Work down and out onto the S face for 20m to reach a narrow rocky couloir. Climb the couloir (1 slab pitch of III) and the broken ground above (stonefall) on the R of a gendarme to a long snow slope leading to the ridge. Follow easy broken rocks to Pt Louis Amédée (2½–4hr). Descend the far side on the R flank to below a gap in the ridge. Climb the step above this gap either by a crack on the L of the ridge (III, good rock) or easier but loose rock on the R. Follow the ridge to a second and less steep step which is climbed on the R side. A short horizontal section leads to the junction with the Innominata Ridge. Continue along a sharp snow crest which can often develop huge cornices on the Frêney side, to a 30m rock buttress. Climb the L side on steep mixed terrain and continue to the summit of Mt Blanc de Courmayeur (4–6hr). Beyond an easy ridge leads to the main summit in 1hr. The rocky summit of Mt Blanc de Courmayeur can equally be turned on the L to reach the easy ridge beyond. 1400m from the foot of the col to the summit of Mt Blanc. 9–12½hr from the Eccles Bivouac Huts, 11–16hr from the Quintino Sella Hut.

115   BROUILLARD INTEGRAL
L Cozzon, L Henry, R Salluard and C Zappelli, 3–5 July 1973

Beginning with the S ridge of the Aigs Rouges de Brouillard, this long and rather tedious undertaking continues over PtBaretti and Mt Brouillard to join Route 114 at Col Emile Rey. It possibly provides the safest way to reach or retreat from Col Emile Rey.

Mont Brouillard 4069m

Rarely ascended but easily reached from Col Emile Rey in 20 min. Routes to the summit are on poor rock and threatened by stonefall.

Punta Innominata 3729m

A Durazzo with J Grange and S Henry, 23 July 1872

A popular peak and famous viewpoint.

116   **SOUTH-EAST RIDGE**
PD+   E Mackenzie with L Croux and C Ollier, 28 Aug 1895

`42`

The normal route, though quite long and a little complicated. It is usually taken in descent. As the rock is not that good the route gives better climbing early in the season when the ridge is still snow-covered.

From the Monzino Hut follow Route H14 towards the Eccles Huts as far as the scree slopes below the S face of the Punta Innominata. Work up R to reach the ridge about ⅓ of the way up (2½hr). Continue up the crest, turning a gendarme and keeping more on the R side towards the top. Reach the fore-summit (3620m, 1½hr) and continue along the mixed ridge to the main summit. 5hr from the hut.

     The ridge can be followed in its entirety from the Col de l'Innominata with an initial pitch of IV just above the col.

117   **SOUTH RIDGE**
AD–   P Preuss and U di Vallepiana, 28 July 1913

`42`

A pleasant and enjoyable route – the best on the mountain.

From the Monzino Hut follow Route H14 towards the Eccles Huts as far as the shoulder (3281m) below the first gendarme on the S ridge. Traverse R on ledges then climb a chimney with one or two moves of IV/IV+. More ledges lead Rwards to the gap behind the first gendarme. Turn the next 3 small gendarmes on the R (III) to reach a gap below a big buttress. Trend across L for 20m to reach a secondary ridge of poor rock and follow it to the fore-summit (4–5hr). Follow the mixed ridge to the main top. 5–6hr from the hut.

Aiguille Croux 3256m

M Mazzucchi with J and H Croux, 25 Aug 1900

This small summit at the end of the Innominata Ridge offers splendid rock climbing in close proximity to the Monzino Hut and has become justifiably popular.

118 NORTH-WEST RIDGE

PD+ M Magni, E Santi and M Tedeschi, 10 Sept 1907

42

A short connection with the Col de l'Innominata.

Follow Route 85 to the Col de l'Innominata. Climb directly up the ridge on improving rock starting with a shattered diagonal crack (III). The last pitch to the summit block is a curious overhang on the Frêney side. 1–1½hr from the col.

119 SOUTH RIDGE

PD+/AD– *The normal route, short but interesting with one superb pitch. In situ*
42 *anchors allow the route to be rappelled in descent.*

From the Monzino Hut go up the Châtelet glacier towards the Col de l'Innominata. Just before reaching the couloir slant up R on easy rock and snow slopes to a small col on the S ridge. A more elegant means of reaching this col is to climb the ridge directly from its base (pitches of III). Climb the great slab above (40m, IV) to reach a shoulder. The main summit is a few minutes above. About 200m, 3hr from the hut.

120 EAST-NORTH-EAST SPUR

VI/A1 P Nava with A Ottoz, 3 Sept 1955

A short difficult route up the impressive rock wall overlooking the Frêney glacier. The approach involves crossing the Col de l'Innominata and traversing smooth slabs along the base of the NE face. Rarely repeated. 250m, 12hr from the hut.

121 SOUTH-EAST SPUR DIRECT

VI/A2/3 G Bertone and C Zappelli, 12–14 July 1967

3

Very sustained climbing up the crest of the spur seen in profile from the Monzino Hut. Lengthy sections of difficult artificial climbing. 300m

122 SOUTH-EAST FACE

V/V+ E Hurzler and A Ottoz, 5 July 1935

42
3

Exposed and generally delicate climbing has made this route a popular classic. It comes into condition very quickly after bad weather. In situ anchors make it possible to descend the route in 10 rappels. 300m, 6hr

Col de Peuterey 3934m

First traverse J Harlin and G Hemming, 27–28 Aug 1961

A feature on the classic ascent of the Peuterey Ridge it is nowadays normally reached from the N side en route to the Frêney face or Upper Peuterey Ridge.

123   **NORTH-EAST COULOIR**
D
44

G and M Herzog with G Rébuffat and L Terray, 15 Aug 1944.
Wintert: R Desmaison and R Flematty, 1 Feb 1967

Though not of high technical difficulty, this route is somewhat exposed to stonefall. A hard frost is essential and it is recommended that departure from the Trident Hut is made early enough to complete the couloir before dawn. Serious.

From the Trident Hut follow Route 77 towards the Grand Pilier (2hr) and climb the couloir crossing several rimayes. Near the top work up L and reach the col via a wide and steep couloir to the L of the rock (3–4hr). 550m, allow 6hr from the hut.

124   **WEST FLANK**
AD/AD+
From the Eccles Huts, follow Route 99 to Col Eccles and go up the snow crest a little way towards the first step. Slant L (facing out) down the steep snow slope leading to the Upper Frêney Plateau, cross a difficult rimaye and traverse the glacier to the col. 2½hr

125   **DESCENT BY ROCHERS GRUBER**
AD+
In bad weather all descents from the upper plateau of the Frêney glacier pose problems. Descending by the Rochers Gruber has the advantage of losing altitude and reaching more sheltered ground rather quickly. However it is exposed to stonefall and the Frêney glacier is badly crevassed, making route-finding difficult in poor weather. This route is not recommended in ascent. Serious.

From Col de Peuterey descend SSW over gradually steepening snow slopes and locate the top of a snow rib which becomes quite steep and very narrow lower down. Follow it to the top of the Rochers Gruber. Good fixed anchors have been left all the way down the crest. Rappel to the rimaye (3600m) and descend the L side of the Frêney glacier, traversing R near the bottom to reach the Col de l'Innominata.

Aiguille Blanche de Peuterey 4112m

H Seymour King with E Rey, A Supersaxo and A Anthamatten, 31 July 1885

A beautiful mountain from almost every angle with its three summits linked by elegant snow crests. The easiest route to the central summit is represented by the first part of the Peuterey Ridge to Mt Blanc (Route 85) making this one of the most difficult of the Alpine 4000m peaks.

Aiguille Blanche de Peuterey: North Face

This presents three excellent ice climbs set in splendid surroundings. The angle of the face is generally not that great and the difficulty and/or danger encountered en route is determined by the state of the central serac barrier, which in recent years has been relatively stable. The remote situation makes all these climbs a serious proposition for their grades.

126
D+
`44`

RIGHT-HAND ROUTE

M Bastien, M Coutin, G Gaudin and P Julien, 6 July 1952

The easiest and safest of the three routes on the face passing the serac barrier on the R and leading directly to the summit. About 700m, 5–7hr from the Trident Hut.

127
D+/TD–
`44`

LEFT-HAND ROUTE

R Chabod and A Grivel, 4 Sept 1933. Winter: L Belfrond and A Ollier, 18 March 1961

The classic route on the face and the most interesting. A long rising traverse is made from the base of the couloir leading to the Col de Peuterey to gain the ice ridge above its lower rocky section. The difficulty of the crux pitch, surmounting the serac barrier, varies from year to year. 700m, 6–8hr from the hut.

128
D+/TD–
`44`

NORTH-EAST COULOIR

P Gabarrou and M Suzuki, 28 July 1975

The fine narrow couloir on the L side of the ridge taken by Route 127 is constantly exposed to ice fall from the serac barrier until the latter can be turned on the L side. 800m, 6–8hr from the hut. Objectively serious.

Aiguille Blanche de Peuterey: South-West Face

A number of routes have been climbed on the rocky pillars overlooking the Frêney glacier. Approaches are long and the rock is poor with serious stonefall. One route may be worthy of attention.

129   **CENTRAL SPUR**
TD   P Olivet and D Roulin, 21–22 Aug 1974

42

This is the pronounced spur on the R side of the great couloir descending from the gap between the SE and central summits. Apart from one section the rock is generally good and the first ascent party thought the climbing in the first 200m to be comparable with the Gervasutti Pillar.

Reach the foot of the spur (stonefall) in 4–5hr from the Monzino Hut. The initial climbing takes place on or near the crest of a superb red pillar (V+ and a little A1). From the gap, above, climb the R side of the spur for 150m on bad rock (V, poor protection). Continue on much sounder and steeper rock (a pitch of V+ and A1) to a huge gendarme on the crest. Turn this and the one above on the R (IV and III) and follow easy rocks to the SE summit. 700m, 15–20hr from the hut.

Pointe Gugliermina 3893m

A very steep and slender rock tower on the SE ridge of the Aig Blanche. It is well known for its fine exposed climbing on the face overlooking the Frêney glacier. The routes catch the sun for most of the day and clear rapidly after bad weather. Although very steep the climbing is not typical of many other granite routes in the range, being more akin to that found on limestone. There are good bivouac sites on the rognon (preferable) and on the Schneider Ledges. Approach via Route 85.

130   **LEFT-HAND PILLAR**
TD+   G Grassi and I Meneghin, 1982

45

This climbs the pillar round to the L of the Gervasutti route finishing up the final ridge. 600m

131   SOUTH-WEST FACE

TD/TD+   G Boccalatte and G Gervasutti, 17–18 Aug 1938. Winter: A
Anghileri, G Lanfranconi, Maccarinelli and Valsecchi, over 4 days
in Jan 1975

45
4

Deservedly classic and one of the finest rock climbs in the range.
Sustained and exposed climbing up the obvious pillar in the centre
of the face. There is some poor rock but it is excellent on the
difficult pitches and the route now sees many ascents. VI– and A1
or VII+ free. 600m in total, 7–9hr

132   SOUTH FACE DIRECT – MOONLIGHT SHADOW

ED1   J Boivin and L Broisin, in 2 days during Oct 1986

45

This climbs the very compact section of the S face to the R of the
previous route, taking an extremely direct line up vertical and
sometimes overhanging rock. Sustained free climbing with pitches
of VII– and one short section of aid. The route was descended by
rappel. 600m

133   SOUTH-EAST FACE DIRECT

ED1   D Belden and A Mroz, 11–13 July 1971. Winter: A Jordaney, M
Machet, R Salluard and C Zappelli, 21–22 Dec 1977

45
4

R of the compact section is a poorly marked pillar. Thissustained
and exposed route on very good rock starts up a prominent crack
line leading to the L side of a huge flake. Essentially free, there are
some short sections of aid climbing, and it still sees few ascents.
600m, About 14hr

DESCENT

Reverse for the most part the lower section of the Peuterey Ridge
(Route 85). This is quite long but can generally be managed in rock
shoes. From the summit rappel to the notch on the NW side in
front of a pointed gendarme called the Epée. Turn it on the R and
slant down broken ground on the Brenva flank, at first L then R to
reach Route 85 several hundred metres lower. Follow this,
descending the Schneider Couloir to near the bottom where a vague
path leads out R to a gap between two conspicuous pinnacles.
Rappel down the chimney on the far side to gain the Schneider
Ledges. 2–3hr

Brèche Nord des Dames Anglaises 3490m

First traverse: S Metzeltin with B Crépaz and P Pozzi, 25–26 July 1960

Normally approached from the Frêney glacier to reach the bivouac hut on the col. See Route 85

134   **BRENVA SIDE NORTH-EAST COULOIR**
AD

This long steep snowy couloir can be climbed from the Brenva glacier in cold and snowy conditions. Otherwise it is very exposed to stonefall. About 500m, 2–4hr. Serious.

135   **FROM BRECHE SUD DES DAMES ANGLAISES**
PD+

First Traverse: A Goettner, F Krobath and L Schmaderer, 30 July 1934

45

An important link in the Peuterey Intégral. See also Photo 47

Climb easy rocks on the crest and then keep on the Frêney side to a shoulder below the vertical walls of Pta Casati. Now climb down steep broken rocks and walls on the Frêney side reaching the icy couloir leading to the Brèche Nord at its junction with the branch from the Brèche Central. Climb it to the col. 2–3hr

Brèche Sud des Dames Anglaises 3429m

136   **FRENEY SIDE**
AD

E Allwein and F Gabier, 31 July 1927

47

The straightforward snow couloir on the Frêney side is very exposed to stonefall. 300m, 2–3hr. Serious. See also Photo 45

137   **BRENVA SIDE**
TD–

First ascent and first traverse R Cassarotto, G Comino and G Grassi, 21 July 1978

A steep and relatively difficult couloir that is very exposed to stonefall. Snowy conditions and a hard frost essential. About 500m, 5hr. Serious.

Aiguille Noire de Peuterey 3772m

Lord Wentworth with E Rey and J Bich, 5 Aug 1877. Winter: H
Hoerlin, E Schneider and H Schroder, 16 March 1929

One of the most beautiful and dramatic rock spires in the Alps
which is also a notorious lightning conductor! It offers a varied
selection of superb rock climbs in the upper grades.

138 **EAST RIDGE**
PD/PD+ E Allegra with L Mussillon and H Brocherel, 27 July 1902

*Although the normal route of ascent, it is almost never used for that
purpose nowadays and serves as the usual descent route for parties
completing the classic routes on the W face and S ridge. It is described in
descent for this reason. It is a long scramble of little technical difficulty
over broken ground but the complexities of route-finding are not to be
underestimated.*

From the summit descend the S face via a series of chimneys and
ledges for 150m. Work L past good bivouac spots to a small
shoulder which marks the top of the first step on the E ridge.
Continue down the R flank on a series of ledges, passing below a
small gendarme, to reach a small amphitheatre between this and a
second lower gendarme. Go straight down a wide couloir and slabby
chimney (good bivouac sites at the base). Slant down L, passing
below a third gendarme, towards the top of a rounded spur. Cross
the spur, descend a huge couloir working L to the top of a second
rounded spur and cross this to another steep and slabby couloir. Go
down this for about 100m, then traverse L to reach the E ridge
below the last big gendarme. Go down the ridge and reach a double
gendarme by a chimney on the R flank. Turn the first of these
gendarmes on the R and the second on the L. Continue on the
Brenva flank to a large square-shaped gendarme. Descend directly
down towards the Fauteuil on a ridge as far as a small notch where it
becomes very sharp. Go down to the R on increasingly steep ground
and descend a loose and narrow couloir for 80m to a shoulder on the
L. Cross the shoulder to the other side and go down grassy slopes
for 100m before working back R. Cross a couloir and continue
almost horizontally for several hundred metres on a vague track, to
reach the snowfield below the SE face. Go down this and follow a
track to the Noire Hut. Over 1100m, several rappels. 5hr

139   **SOUTH-EAST FACE DIRECT**
TD+   G Bianchi, M Canali, E Galimberti and T Nardella, 7–9 Aug 1976

46

This starts directly below the summit by climbing the central couloir, which is often snowy and very exposed to stonefall. Reach the foot of the huge steep walls above and climb them directly on generally good rock (IV to V+ and several pitches of A2) to an enormous terrace. Continue up the R wall of the great dièdre above (A1) then move out R, finally climbing up the crest of a prominent tower (V then IV). 1000m. The route was left fully pegged.

140   **POINTE BRENDEL SOUTH-EAST FACE**
TD   U Manera and I Meneghin, 15–16 Aug 1981

46

A fairly direct route on good granite. It is not sustained but offers some fine free climbing and one difficult overhanging aid pitch. No gear was left in place.

Start on the R side of the couloir separating Pts Brendel and Bich (1½hr from the Noire hut) and scramble up easy ground below the steep walls of Pt Brendel. Keep on the R to avoid stonefall in this lower section but near the top work across to the L-hand side and reach the base of the very prominent R-ward slanting crack that cuts across the first part of the wall. Climb it with increasing difficulty for 4 pitches (IV to VI) then slant up R on easier ground (III and IV) to a series of slabs. Cross these to the R (V then IV) to reach a R-ward slanting dièdre, which runs parallel to the original crack and leads up to the central, overhanging section of the wall. Climb the dièdre (V+) to a comfortable terrace at the base of the overhangs (bivouac).

    Climb the black roofs by a series of L-ward slanting cracks (A3 then V+). The wall becomes less steep and is climbed by bearing L for 100m (IV then III), to reach a horizontal ledge at the base of the final slabs. It is possible to escape here as a traverse line L leads to the gap between the Pts Brendel and Welzenbach.

    Climb up directly on smooth slabs (V+ with several aid moves) then traverse an area of less steep slabs to the L and climb a clean dièdre (A1 and V). A long crack in the slab above (V and VI) leads to the S ridge at the top of the Demi-Lune pitch. 18hr, c700m

Descend most conveniently utilising the gully between Pts Brendel and Welzenbach (see route 141). Allow 3–4hr.

141 **POINTE WELZENBACH SOUTH-EAST PILLAR**

TD M Bernardi, G Grassi and F Salino, 1 Aug 1980

46

A very fine climb on excellent rough grey granite with great exposure in the upper section. It is recommended that a few blade pegs are carried.

The base of the pillar is very obvious and is reached from the Noire hut in 1hr. Climb up the R side of the spur for 150m (III and III+) until it becomes steeper, then follow the crest and finally the L flank for a further 80m (IV and V−) in dièdres and cracks. The ground now becomes less steep and the crest is followed easily to the foot of the vertical 300m upper buttress.

     Move up L for 30m and climb a prominent dièdre (20m, V+). Go up and L on narrow ledges then climb a little way up a dièdre-crack (V) before moving L across a vertical wall (V+) and climbing to some ledges above (V). Reach the crest of the spur on the R (IV), climb a compact slab (V+) followed by a ramp (IV) to a shoulder below smooth vertical walls. Move up and L along flakes then climb a light coloured wall (VI). A thin crack on the R (VI+) leads up to overhanging rock. Move L on a flake (V+) to reach and climb a short dièdre (VI). Move up R to the crest of the spur (IV−) where the granite is black and climb a fine series of cracks and an overhang (V) before slanting up L to a dièdre-couloir which is followed to its end (III and IV). On the L an obvious yellow dièdre (V+, but not to be confused with the one on the R flank of the spur) leads to a short smooth slab on the R. Climb it (V−) to ledges and continue up easier cracks to the summit. 550m, 6½hr.

Descend by rappel to the gap between the Pts Welzenbach and Brendel then make 12 further rappels, at first down the gully then more towards the lower part of the ascent route, to the base of the pillar. Allow 3–4hrs

142 **SOUTH RIDGE**

TD K Brendel and H Schaller, 26–27 Aug 1930. Winter: T Gobbi and

46 H Rey, 26–27 Feb 1949

One of the most famous climbs in the range and an established classic. The technical difficulties are not that great and there are long sections of easier pleasant climbing all on generally excellent rock. The route is very long with over 2500m of actual climbing, though only 9 or 10 pitches are IV or more. It is necessary to move well together or solo on the easier sections in order to complete the route in a day. There are a fair number of good bivouac sites in the upper section and on the descent of the E ridge.

From the Noire Hut cross the Fauteuil des Allemands and go up the moraine to the foot of Pt Gamba (2675m, 1hr). Climb 60m up the rocks of the E spur, then a slab on the R (IV), continuing up grassy cracks and working slightly L to reach a series of ledges (80m, III). Follow these ledges up to the R and into the couloir running down from the gap above Pt Gamba. Climb the couloir for 30m, then the rib on the R that divides it into two branches, and after 50m cross the R-hand couloir. Work up R on some grassy ledges to reach the crest of a rib coming down from the Second Tower. Climb it easily to a steep step near the top (2hr).

Turn the step on the R (III) and climb chimneys to near the top of the tower (IV). Climb a wall (IV) and work up R returning to the ridge below an overhanging block. Climb this, normally using a shoulder (IV), and descend a little slab to the gap between the two gendarmes forming the top of the Second Tower. Turn the second gendarme on the R and continue along the crest. Turn another little gendarme on the R followed by a slab above the gap beyond (III+) to a step. Slant up ledges on the R for 10m to the base of a large slab. Climb it (IV+) working L and continue for 2 pitches to the summit of Pt Welzenbach (3355m) via slabs and chimneys (III, 3–4hr).

From a point 20m down the E flank make a vertical rappel to the col. Traverse slightly R and go up a couloir for 25m (III). Return Lwards up a slabby ramp (III+) and onto the L side of the crest. Go up this to a steep step – the Ressaut en Demi-Lune. Climb this directly past two huge cemented pegs (IV+ and V) for two pitches then continue more easily to the top of Pt Brendel (2hr).

Descend on the L side to the next gap which is divided by a tower of red rock. Turn it on the L and climb the chimney that separates it from the Fifth Tower (IV−) then climb the steep wall above, trending L to reach the bottom of a large dièdre (V). Climb it with an awkward and exposed exit R at the top (V+) and continue much more easily to the top of the Fifth Tower – Pt Ottoz (3586m) which can be by-passed by a traverse on the R. From the gap beyond the tower continue easily to a high steep step and climb it just R of the ridge over two small overhangs (V). Slant up R for 15m and climb a chimney (IV) to reach the L side of a huge detached block. Climb straight up for 3m (IV) then slant L to the ridge and follow it to a shoulder (bivouac site). Traverse up R for 30m to a couloir and climb it and its continuation chimney to the top of Pt Bich (3–4hr).

Make a long rappel into the gap and after descending a little on the R climb broken rock first R then back L to regain the ridge. Follow it for 80m to the summit (1hr). 1200m, 12–14hr from the hut.

143 **NORTH RIDGE**

A Goettner, F Krobath and L Schmaderer, 29–30 July 1934

The descent of this precipitous ridge is obligatory for parties engaged in the Peuterey Intégral and is made entirely by long and dangerous rappels with impressive exposure. It is best to complete it early in the morning. Serious.

From the main summit make 2 rappels down 60° slabs to the top of a vertical step. Make 2 more rappels (free to start) down the W side of the step but close to the ridge. Descend a shoulder then rappel down a huge 200m chimney on the W flank which is often overhanging and seriously exposed to stone and ice fall. Traverse R (N) from the base and rappel down slabs and walls to the snowy couloir of the Brèche Sud des Dames Anglaises. Climb it to the col. 4–5hr

Aiguille Noire de Peuterey: West Face

A vast and imposing rock wall overlooking the serac-torn Frêney glacier. There are a number of demanding routes on the ribs and buttresses, several of which remain unrepeated. The face has large areas of both good and bad rock but only one route has gained popularity.

The routes are best approached via the Col de L'Innominata (Route 85) or by gaining the lower Frêney glacier via a traverse underneath the Aig Croux (3–4hr).

144 **POINTE WELZENBACH WEST FACE**

TD+

47

G Bertone, M Claret and R Desmaison, in 2 days during Sept 1973

A direct line up this face giving a very fine mixture of free and artificial climbing on excellent rock.

Reach the large snow patch below the main part of the face via a black overhanging dièdre on the L (sustained V and A1). Follow easy ledges up to the couloir separating the Pts Brendel and Welzenbach and climb it for 100m (III). Move out R to a huge flake and climb directly to the S ridge which is gained 3 pitches below the summit (sustained V and A1/2). 450–500m

145 POINTE BRENDEL WEST FACE
ED1 M Claret and R Desmaison, 13–15 Aug 1973

47

The upper half of this route gives sustained slab climbing finishing on the S ridge at the foot of the final buttress. See also Photo 42

Follow the previous route to the large snow patch then slant up L on ledges and broken ground towards the crest of the pillar. In the middle of the wall directly below the summit climb a R ward sloping dièdre/ramp and continue up steep slabs first L then R to the S ridge. 600m

146 POINTE BICH WEST FACE DIRECT
ED2 J Couzy and R Desmaison, 3–4 Aug 1957

47

This fine line on essentially sound rock gives some demanding artificial climbing especially in the last 250m. See also Photo 42

Climb just R of the crest of the smooth vertical spur that lies R of Route 147 to rejoin the latter at the ledge system leading up to the S ridge. Follow this for 3 pitches to a huge dièdre on the steep L wall and climb it to the fore-summit of Pt Bich (sustained VI and A2). 650m

147 POINTE BICH (BOCCALATTE ROUTE)
TD+ N Pietrasanta and G Boccalatte, 1 Aug 1935

5

A brilliant piece of free climbing on excellent rock. Unfortunately the climbing is not homogeneous and finishes some considerable distance below the summit. Despite the quality, this route has not gained popularity. The cracks will remain wet if the upper ledges still contain snow. 500m, 10hr to the ridge.

148 WEST FACE DIRECT (RATTI-VITALI) ROUTE
TD V Ratti and L Vitali, 18–20 Aug 1939. Winter: A Bozzetti and L Pramotton, 31 Jan–2 Feb 1967

47
5

A magnificent climb and a well-established classic on generally good rock. The difficulties are concentrated in the upper 200m and give delicate rather than strenuous climbing with plenty of exposure. There is one spectacular artificial pitch. The route is no longer a particularly serious proposition as good fixed anchors, established by the Courmayeur guides, allow a rappel retreat from almost any point on the climb (20 rappels from the summit). 650m, 10hr

Pointe Gamba 3067m

P Preuss and U Di Vallepiana, 20 July 1913

A lovely rock spire at the foot of the S ridge of the Aig Noire.

149   **SOUTH RIDGE AND EAST FACE**
III

The easiest route of ascent and a worthwhile little climb on good rock.

46

From the Noire Hut cross the Fauteuil and climb the couloir to the
N gap of the Col des Chasseurs (1hr). The col can also be reached
from the Monzino Hut by crossing the very crevassed Frêney
glacier directly opposite and climbing steep loose grassy rock
(1½hr).

    Climb up the S ridge to the foot of a steep wall and turn it on
the L. Climb a 10m chimney then broken rocks on the L side.
Traverse horizontally L for 25m and climb cracks to a small
shoulder on the ridge. Now descend 50m on the E face and traverse
along grassy ledges to a small spur descending from the summit.
This point is just up to the L of the ledges on Route 142 and it is
more popular to reach the spur via that route.

    Climb up the spur for 40m then traverse L and climb directly
up to a gap in the ridge 50m below the summit. Pass a little to the R
of the gap and slant up towards the summit via a slab and a final
chimney of loose blocks. 300m, 4–5hr from the Noire Hut.

150   **SOUTH RIDGE DIRECT**
V

A Frattola and T Gobbi, 2 July 1944

47

A fine climb on good rock which is not often done.

Climb the steep wall avoided in Route 149 by a diagonal crack (V).
Continue above the shoulder to a smooth nose of rock and make a
10m rappel into a small couloir on the Frêney side. Climb this and
the walls above to the ridge (IV). Continue more or less directly up
the ridge (pitches of IV, sustained) to a terrace below the final
barrier of yellow overhanging rock. Just L of the ridge climb a
strenuous groove with an overhang (V) and reach the summit.
350m, 5–6hr from the hut.

Col des Chasseurs 2740m

A quick link between the Noire and Monzino Huts but the Frêney
side is steep and unpleasant. See Route 149.

Mont Rouge de Peuterey 2941m

This final rock bastion at the end of the S ridge of the Noire has a selection of easily accessible climbs on the vast slabby SE face rising to the N of the Frêney chalets (1589m). The rock is often poor and can be lichenous and grassy. The best descent is to scramble down the ESE ridge to the Fauteuil des Allemands.

151   **SOUTH-EAST FACE BRITISH ROUTE**
VI   J Brown and P Crew, Aug 1968

Takes a huge depression to below some enormous overhangs which it passes on the L (VI). Steep walls (VI) lead to easier climbing 300m below the summit. Not sustained at the grade. 1100m, 6–8hr

152   **SOUTH-EAST FACE ITALIAN ROUTE**
V/A1   A Fossati, G Patelli and M Piazza, 6–7 Aug 1976

A sustained climb to the R of the last route. 1100m

There are two worthwhile climbs on the NE face which is easily reached from the Noire Hut in ¾hr

153   **NORTH-EAST FACE DIRECT ROUTE**
IV/IV+   T Gobbi and N Serralunga, 13 June 1944

Takes the line of the obvious chimney directly below the summit until this disappears at half height. The spur to the L is then followed. 400m, 4hr

154   **NORTH-EAST FACE OTTOZ ROUTE**
IV   A and O Ottoz, 1933

A couloir descends from the gap between the second and third towers on the N ridge. The climb more or less follows this to reach the top of the third tower. 400m, 3hr

Mont Maudit 4465m

W Davidson and H Seymour Hoare with J Jaun and J von Bergen, 12 Sept 1878

This superb summit, the second highest in the range, offers a wide variety of very fine routes on both rock and ice. See Route 62 for a traverse of the main ridge (normal routes).

155   **NORTH-WEST RIDGE FROM COL DU MONT MAUDIT**
PD   G Morse with E Rey, 21 Aug 1895 in descent

`37`   A nice little rocky ridge followed by a snow crest leads to the summit. ½hr

156   **NORTH SLOPE**
PD+   P Cassan, P Kornacker and H Kuhn, 31 July 1901

`37`   A fine little route on snow or ice that climbs directly up the slope above the snowy cwm between Mt Maudit and Mt Blanc du Tacul (see Route 62). The rimaye here is often easier to cross than that below the Col du Mont Maudit. Average angle 45°, 1½–2hr

157   **NORTH-EAST RIDGE FROM COL MAUDIT**
PD   J Masterman with A and B Supersaxo, 31 July 1898

`37`   *A lovely little ridge, with continuously interesting climbing.*

From the snowy cwm of Route 62, between Mont Maudit and Mt Blanc du Tacul, walk up towards Col Maudit and climb mixed ground to reach the ridge halfway between the Col and a prominent shoulder. Follow the ridge over the shoulder (4336m) and continue to the summit tower. Turn it on the R and climb the W side to the top. 3hr

Mont Maudit: South-East Face

A vast face overlooking the Brenva glacier and offering a number of very fine routes. The climbing is generally mixed and all routes suffer from a quick deterioration in snow conditions after dawn. It is essential to start a number of the routes very early and in some cases finish early in order to enjoy them at their best. The rimaye can often prove quite difficult.

Mont Maudit: South-East Face: South-West Shoulder 4361m

158   **BICENTENNIAL COULOIR**
TD/TD+   G Grassi and R Fiava, 10 July 1986

`48`   This route lies immediately L of the SE ridge and has some short vertical ice pitches.

159   **SOUTH-EAST RIDGE**

TD–   B Domenech and E Hanoteau, 1974

48

This excellent mixed route, thought to be superior in quality to the classic Frontier Ridge (Route 174), follows the crest of the ridge, climbing the rock buttress at half height to the right of a deep couloir. The upper snow crest is 40°–50°. 700m, 7hr

160   **EAST PILLAR**

TD+   G Grassi and G Groaz, 26–27 Aug 1978

48

Hard free climbing up the huge dièdre in the centre of the face. The rock pillar itself is 400m high and comprised of magnificent granite.

From the Brenva glacier climb the snow slopes for 150m (40°–50°) and reach the base of the dièdre in 2 pitches (IV/V). Climb the dièdre for 150m (V and VI) and exit R via an icy runnel to a good terrace. Traverse L out of the dièdre and climb up blocks (IV+) followed by a system of cracks (IV) to reach the crest of the pillar on the L. A reddish slab (IV+) leads to large terraces at the base of a prominent red pillar. Traverse across a narrow ledge and smooth slabs (V) to reach an exposed stance on the L side of the pillar. Climb up a slanting dièdre, avoiding an overhang on the L, to reach a series of ledges (V, V+). Continue for 3 pitches (IV then mixed) to reach the snow crest of Route 159 and follow it to the summit. 650m, 12–16hr

161   **EAST FACE**

D+   L Griffin and C Torrens, 4 Aug 1975

48

An interesting mixed route requiring a hard frost and an early start. There is a slight risk of stonefall from the upper buttresses.

The initial rock buttress is climbed a little L of centre in an icy chimney/couloir (IV, mixed). A fine snow crest and steeper ice slopes (55°+) lead up L to the final buttress which is steep and rather loose (IV). Follow the snow ridge to the summit. 650m, 10–12hr

162   **COUNTRI COULOIR**

TD   R Beglinger and J Fantini, 4 Aug 1979

48

The top gully contains a 40m vertical ice pitch. The slanting ice ramp is 60°. 650m, 9hr

163   **EAST SPUR**

D+/TD–   E Ferrario and A Oggioni with W Bonatti, 20 Sept 1959

`48`

Rarely climbed, the crux of this route is a narrow icy couloir on the L side of the spur at about ⅓ height followed by an icy dièdre (V) that leads back R to the crest. Surmounting the cornice can often be quite time-consuming. 650m, 9hr

164   **EAST COULOIR**

D   P Bonnenfant and M Simonet, 26 July 1961

`48`

A straightforward snow/ice couloir which is constantly threatened by stonefall from the flanks and ice fall from the enormous cornice at the top. Surmounting this obstacle can be very difficult. 650m, 5–6hr. See also Photo 49

Mont Maudit: South-East Face Proper

165   **CRETIER ROUTE**

TD–   L Binel, R Chabod and A Cretier, 4 Aug 1929. Winter: J Balmat, D

`49`   Ducroz, M Dandelot and J Jenny, 22–24 Dec 1975

A magnificent mixed climb and the classic route on the face taking the most elegant line up this complex wall. The climbing is almost continuously difficult on both rock and ice. Knife-edged crests can develop and in snowy years, large and precarious mushrooms can form. Though technically harder than any of the Brenva Face routes and accomplished much less often, it is not as serious. The climbing on the crest of the ridge is objectively safe. See also Photo 48

Reach the foot of the face in 1hr from the Trident Hut. Climb a chimney line immediately on the R of the couloir, to the crest of the pillar (IV). Continue up the slabby crest (III and IV) and a difficult smooth chimney (IV+). Turn the last step on the R and continue up a narrow snow crest and the rock step above, until a steep icy ramp leads up L to the crest of the main spur. Just above is a small shoulder with an overhanging cornice. Turn this on the L and climb the crest of the spur, steep and rocky (some IV), to the exposed (sometimes double corniced) snow crest. Follow this to reach the SW ridge not far from the summit. 750m, 7–10hr from the hut.

166   DIRECT START

TD–/TD   R Aubert, R Dittert and F Marullaz, 28 July 1937

`48`   This reaches the crest of the lower buttress by some very steep rock-climbing on the L flank. Continue up the ridge turning any obstacles on the L. See also Photo 49

167   POLISH ROUTE

TD   J Bougerol and A Mroz, 17–19 Aug 1971

`49`
`6`   A fine direct route that has almost become a modern classic. The difficulties are essentially on rock and give entirely free climbing on good granite. The couloir that must be crossed to reach the central rock band is exposed to rock and ice fall. 750m, 10–15hr. See also Photo 48

168   GABARROU-MARSIGNY ROUTE

TD+   The succession of steep ice-falls that are contained in the narrow
`48`   couloir lying to the L of the initial pillar of Route 165 and the upper section of Route 167 were climbed by P Gabarrou and F Marsigny 2 Aug 1987 to produce what they considered to be one of the most splendid gully climbs in the range, with several poorly protected vertical pitches. Unfortunately the conditions required to render this climb at all attractive seldom occur. 650m, 15hr. See also Photo 49

169   CZECH DIRECT ROUTE

TD/TD+   L Chrenka, V Launer, F Piacek and P Tarabek, 25–27 July 1975

`49`
`6`   Takes a direct line up the central walls. It is not sustained and there are areas of poor rock. Long sections of the route are exposed to stonefall. V+ and A1, 750m

170   BONATTI ROUTE

TD   R Gallieni and A Oggioni with W Bonatti, 6–7 Aug 1959

`49`
`6`   After the initial compact rock buttress (V and V+) the route gives difficult mixed climbing with several steep icy runnels and is seriously exposed to stone and ice fall. 750m

171   KAGAMI SPUR – POLISH START

TD   L Sados and R Zawadzki, 5–6 Aug 1963

`49`   *The original start climbed the L flank of the pillar near the central couloir and is seriously exposed to stonefall. The direct start on essentially good rock leads to pleasant mixed climbing on the upper ridge. The last*

150m however can often prove very taxing. A very safe line that does not seem to have become popular.

Start at the lowest point of the spur. Slant up R easily and climb an overhanging chimney, then a crack to the top of a triangular block (V+). Trend up L in cracks and a chimney (VI) and work up to an overhanging groove on the R of some steep walls. Climb it and the narrow chimney above to a good ledge (V+). Slant up R and take a series of chimneys (overhangs, some loose blocks, V+) to the top of the buttress (7hr).

Follow the crest of the spur to the top. If the final step proves too difficult it is possible to rappel into the couloir on the R and climb a chimney on its R side to the summit ridge. 650m, 13hr from the hut.

An important variation has been made just L of the crest of the lower pillar via a prominent chimney couloir (IV and V).

172 RENCONTRE AU SOMMET
TD–/TD G Grassi, P Marceso, F Marsigny and M Rossi, 11 July 1985

49

This is the couloir immediately to the R of the Kagami Spur. The first few pitches rarely form in the summer months and the first ascent was done at night on frozen meltwater. The first 50m is 75°–80°. 650m

173 SOUTH-EAST FACE OF NORTH-EAST SHOULDER
TD– (4336m)

49 P Gabarrou and P Steiner, 7 June 1981

Excellent climbing with technical difficulties on mixed ground in the two L ward slanting ramps (65°–75°). Prerequisites to the climbing include a heavy covering of consolidated snow and a hard frost. It is essential to start very early at night. 650m, 7hr

174 FRONTIER RIDGE
D M von Kuffner with A Burgener, J Furrer and a porter, 2–4 July

50 1887. First calendar winter ascent: J Georges and B German, 18–19 Feb 1975

One of the finest ridges in the range and a major classic. It is a long mixed route at high altitude that is objectively safe. The difficulties are fairly sustained and mainly on snow/ice in magnificent surroundings. See also Photo 49 and 52

From the Col de la Fourche Hut follow the narrow ridge to the foot of the first step (mixed, then snow). (This can sometimes be quite tricky and time-consuming in which case it is possible to reach the same point from either the Brenva glacier or Maudit Cirque wide and easy snow couloirs, the one on the Brenva flank being shortest and easiest). Turn the lowest rocks on the R, slant back L in a couloir/ramp line to the snowy crest and follow it over a shoulder to the base of a large red gendarme – the Pt de l'Androsace. Turn it, and the small rock teeth that follow, on the Brenva flank and return to the ridge at a small snow saddle. It is possible to traverse the Pt, starting by a deep chimney on the R (IV) and from the summit rappeling 20m down the far side. Above is the upper step. Climb it on the L flank by a slanting couloir. At the top climb up a little to the R than slant back L to reach the ridge 100m below the NE shoulder. It is possible to escape R from here into the snowy cwm of Col Maudit. Continue over the shoulder (4336m) following Route 157 to the summit. About 800m, 5–7hr from the hut.

Mont Maudit: East Face

This easily accessible face overlooking the Maudit Cirque is characterised by a number of well-defined rock pillars leading to the Frontier Ridge. In suitable conditions the intervening couloir lines give very fine ice climbing. The bottom of the routes can be reached in 2hr from the Torino Hut, ½hr longer from the Midi.

175   **COULOIR DU CHOUCA BLANC**
AD+   J Asselin and P Gabarrou, 30 May 1985

50

In springtime this offers a fine variation start to the Frontier Ridge. An ice gully of 60° and some mixed climbing in the middle section. 450m, 2hr

176   **GUILLOT PILLAR**
TD–   F Guillot and P Lamarque, 10 Aug 1973

50

This takes a line of cracks up the centre of the pillar (V and V+) on good rock. Rappel to the little snowy saddle beyond and continue up mixed ground in a similar line to that taken by the previous route. 450m

177   **COULOIR DE LA CONSOLATION**
D/D+   P Gabarrou and C Stratti, 24 March 1985

`50`

Climbs a large snow slope L of the prominent Androsace Pillar. The upper section, just L of the pillar, contains some short but very steep icy sections. 450m, 4hr

178   **ANDROSACE PILLAR**
ED2   G Bertone and C Zappelli, 2–3 Sept 1964

`50`

A very sustained and direct route following a line on, or close to, the crest of the spur. There have been very few repetitions. The lower section has only been climbed with much aid in a series of overhanging dièdres, cracks and roofs (sustained V and A1/2 with several pitches of VI). The upper red towers, climbed directly on the crest (V and V+), are followed by some demanding mixed climbing and an overhanging dièdre (VI) before easier rock leads to the summit. 500m, Allow 2 days.

179   **ANDROSACE COULOIR**
TD–   G Comino and G Grassi, 21 June 1979

`50`

The icy couloir immediately R of the Pillar. The crux is an 80°–90° ice pitch. 600m, 6–8hr

180   **CENTRAL SPUR**
TD–   P Gabarrou and P Pibarot, 13 July 1987

`50`

The first ascent party found very enjoyable climbing in atmospheric surroundings. The rock is excellent except at the start and once established on the crest the climbing is objectively safe. It is essential to reach the base of the spur before dawn.

Cross the rimaye (often very difficult) and climb a short snow slope to the foot of the spur. 3 pitches (III and IV with a short dièdre of V+/VI on the third) lead to the crest of the spur which is rocky at first, then snowy but can be followed easily to the first steep step. Climb up for 3 pitches (IV and IV+) then finish up the L flank of a 50m monolithic buttress in a series of cracks (V and V+). Follow the ridge, less steep, for 2 pitches (III). Climb a second monolithic buttress by a short steep ice gully on the L flank, followed by a rock pitch culminating in a superb slab (V) which leads to the top of the spur. 2 or 3 pitches along the spiky granite crest are needed to gain the NE shoulder. 600m, 8hr

181   **CENTRAL COULOIR**

TD   P Gabarrou and B Maquennehan, 30 July 1978. Winter: H Bouvard

50   and P Gabarrou, 16 Feb 1986

The first of the big couloirs completed on this face. Above the initial ice slope the major difficulties are centred around a steep ice wall at half-height and some extremely steep runnels towards the top. 600m, 10hr

Mont Maudit: Three Gendarmes c4050m

To the L (S) of Pt 4032m (an isolated gendarme on the ridge close to Col Maudit) is a group of 3 pointed gendarmes with prominent rock pillars descending to the Maudit Cirque glacier.

The climbs are quite short, easy of access and are well-equipped with in situ protection and fixed rappel anchors for descent down the route. All the difficult sections are generally on very good granite.

182   **LEFT-HAND COULOIR**

TD/TD+   G Grassi, A Fare and C Longhi, 1984

50   The couloir immediately L of the L-hand pillar gives very sustained ice climbing in the upper vertical section. 400m

183   **LEFT-HAND PILLAR**

TD   G Grassi and I Meneghin, 19 Aug 1984

50   *Excellent climbing on good rock with a well-equipped rappel descent.*

Climb the couloir on the R of the pillar (IV) until it is possible to work up onto the R side of the crest (V+ to VI+). At half-height move round onto the L flank and climb up a succession of steps (IV). Continue R up a huge crack in the upper section (IV and V), joining the crest a few pitches below the top. 400m, 7hr

184   **CENTRAL PILLAR DIRECT**

TD−   C Carli and J Chassagne, 26 Aug 1981

50
8   Difficult climbing low down on the crest (IV) gives way to more straightforward rock which can often be verglassed in the upper section. The easy ground above the fourth pitch is a little loose and the line of the route was descended by rappel. There is one short roof of A2. 400m, 6–9hr

185 **CENTRAL COULOIR**
TD–   G Comino and G Grassi, Summer 1979

50   400m

186 **RIGHT-HAND PILLAR**
TD–   P de Galbert and C Jaccoux, 24 Sept 1970

50   Climbs the couloir on the L of the pillar until it is possible to work
up R to below the vertical upper section. Climb this just R of the
crest for 4 pitches (V and VI, some loose rock) then regain the crest
and reach the summit in 2 further pitches (IV+). 400m, 4–5hr

Col Maudit 4035m

First traverse: T Graham Brown with A Graven and J Knubel, 1
Aug 1932

Between Mt Maudit and Mt Blanc du Tacul. The central serac
barrier (80°) was climbed direct on 4 July 1979 by G Comino and G
Grassi. This can sometimes appear to form a stable unbroken
barrier – the choice is yours. TD

187 **DESCENT TO CIRQUE MAUDIT GLACIER**
AD–   *This provides a useful and safe descent and was completed in this fashion
by the first traverse party.*

From Col Maudit reach the top of the spur that forms the true L
bank of the wide couloir descending from the col. Go down the spur
keeping to the R (S) flank. There is one difficult chimney/couloir
section. Above the final steep buttress traverse L (E) into a couloir
and go down this (stonefall) crossing the rimaye to the glacier.
450m, 2½–3hr

Pointe Durier 3997m

188 **MAZEAUD-TSINANT ROUTE**
TD   P Mazeaud and A Tsinant, 29–31 July 1963

37   *This conspicuous red tower (3997m) high on the NW face of Mt Maudit
overlooking the upper Bossons glacier gives a short rock route with an
approach that is probably unjustifiably long and complicated. It has
rarely been repeated.*

Reach the base of the pillar directly from the Grands Mulets or from Col Maudit by a rappel descent of the very steep couloir on its N side. Both approaches finish with 200m of difficult mixed climbing to reach the base of two parallel cracks that rise steeply to the N ridge. Climb these and continue up the ridge to the top (sustained VI and A2). 200m on the pillar.

Mont Blanc du Tacul 4248m

Due to the ease of access provided by the Aig du Midi téléphérique, this has become one of the most popular high mountain venues. The NE face has probably the finest collection of rock, ice and mixed routes in the range. Many of the climbs are easily possible in a day from the first téléphérique but most parties will prefer an earlier start and a more leisurely approach from an overnight bivouac in the vicinity of the Midi. The rock is generally excellent on all the routes except for the last 200m where it becomes quite loose and shattered. However this is usually easy ground. The mountain is very popular for winter climbing and many of the couloirs are regularly ascended each year.

Descent is usually effected by the normal route (Route 189) but when this becomes too dangerous it is advisable to go down the N ridge to the top of the N face triangle where a fixed rappel descent will be found down the W flank next to the snow/ice slopes of the NW face.

189
PD–
55

NORTH-WEST FACE
One or more members of the Hudson–Kennedy party, 8 Aug 1855

The normal route which in good conditions is quite straightforward and a nice introduction to alpine snow climbing. However it can become very avalanche-prone and in winter windslab is a common occurrence. Several long and wide crevasses may have to be negotiated and at the bottom a rimaye can be difficult to cross. In this case a ladder is often found in place. See also Photo 37

From the Col du Midi slant up R on the NW face avoiding small seracs and crevasses to the flat shoulder at the base of the W ridge. Follow the easy-angled ridge to the rocky summit. 700m, 2½–3hr, 1½hr in descent.

190   **DIABLE (SOUTH-EAST) RIDGE**
D+   M O'Brien and R Underhill with A Charlet and G Cachet, 4 Aug
52   1928. Winter: E Stagni and M Galley with R Lambert, 9–10 Feb
1938

*This classic ridge traverse is one of the finest of its class in the Alps. The
route is long, the climbing of the five Aigs du Diable delicate and exposed
and the difficulties are mostly above 4000m. Serious. See also Photo 53*

From the Torino Hut or the Aig du Midi follow Route H17 into the
Maudit Cirque (1½ or 2hr). Go up R to the foot of a couloir in the
SW flank of the Diable Ridge. This is the second couloir after the
Clocher (3853m) at the lower end of the ridge. Cross the rimaye at
c3580m and climb the couloir, slanting L over snowy rocks and
subsidiary couloirs to reach the Col du Diable (3955m, 2hr). It is
also possible to climb the steep snow/ice couloir directly below the
Col du Diable.

    Follow a thin snow ridge then traverse L on easy ledges round
the Corne du Diable to the gap beyond. Now climb the Corne
(4064m. III) and return by rappel. Climb a smooth slab (IV+) and
easier rocks to the top of Pt Chaubert (4074m). Descend the NW
face of this pinnacle by 3 rappels to the second lower gap below Pt
Mediane (1½hr).

    Follow ledges up to the base of a large open dièdre. Climb the
back of the groove for 15m (IV) then traverse R to a notch in the
R-hand ridge (IV). Climb a crack L of the ridge for 15m (IV) to a
narrow platform. Follow a ledge R onto the NE face and climb up
steep slabs to rejoin the ridge (IV). The large dièdre could also be
climbed directly to this point (IV+).

    The summit of Pt Mediane is composed of 3 blocks resting
against each other to form 2 windows. Go through the L-hand
window and reach the top (4097m).

    Now rappel 30m into the Brèche Carmen from the L-hand
window. A little to the R of the ridge climb up cracks (IV) then
make a rising traverse R to a platform between the two summits of
Pt Carmen. Climb the sharp E ridge to the W summit (4109m, 1hr)
and return to the platform where it is possible to make 2 rappels
down a chimney on the SW side and continue easily to the Brèche
du Diable. Follow the ridge easily, passing under the Isolée which
lies off the ridge to the L and reach the gap beyond – the Brèche de
l'Isolée. Descend a couloir on the L side for 15m and reach the NE
face of the Isolée by a short traverse. Climb cracks to about 5m

below a huge flake then traverse L below a bulge and reach a flake running across the S face. Follow this to a short groove and climb it and the wall that follows to a good platform (sustained IV). Reach the top easily (4114m) in 30m. Return to the platform and make a 25m rappel back to the Brèche de l'Isolée (2hr). Follow the ridge, a little R of the crest, until the last step. Turn this on the R easily then climb back L up a rocky ridge. Continue more easily to the summit (1–2hr). 11–13hr from the Torino Hut.

Mont Blanc du Tacul: Col du Diable 3955m

There are several alternative routes for reaching this col lying just to the SE of the Aigs du Diable. All are longer and harder than that just described but provide interesting climbing.

191
AD

53

VIA BRECHE DU CARABINER AND AIGUILLETTES DU TACUL

The substance of this route was ascended by A Hess with L Croux and F Ollier, 25 Sept 1898

This provides a longer and more interesting approach to the Aigs du Diable by climbing the lower ridge. See also Photo 51 and 60

From the Torino or Midi station reach the couloir between the Grand and Petit Capucin and climb it to the top – the Brèche du Carabiner. Make a short descent onto the hanging glacier to the N and then climb ice slopes and a small rocky rib to the gap between the two Aiguillettes (4hr). Traverse the NW point (3913m) and continue along the sharp mixed ridge to the Col du Diable. About 5hr from the Torino Hut.

192
AD+/D

51

NORTH-EAST FACE LEFT-HAND COULOIR
First descended by B Macho, 28 Dec 1975

The NE slope of the Col du Diable is split by a long rocky spur descending to the glacier bay on the W side of the Pyramide du Tacul. Cross the rimaye and climb up a 55° ice slope. Higher up cross the rocky spur on the L to reach the hanging glacier (this point can also be reached more easily from the Brèche du Carabiner). Climb the wide couloir just L of the spur to the col. 550m, 4–6hr. See also Photo 53 and 60

193 **NORTH-EAST FACE RIGHT-HAND COULOIR**
D+   R Chéré, 20 July 1974. Winter: B Macho, 28 Dec 1975

`51`

After climbing the 55° ice slope mentioned above, slant up R and
gain a narrow couloir leading to the Col du Diable. 550m, 4–6hr.
See also Photo 53 and 62

194 **CORNE DU DIABLE EAST-NORTH-EAST COULOIR**
TD–   J Lafaille, 12 Feb 1985

`51`

The curving couloir in the ENE spur descending from the Corne du
Diable and joining the Diable Couloir at ⅔ height. 70°–75° then
60°. See also Photo 62

Mont Blanc du Tacul: North-East Face

195 **DIABLE COULOIR**
D   G Antoldi, G Boccalatte, R Chabod, M Gallo and P Ghiglione, 31
Aug 1930. Winter: H Agresti and J Fanton, 9 March 1968

`53`

*A classic snow and ice route which is slightly steeper than the Gervasutti
Couloir. The average angle is 49° but the upper slopes are 55°. Near the
top a rocky spur descending from the SE ridge divides the couloir into two
branches. The principle objective dangers, stonefall and avalanche, can
be avoided by reaching the base of the spur before dawn. See also Photos
62 and 51*

Reach the rimaye below the couloir in 2–2½hr from either the
Torino Hut or Midi station. Above, the narrows are either climbed
directly or on steep rocks to the L for 70m. In the upper section the
L flank provides the shortest and easiest finish. The R flank is more
elegant but steeper and in bad conditions the rocky spur can be
climbed directly (IV). Finish up the SE ridge to the summit. 800m,
6–9hr

196 **DIABLE PILLAR**
TD   E Cavalieri, P Ravaioni, E and G Vaccari, 11–13 Aug 1963. Winter:
S Avagnina, G Comino and A Nebiolo, 27–28 Dec 1975

`53`

*A magnificent climb over varied terrain which has not gained popularity.
The pillar itself, a 250m tower of red granite, is situated high on the R
side of the Diable Couloir and the approach will be exposed to a little
stonefall. See also Photo 51*

In good conditions the easiest and most elegant way of reaching the pillar is to climb the Diable Couloir to its foot (3hr). Otherwise climb the first 2 pitches of Route 198 and slant up L crossing couloirs and the base of the Sans Nom Pillar (III to V)(6hr).

Start on the L of the crest below a red tower topped with a conspicuous block. Climb slabs (III and IV) returning R to the crest below a vertical smooth wall. Traverse R on a ledge and reach a wide crack leading to a terrace (35m, V+). Climb up to the L on slabs and in dièdres then back R to a system of cracks leading directly to the R-hand crest of the pillar 30m below the summit (V and A1 sustained).

Reach the top easily, descend the snow crest on the other side and follow the ridge (III and IV) to the final grey tower on the Boccalatte Pillar. Climb this (IV+/V) and reach the summit. 880m, 12–15hr.

197	**SANS NOM PILLAR**

TD   G Cossino, G Grassi, F Piana and A Zimaglia, 19 July 1977

Another excellent climb on very good granite that has been compared in style and quality to the Gervasutti Pillar. 800m, 12–14hr. See also Photo 51

The ephemeral couloir to the R of the pillar fell to Grassi and party on 23 July 1987. 400m of sustained ice climbing. 800m to the summit. ED2

Mont Blanc du Tacul: North-East Face continued opposite

Mont Blanc du Tacul: Three Points Pillar 3885m

This tower of perfect granite is effectively a summit in its own right and although it is possible to continue to the summit of Mt Blanc du Tacul, it is not a logical continuation. Descent is made by rappeling the route of ascent (in situ anchors and slings) in c3hr.

198	**EAST-NORTH-EAST FACE ORIGINAL ROUTE**

VI/A1   E Cavalieri, A Mellano, R Perego and B Tron, 13–14 Aug 1959

A beautiful climb on compact granite and the classic of the face. It is more difficult than the Gervasutti Pillar but not so serious as a rappel descent is possible from each stance. The route is very popular and clears rapidly after bad weather. 400m, 8hr. See also Photos 51 and 53

199   **EAST-NORTH-EAST FACE DIRECT**
VII–

J Hagenmuller and S Koenig, June 1979

`56`
`9`

Another excellent climb up a series of cracks to the R of the
previous route. It is not at all sustained at the grade. 400m. See also
Photos 51 and 53

200   **TOBOGGAN**
VII

M Piola and P Steiner, 25–26 June 1986

`56`
`9`

Hard and sustained free climb starting up the R side of a flake in the
centre of the face then making a 5m pendule R to gain a line of
cracks leading up to the conspicuous roof at ⅓ height. Above the
route follows the big red wall in the centre of the pillar and has
unavoidable pitches of VII. 400m. See also Photos 51 and 53

Mont Blanc du Tacul: North-East Face continued

201   **SUPERCOULOIR**
ED2

J Boivin and P Gabarrou, 18–20 May 1975. First winter ascent to
the summit of Mt Blanc du Tacul: P Berhault and P Martinez, 3–4
March 1979

`56`

*This magnificent ice route rapidly achieved the reputation of being one of
the finest couloir climbs in the Alps and has justifiably become a popular
modern classic. It is very exposed to stonefall and is technically quite hard
but the difficulties end after 400m and good rock belays (rappel points)
can be found throughout. In most summers the ice disappears and the
couloir becomes a rubble chute which means that, in general, ascents take
place from winter to early summer. See also Photos 51 and 53*

Climb the initial steep and verglassed wall below the couloir slightly
on the L for 2 pitches (V and A1). A third pitch leads R over an icy
overhang and up a 45° snow slope to the foot of the narrow icy
couloir. This same point is often reached by climbing the first 3
pitches of the Gervasutti Pillar to easy ground and then making a
straightforward traverse L along a snowy ramp. The overall grading
of the route is thus reduced (ED1) but this method has the
advantage of allowing rapid access to the ice climbing.

Climb the couloir generally on the L side for 300m (Scottish 4
to 5). The first and last pitches are considered the most difficult.
The angle now eases and the couloir becomes more open. Climb up
snow and mixed ground for 150m to join the upper section of Route
203 and follow it to the summit. 800m, 12–15hr

202   **ANUBIS**
TD   B Domenech, C and Y Remy, 20 Aug 1984

`56`
`10`

A pleasant free climb up the L flank of the Gervasutti Pillar and worth considering if the pillar itself is very crowded. 800m, 8–12hr. See also Photos 51 and 53

203   **GERVASUTTI PILLAR**
TD   P Fornelli and G Mauro, 29–30 July 1951. Winter: D Rabbi and G Ribaldone, 27 Feb–2 March 1965

`56`
`10`

This slender pillar gives one of the finest rock climbs in the Alps. The lower part of the route is sustained open climbing on magnificent granite with surprisingly little exposure. It clears quickly after bad weather though the upper mixed section can become awkward when very icy. At the height of the season the route will attract many parties and an early approach is advisable. See also Photos 51 and 53

At the foot of the final step on the pillar follow a diagonal ramp line on the R for 2 pitches (icy) and finish up a 20m crack to a col (IV+). Traverse L and descend for 10m to reach the base of 2 high chimneys below a double tower. Climb the L chimney (IV+, icy) to reach the base of the large red tower above. This can be climbed directly (V+, see Route 205) but it is more usual to climb broken rocks on the L beside the upper section of the Supercouloir to reach the saddle behind the red tower. Climb up the ridge for 100m to a 30m high grey tower. Climb this direct (IV+/V–) and follow an easy snow slope to the summit. 800m, 8–12hr

204   **CENTRAL SPUR – BOCCALATTE PILLAR**
D+/TD–   G Boccalatte and N Pietrasanta, 28 Aug 1936. Winter: P Béghin and R Reymond, 17–19 March 1972

`56`
`11`

A fine natural line and an established classic, though climbed far less frequently than the Gervasutti. It has more of a mountaineering atmosphere and indeed can give a particularly good winter ascent. The sustained rock climbing on the crest of the pillar can be avoided in certain conditions by climbing in the couloir on the L (D–/D). Turning the 200m high Tour Carée on the steep and icy rocks of the N flank usually provides the crux. Serious. 800m, 6–8hr. See also photo 51

205   **RED TOWER FINISH**

TD   R Michon del Campo with G Rebuffat, 7 Aug 1946

56

This is really the true and certainly the most logical finish to the Boccalatte Pillar. It is highly recommended giving fine exposed climbing on magnificent granite. See also Photo 53

206   **CENTRAL PILLAR DIRECT**

ED1/2   J Coqueugniot and F Guillot, 1 July 1968

56

This follows the true crest of the Boccalatte Pillar from its base. It gives very good free climbing and is more difficult and sustained than the Gervasutti Pillar. See also Photo 51

The base of the lower spur is reached just R of a narrow couloir at c3400m. Climb the crest (III and IV with 1 pitch of V) and after a snowy section climb a very steep buttress by a strenuous overhanging chimney on the R side (VI). Continue to the junction with Route 204 and follow it (V and V+) to the monolithic tower near the top. Make a long diagonal rappel to the foot of the Tour Carrée and climb up the L side in a huge dièdre (V+). Below some roofs, traverse R (V+ and VI) to reach a chimney (IV) and continue up cracks to the summit of the Tour (very sustained V+ and VI). Climb over the following tower and reach the foot of the Red Tower and follow Route 205 to the summit. 800m, 12–15hr to the summit.

207   **QUILLE COULOIR**

D+/TD–   R branch: B Macho, 16 May 1973. L branch: R Barton and R Shaw,

56   28–30 Dec 1973

This is the wide couloir between the Boccalatte and Quille Pillars. The upper section usually provides difficult mixed climbing and as there is considerable stonefall danger it is best attempted in the cold snowy conditions of winter or spring.

      Shortly after half-height the couloir divides, the R branch giving a more snowy finish onto the NE spur at the grade given while the L gives a harder and more direct line (TD). 800m. See also Photo 51

208   **QUILLE PILLAR**

TD/TD+   D Mollaret and Y Seigneur, 3–4 April 1965. Winter: J Droyer and J

53   Pommaret, 25–26 Feb 1975

A very good free route with interesting mixed climbing both above and below the pillar. It is essential to be at the foot of the pillar before dawn as the Quille Couloir is seriously exposed to stonefall. See also Photo 51

Climb the Quille Couloir and the crest of the mixed rocky spur leading to the L edge of the Pillar. Climb cracks and chimneys just R of the crest moving back L at half-height and climbing an overhanging dièdre to reach, on the R, a good terrace on the crest (V then VI and VII).

Continue up steep cracks more or less on the crest to the top of the Quille. Make 2 rappels and a rising traverse on the L side of the ridge to avoid a steep buttress, then climb a snowy couloir to the NE spur and follow it to the summit. 800m

209   **NORTH-EAST SPUR**

D+/TD–   C Aureli, E Cavalieri, E Montagna and S Sironi, 11–12 Aug 1965

54

This fine mixed climb follows the ridge on the L side of the Gervasutti Couloir and has been rather overshadowed by its more popular neighbours. See also Photo 51 and 56

Slant up and R from the lowest point, climbing a rock/snow couloir to the crest of the spur. Continue up the crest, passing 2 steep gendarmes by icy climbing on the R flank, to a terrace at the foot of some smooth walls. Climb these, slightly on the L, by smooth and strenuous cracks to the top of the buttress (V and V+, then IV+) which is above the top of the Quille Pillar. Continue along the crest to a large gendarme and climb it directly before turning its top on the L side (IV). Follow the spur to the summit. 800m, 12hr

210   **GERVASUTTI COULOIR**

D–   L-hand (direct) finish: R Chabod and G Gervasutti, 13 Aug 1934.

54   R-hand finish: L Lachenal and L Terray, May 1948. Winter: A Marchionni, L Mazzaniga, A Mellano, R Perego, G Ribaldone and A Risso, 25 Feb 1962 .

The obvious and elegant couloir is an established classic and can be a straightforward snow climb in good conditions. The average angle is 48° but the exit slopes are steeper. The route is very exposed to falling stones and ice from the top seracs so the climb is best done at night and in cold conditions. Due to its easy approach and quick descent it has become one of the most popular winter climbs in the range. It is normal to take the easier R-hand exit. The L-hand exit is steeper with a couple of hard ice pitches (D+, Scottish 3). L-hand finish: 800m, 8–9hr. R-hand finish: 670m, 5–7hr. Both are serious. See also Photo 51

211   **JAGER COULOIR**
D   P Barthélémy and C Jager, 12 June 1964. Winter: W Cecchinel, 17
54   Jan 1971

A popular climb in both summer and winter. It is much narrower and slightly steeper than the Gervasutti Couloir but in cold and snowy conditions, the objective danger is negligible. 600m, 55°, 5–6hr. See also Photos 51 and 53

212   **KOREAN PILLAR**
TD–   P Vance and J Yu, 17 June 1977
54   *This climbs the rocky pillar that lies between the Jager and Hidden Couloirs and gives interesting climbing on both rock and ice. See also Photos 51 and 53*

Climb the Jager Couloir to ⅓ height then slant up R in a steeper couloir (60°) to reach the E crest of the pillar from the R side, above the first step. Climb the second step directly and the third on the L flank. IV to V+, 600m, about 12hr

213   **HIDDEN COULOIR**
TD   S Billane and L Griffin, 30–31 Dec 1973 and 1 Jan 1974
54   *The lower section of this climb appears to be rarely in condition. See also Photos 51 and 53*

Mixed climbing leads to the steep icy runnel. Climb this in 4 pitches (Scottish 4/5) to reach the upper, wider 60° couloir (this can be approached much more easily from the Jager Couloir; W Cecchinel and C Jager, Jan 1977). Climb the couloir and finish up the rock rib on the R (IV). 550m

214   **CECCHINEL PILLAR**
TD–/TD   W Cecchinel and C Daubas, 11 Aug 1973. Winter: Y Vaucher and S
54   Schafter, 26–29 Feb 1976

A fine climb that is reasonably popular with continuous interest throughout its length. The lower section can be a little loose at times but above, the rock is excellent giving exposed mixed climbing on a fine granite tower. See also Photos 51 and 53

The top of the first step, Pt 3544m, is reached by a couloir on the L side in 4 pitches (III). Climb on or near the crest of the spur in cracks, dièdres and short icy couloirs for 7 pitches (IV and V) to a vertical step. Climb it on the R side via a flake and some cracks (V) and in 2 further pitches reach the crest (IV, mixed; this point can also be reached from the top of the easy snow slopes of the

115

Albinoni-Gabarrou Couloir in 4 pitches of excellent mixed climbing). Climb the crest then the R side for 3 pitches (III/IV−). A long pitch leads back L to ledges below a compact granite pillar. Climb this direct by a system of cracks (IV+ and V) then follow the snow crest with several rock steps (III) turning difficulties on the R. A short rappel leads to a narrow horizontal section after which easy climbing leads to the top. 650m, 10hr

215	**ALBINONI-GABARROU COULOIR**
TD	J Albinoni and P Gabarrou, the night of the 4–5 July 1974. Winter:
54	R Thomas and K Wilkinson, 9 Feb 1976

This modern classic gives an excellent series of steep and sustained ice pitches in its upper half. The base of the couloir can be reached in 1hr from the Midi Station and the climb has become a popular winter excursion. In summer the couloir catches the morning sun and the climb should be completed largely at night during a good frost. See also Photos 51 and 53

Climb snow and ice (45°–50°) for 250m until the couloir splits. Take the prominent L fork which gives 4–5 steep ice pitches (Scottish 4) leading to easier mixed ground. 550m, 6–9hr

216	**MODICA-NOURY SUPERGOULOTTE**
TD+	S Modica and A Noury, 23–24 June 1979

| 54 | This climbs the R fork of the couloir mentioned above; steeper and narrower with a 20m vertical section (Scottish 5). 550m. See also Photos 51 and 53 |

217	**MARTINETTI PILLAR**
TD−/TD	M Martinetti and C Mollier, 23 Aug 1960

54

Continuously good climbing on excellent rock with a superb tower of steep red granite to finish. Undoubtedly the best rock route on this part of the face but it can often be very verglassed especially in the lower section. From the summit it is possible to traverse NE along the top of the rocky walls to reach a fixed rappel descent leading down into the glacier bay between the Martinetti Pillar and Pt Lachenal but it is easier and more aesthetic to continue up the N ridge to reach the summit of Mt Blanc du Tacul in less than 1hr. The climb is considerably harder in anything less than perfect conditions. See also Photos 51 and 53

On the R side of the pillar and about 60m above the rimaye slant up L on ledges (III) to reach a huge dièdre and climb it (V then III and IV) for 120m to a series of terraces. Traverse L 15m (IV) and climb the crest (IV+) to reach flakes on the R that lead to a dièdre (V). Climb it, traversing under the roof (V+) and continue to the base of some vast slabs (V). Climb these slabs and walls (IV then V+) for 70m to a small notch below the steep red summit tower. Above are 2 walls split by a vertical crack. Climb the R wall for 5m, then the crack to the roof (VI). Climb the wall on the L round the roof returning R when above it (VI, very exposed). Traverse L and climb a slanting dièdre (V) returning R at the top to climb a smooth bulge (VI). Above a thin slanting crack (V) followed by a dièdre (IV+) leads to the top of the pillar. Continue up the easy snow slopes to the N ridge. 450m, 10hr

218   **HAGENMULLER-KOENIG PILLAR**
V/VI   J Hagenmuller and S Koenig, June 1979

53

The small pillar to the R of the Martinetti. Good rock, 350m. See also Photo 51

Mont Blanc du Tacul: North Face Triangle

Superb ice or mixed climbing, quick access from the Midi Station (½hr), good views, a non-serious atmosphere and an easy descent all combine to make this little face extremely popular in both summer and winter. It is easy to continue up the N ridge to the summit of Mt Blanc du Tacul in 1hr but most parties traverse up and R to reach the normal route (189). In winter or when the traverse is dangerous rappel down the W flank alongside the snow slopes of the NW face. All the routes can be completed in about 3hr.

219   **HANGING GLACIER**
AD–   C Cassin and G Menard, R Girod and J Méchoud, A Faure and J
55   Luc with A Contamine, 8 Aug 1969. Winter: P Martin and Y Vaudelle, 18 Jan 1976

Totally on snow and ice with some steep serac pitches. 350m

220   **NORTH COULOIR**
AD–   P Labrume, J Martin and M Negri with A Contamine, 5 Aug 1962.
55   Winter: E Barbeto, M Barbeto, A Bonomi and L Ratto, 12 Feb 1967

Climbs directly up a couloir between the Hanging Glacier and the L edge of the rocky triangle. 350m

221   **LEFT EDGE**

AD

55

G Gren, G Grisolle, A Poulain and M Ziegler with A Contamine, 4 July 1968. Winter: I and H Agresti, 29–30 Dec 1969

One of the nicest routes on the face. Sustained mixed climbing. 350m

222   **DIRECT**

D

55

P Gabarrou and D Marquis, 5 June 1977

Very sustained climbing but it is possible to avoid the most difficult pitches. 70°, 350m

223   **CONTAMINE-MAZEAUD ROUTE**

AD+

55

A Contamine and P Mazeaud, 21 July 1963. Winter: B Gysin, Feb 1973

Under good conditions this becomes a little gem and an ice-climbing classic. Exit R under the final wall. Short sections of Scottish 3, 350m

224   **WEST PILLAR**

D+

55

M Chabert, J Coqueugniot, B Dineur and B Gaschignard, July 1972

A good rock climb in dry conditions. Some ice pitches of 65° will be encountered. Pitches of V and V+

On the L side of the pillar is 'Hot Chocolate' which follows a line of steep narrow ice runnels for six pitches. Although not often in condition it is thought to be one of the best routes on this face. Sustained climbing at 55–75°, Scottish 4. It reaches the crest of the spur at the top of the Chèré Couloir and the latter can be descended in 4 rappels. First ascent L Brunner, G Dunser and W Muxel, 2 July 1985. 5hr

225   **CHERE COULOIR**

D–/D

55

R Chèré and J Tranchant, 18 Aug 1973. Winter: R Ghilini and B Pasche, Feb 1975

The most popular route on the face and a modern classic. The crux pitches are short and steep (75°, Scottish 4) and have excellent rock belays (bolts). Fixed anchors allow the couloir to be descended easily by rappel. 70°, 350m

Aiguille de Saussure 3839m

226   **WEST FACE**
V/V+   J Balmat and C Mollier, 21 Sept 1970

37

A nice little climb on excellent rock which is essentially free. The isolation of the route combined with the lengthy and somewhat complicated approach (PD/AD) has ensured few repetitions.

Follow Route 189 and continue to the cwm between Mt Maudit and Mt Blanc du Tacul. Slant down to the NW over complicated crevassed ground to the foot of the face (3hr. This point can also be reached more or less directly from the Grands Mulets). Start by climbing a 60m Lward slanting dièdre and climb fairly directly up the face to the base of a Rward slanting dièdre/chimney that leads to the crest of the ridge in the upper section. Climb it and the ridge above to the summit. 250m on the pillar, 5–7hr

Satellites of Mt Blanc du Tacul

Some of the most popular rock climbing in the range takes place on these sun-drenched and easily accessible rock towers in the Vallée Blanche. The situation is generally not serious as many of the routes are short and have rappel descents. They clear quickly after bad weather and are very often climbable in late winter and spring.

Point Lachenal 3613m

Reached in 1hr from the Midi Station, the SE face, in striated orange granite, offers a fine selection of rock climbs with essential protection in situ. From the top either descend easy snow slopes to the N or rappel the Contamine route.

227   **MACROSCOPE**
VII–   A and G Long, 19 July 1982

57
12

Strenuous crack climbing on the crest of the spur.
250m

228   **CONTAMINE ROUTE**
VII+   A Contamine, P Labrunie and R Wohlschlag, 30 Aug 1959

57
12

One of the most popular routes in the range. Not sustained but free-climbing the crack in the 50m wall is quite demanding. 250m

229   **HAROLD AND MAUD**
VII+   J Afanassief and D Escande, 16 July and 3 Sept 1979

57
12

A steep and strenuous crack line but not sustained at the grade. 250m

230   **CECCHINEL-JAGER ROUTE**
V/A1   W Cecchinel and C Jager, 21 April 1968

57
12

Takes the line of the big dièdre and the chimney in the upper section of the face.

231   **MARYLENE**
V/V+   G Margotat and P Sombardier, 23 Aug 1978

57
12

Another very popular route offering varied climbing. See also Photo 51

Point 3664m

232   **SOUTH FACE**
III/IV   A Perez and F Audibert, 11 July 1971

53

This is situated to the W of the Pt Lachenal, and the S face is reached by walking up the glacier cwm between the former and the E face of Mt Blanc du Tacul (slight danger from serac fall).

    The route takes a line of cracks in very good granite starting to the R of the lowest point of the rectangular face. There is one move harder than the grade given. 150m, 1½hr

---

Gros Rognon 3541m

233   **SOUTH-EAST PILLAR**
V/A1   P Giroud and P Vollin, 27 April 1975

A nice little direct route which clears very rapidly after bad weather.

Start just to the R of the lowest point of the SE Pillar (3276m). Climb straight up for one pitch (V with 2 aid moves). Climb up to a large block (V). Climb a wall moving L at the top (2 aid moves) then a dièdre and follow the crest of the pillar in 4 or 5 pitches to the top (IV then III). 200m, 3hr

Descend broken rocks to the W in ¼hr

Pyramid du Tacul 3468m

R Chabod and M Mila, 2 July 1934

A very popular summit of excellent granite.

234   **NORTH-NORTH-WEST RIDGE**

III   First ascent party

51

From the Vallée Blanche reach the snowy saddle between the Pyramid and the Chat by climbing the glacier slopes to the N (2hr from the Midi Station).

    Climb the ridge, snow then a rounded and rocky section with a steep buttress climbed from L to R (III). Easier climbing leads to the summit. 130m, 3hr

235   **SOUTH-EAST WALL**

V/A1   P Nava with A Ottoz, 4 Aug 1953

53

This gives very interesting climbing but it is not as popular as the more modern routes on the NE Face. See also Photo 51

Start 100m up and L of the base of the E ridge and climb steep cracks to a very big terrace (V). Traverse R through a letterbox and continue horizontally on a slab (V, A1). Climb up to a roof, traverse L and take a wide crack to some terraces (V, A1). Climb straight up to another roof (IV) and traverse R to the E ridge (A1). Follow this easily to the summit. 150m, 4–5hr

236   **EAST RIDGE**

IV/IV+   E Croux, L Grivel and A Ottoz, 29 July 1940

53
14

A very popular classic. Good in situ anchors allow the route to be descended from the summit in 8 rappels. 270m. See also Photo 51

237 **D'ENTREE DE JEU**

V/VI   B Domenech, C and Y Remy, 24 July 1985

13

Climbs directly up a line of dièdres to the E Ridge. Bolts and pegs in place. 250m

238 **RONFLEUR PARADOXAL**

V   B Domenech, C and Y Remy, 22 Aug 1984

13

A system of cracks on the L of the clear grey walls starting up the R side of a flake. 250m

239 **ARMES EGALES**

V/VI   B Domenech, C and Y Remy, 21 Aug 1984

13

A system of cracks between the grey walls on the L and broken rock to the R. 250m

Le Chat 3500m

This rock tower behind the Pyramid du Tacul gives a short interesting route on excellent granite.

240 **EAST RIDGE**

VI   P Nava and G Bertone, 2 Sept 1972

53

Follow Route 234 to the snowy saddle and cross ledges on the S Face to below a dièdre which is situated to the L of the large pillar forming the E Ridge. Reach the dièdre and climb it then continue up the ridge, via a steep crack, to the summit block. Descend the route by rappel. About 100m, 3hr. See also Photo 51

Pointe Adolphe Rey 3536m

N Pietrasanta, G Boccalatte, R Chabod and G Gervasutti, 16 July 1935

A very popular climbing ground that has come under close scrutiny from the modern rock alpinist.

241   WEST RIDGE AND NORTH FACE
AD+   First ascent party

`53`

This short route has an air of seriousness and is best attempted when the N Face is very dry. See also Photo 51

From the Midi Station reach the couloir descending from the gap between the Pointe and the Petit Capucin. Climb to the gap by steep broken rocks on the R side of the couloir (2hr). Go up the W Ridge to a vertical step then traverse onto the N Face and make a short diagonal rappel into an icy couloir. Climb L to a block then take a steep thin crack for 15m before traversing L across a rib. Slant up R on steep rock for 35m and after a slab traverse L over friable rock for 15m to a chimney. This leads to a shoulder on the E Ridge. A short vertical step and easy ground leads to the summit. 200m, IV and IV+. 3½hr from the Midi.

The ridge can be descended on the crest in 3 rappels, but it is easier to rappel the S Face. Go down the ENE Ridge for 1 pitch to the base of the summit block. Make a 25m rappel on the S Face then scramble down Rwards to above a roof. Rappel down the side of a huge chimney to reach the foot of the approach couloir. 1hr

242   NORTH-EAST RIDGE
V+/VI   R Guillaume and L Terray, 15 Sept 1958

`53`
`15`

A fine climb though somewhat over-shadowed by its more popular neighbours. See also Photo 51

The route starts R of a short wall in an obvious break filled with loose rock and follows more or less the line of the crest in cracks and chimneys with a few aid moves over roofs. 320m, 5–7hr

243   EAST-SOUTH-EAST SPUR (SALLUARD ROUTE)
V+   T Busi with F Salluard, 6 Sept 1951

`58`
`15`

An established classic and possibly the most frequented climb on the peak. Steep strenuous climbing on excellent rock. 300m, 5–7hr. See also Photo 53

244   PAS D'EDELWEISS POUR MISS WILKINSON
V+/VI   C and Y Remy, 1 Oct 1985

`58`
`15`

Takes a line of dièdres L of the Salluard Route. 250m, 5hr. See also Photo 53

245 **GREAT RED DIEDRE (BETTEMBOURG ROUTE)**
VII   G Bettembourg and H Thiverge, 24–25 April 1975

`58`
`15`
A modern classic. Climbed completely free, the first pitch is a strenuous layback (VII), thereafter V+/VI. Fixed anchors allow the route to be descended in 6 rappels from the top of the dièdre. 200m to the junction with the Salluard, 300m to the summit. 6–8hr. See also Photo 53

246 **LE CORSAIR**
VII–   B Domenech, C and Y Remy, 23 July 1985

`58`
`15`
A superb route that gives some excellent steep and thin slab climbing. Pegs and bolts in place. 300m to the summit, 6–8hr. See also Photo 53

247 **GERVASUTTI ROUTE**
V/VI   G Gervasutti and G Paney, Aug 1944

`53`
`15`
Another fine traditional free climb that is still quite popular. It roughly follows the line of the dièdre which divides the grey rock on the L side of the face from the red rock to the R. 250m, 5hr. See also Photo 58

248 **JE PEUX VOIR LE SOLEIL DEBUT**
VII–   C and Y Remy, 3 Oct 1985

`53`
`15`
Takes a fairly direct line up the grey rock on the L side of the face. Well-equipped with in situ pegs. There are several aid moves. 250m, 6hr

Petit Capucin 3693m

L de Riseis with A and H Rey, 25 Aug 1914

Another fine little rock peak though less frequented than its neighbours.

249 **SOUTH FACE AND WEST RIDGE**
PD   G Boccalatte and R Chabod, 17 Aug 1929

`53`
This is the normal route of ascent and descent. Nowadays it is almost entirely used as a way off the peak by parties making ascents of the E Face. It is described in this direction.

From the summit climb down the W Ridge and descend a 60m chimney on the S Face. Follow easy ledges to the gap between the Roi de Siam and the Petit Capucin and descend a snowy couloir in 3 pitches to the SW. Scramble down R into the wide couloir descending from the Brèche du Carabiner and use this to reach the glacier. 250m, 1hr

250   NORTH-EAST RIDGE DIRECT
V/VI/A1   G Ribaldone and G Vaccari, 28–29 July 1965

62

Climbs directly up the pillar rising above the glacier bay on the N side of the Petit Capucin to join the upper part of the E Face 5 pitches from the summit. Sustained climbing. 400m

251   EAST FACE
IV/V   C Arnoldi, G Gagliardone and G Gervasutti, 16 Aug 1946

62
16

An established classic and one of the best climbs of its standard in the Vallée Blanche.

Follow Route 241 to the col between the Petit Capucin and Pt Adolphe Rey then traverse horizontally over steep icy rocks for 70m to some ledges below the crack indicated on the topo. 250m, 5–6hr from the Midi Station.

252   SOUTH-EAST FACE VIA ROI DE SIAM
IV/V–   G Manet and M Courcelle with J Fontaine and J Streng, 30 July 1967

53
16

Varied climbing on very sound granite but broken by two or three big ledges. From the summit of the Roi de Siam (3632m) make a 30m rappel into the gap beyond and via Route 249 reach the top. 250m, 4hr

Grand Capucin 3838m

This superb tower is probably the most famous granite monolith in the range. Although once the stamping ground of serious artificial climbers, the rise in standards has now created a selection of fine free rock routes of the highest quality; one or two are as difficult as anything in the western Alps. Descent is normally effected by 9–10 rappels down the S Face which allows parties to return to the start of their routes without having to set foot on the snow. Most routes can be completed in a day carrying minimal gear, thus reducing the overall effort and seriousness of the enterprise. However the approach routes on the L of the face can be subject to stonefall and the Capucin is very exposed to the changing moods of the weather. It has an awesome record as a lightning conductor! To be caught high on the peak in a storm can be a very serious proposition.

253 DIRECTE DES CAPUCINS

ED2   E Bellin, J Boivin and M Moioli, 9–10 July 1983

59
17

This tremendous route follows a continuous system of cracks that split the R side of the E Face. The difficult climbing takes place in wide cracks for which suitable protection should be carried.
VII+/VIII–. 450m, 10hr

254 EAST FACE ORIGINAL ROUTE

TD/TD+   W Bonatti and L Ghigo, 20–23 July 1951. Winter: G Alippi, R Merendi and L Tenderini, 27 Feb–1 March 1959

59
17

The ascent of this now classic route was a famous milestone in the climbing history of the Western Alps. Sustained climbing with great exposure. With the normal amount of in situ gear it is possible to climb most of the route artificially. It has however been climbed completely free on several occasions when it becomes ED3 with sections of VIII/VIII+. Most parties however still use some aid to bring the technical level to a more reasonable V+/VI and A1. 350m from the terraces, 10hr. See also Photo 60 and 51

255 L'ELIXIR D'ASTAROTH

ED3   M Piola, P Steiner and R Vogler, 18–20 Aug 1981

59

This takes an elegant line directly up the E Face on magnificent granite. Climbed completely free at VIII with 1 pitch of A3 (skyhooks and copperheads). Even with aid there are unavoidable sections of VI+ and one bivouac will almost certainly be necessary. 450m

256 GULLIVER'S TRAVELS

ED3   M Piola and P Steiner, 18–19 July 1982 after
60   preparation.Panoramix: M Pedrini and S Vicari, 22 July 1983
17

A modern classic of considerable technical difficulty (VII+/VII–) with all essential protection in place. If lengthened by reaching the terraces via the first 3 pitches of Elixir d'Astaroth and finishing with the Panoramix variation directly (IX/IX+) through the large roof, the climb becomes one of the most demanding in the Mt Blanc range. There is unavoidable VI+ climbing. 300m, 8–12hr. See also Photo 59

257   **SOURIRE DE L'ETE**

ED1   G and R Vogler, 24–25 Aug 1981. Winter: G Hopfgartner, M Piola
and P Steiner, 1 Jan 1984

`60`

The first 7 pitches give fine free climbing (VI+/VII) with essential
protection in place. Above lie 3 pitches of sustained A2 but it is
possible to avoid these by finishing up the Swiss Route. 350m,
8–12hr

258   **SWISS DIRECT**

TD+   C Asper, M Bron, M Grossi and M Morel, 24–26 July 1956.
Winter: A Marchiaro and G Ribaldone, 21–23 Feb 1965

`60`
`17`

Originally climbed largely by artificial means, the free version of
this route has become a modern classic. Although not as popular as
the Bonatti it sees many ascents and there is considerable in situ
protection. The technical difficulties are lower than on other routes
on this face. VII. 300m, 6–8hr

259   **O SOLE MIO**

ED1   M Piola and P Steiner, 21–22 April 1984

`60`
`17`

An entirely free ascent (VII/VII+) is considered by some to offer
the finest climbing on the Capucin. It takes the S pillar just L of the
Swiss route and escape is possible onto this route in a number of
places. There is unavoidable VI/VI+ climbing. 300m, 8–10hr

Descent: From the summit descend O Sole Mio to the huge terrace
halfway up the Swiss route (4–5 rappels). Rappel the big dièdre of
the Swiss route to the terraces bordering the Couloir des
Aiguillettes. It is possible to continue rappeling down the rocks on
the flank of this couloir to the glacier.

Le Trident 3639m

A and M Damesme and J de Lépiney, 13 Sept 1919. Winter: E
Stagni, I Gamboni, J Martin and R Wohlschag, 12 March 1966

A fine rock tower at the end of the Clocher Ridge with a prominent
forked summit.

260 **NORMAL ROUTE VIA EAST FACE**

IV/V First ascent party

A classic route with magnificent rock in the upper section. The lower section is quite vague and locating the correct line is difficult. Some of the rock needs careful handling. See also Photo 59

Reach the foot of the snowy couloir separating the Trident from the Clocher, in 2hr from the Midi Station. Climb the couloir for 60–80m, then the rocks on the R (III and IV) to reach a large balcony. Climb a crack slanting up R to the foot of a big chimney bounded on the R by the S Ridge (IV). Climb the chimney (IV/V) and its continuation, a dièdre which lies just L of the crest and is overhanging at the start (V). Cross the S Ridge and slant up R on easy ground for 2 pitches (III) to reach some terraces (sometimes snowy) below the final wall. Climb straight up the wall in a strenuous chimney (IV+) and wide cracks to a good platform 30m below the notch between the S and central summits. Continue straight up for 12m then traverse R and climb a crack to the Central summit (IV+). Descend to the notch and reach the S summit by an exposed traverse on the E Face (IV).200m, 3hr

Descent: Make two rappels down the E Face to the terraces. Climb or rappel down these to the top of a couloir/chimney and make 1 rappel down this to the Couloir des Aiguillettes. Follow this to the glacier. 1–1½hr

Chandelle 3561m

A small yet striking pinnacle.

261 **SOUTH FACE**

VII/VII+ W Bonatti and R Gallieni, 3–4 Aug 1960. Winter: G Bertone and R Pellin, 18–19 Jan 1967

The South Face, now ascended completely free, has quicklybecome a little classic giving very exposed and sustained climbing.150m, 6–8hr

Petit Clocher 3692m

262
VI

NORTH RIDGE
B Denjoy and P Bodin, 12 July 1981

This lies halfway along the connecting ridge between the Trident and the Clocher. The N Ridge gives a short but very sustained free climb (V and VI) with 1 artificial pitch to finish. 130m

There are mixed artificial and free climbs on the E Face.

Clocher 3853m

First ascent: T de Lépiney, P Picard and P Tézenas du Montcel, 19 Aug 1926

The final bastion at the end of the SE Ridge of Mt Blanc du Tacul. A superb S Face finishing about 100m below the summit offers many modern free routes.

263
AD+
62

SOUTH-EAST SIDE
Essentially the route taken by the first ascent party, this gives interesting mixed climbing with some stonefall danger.

Climb the couloir between the Trident and the Clocher which leads to the Brèche du Trident. Traverse into the Couloir des Aiguillettes and climb it, mainly on the L side, to the Brèche du Clocher, a col to the N of the summit (3805m). Slant up L on easy rocks for 20m to a wall. Take a jagged crack (20m, IV). Traverse L along an icy ledge to a chimney and climb it to a ledge on the E Ridge close to the summit. Large blocks and a crack (III) lead to the top. 450m, 5½hr from the Midi Station.

Clocher: South Face

There are many excellent routes here which often follow strenuous crack lines. The best descent is to rappel Borithorn which has fixed anchors at the top of each pitch.

264   RED PILLAR
VII+   E Alexandre and J Boivin, 8 Aug 1980

| 60 |
| 19 |

The smaller prominent pillar to the R of the face. 250m

265   BORITHORN
VII   E Alexandre and J Boivin, 26 Aug 1978

| 60 |
| 19 |

An excellent climb, very direct, which is sustained at V and V+. There is one short crack of VII. 350m

266   PROFITEROLE
VIII−   J Boivin and C Profit, 18 Aug 1980

| 60 |
| 19 |

Good climbing though non-homogenous, mainly IV and V with 1 hard pitch, a 25m layback (VII) followed by a roof (VIII−).

Tour Ronde 3792m

J Blackhouse, T Carson, D Freshfield and C Tucker with D Balleys and M Payot, 22 July 1867. Winter: U Mautino with J Petigax and C Croux, c1895

A delightful peak which is very popular and is frequently ascended in winter. As a viewpoint it is probably one of the finest in the range, standing opposite the full sweep of the Peuterey Ridge and the magnificent Brenva Face.

267   SOUTH-EAST RIDGE
PD   First ascent party in descent

| 62 |

This is the normal route of ascent and is quite short. The climbing is both pleasant and varied and makes an excellent introduction to alpine mountaineering.

From the Torino Hut cross the Col des Flambeaux, go round the base of the Aig de Toule and follow the glacier cwm on the E side of the Tour Ronde to the Col d'Entrèves (1½hr). Follow the snowy SE Ridge, at first on the R side then turn a series of gendarmes on the L. Reach a (snow) saddle (Col Freshfield 3625m) and from there climb directly to the summit at first on rock (I–II) then a snowy slope and finally more rock. 3hr from the hut.

Many parties climb direct to Col Freshfield from the glacier cwm. This route is often followed in descent but is subjected to stonefall in periods of little snow cover.

Note: It is possible to reach the summit directly from the Brenva Bivouac on complicated glacier terrain and steep snow slopes, but nowadays this is very rarely followed.

268   GERVASUTTI COULOIR
AD   R Chabod and G Gervasutti, 27 July 1934

61

A popular little classic which in good condition is often used for descent. The slope is a fairly uniform 48°. At the top turn the summit tower on the N side and climb it from the E. 250m, 3½hr from the Torino Hut.

269   WEST FACE 1973 ROUTE
V/V+   First ascent party unknown, 1973

61
20

Good strenuous climbing on solid rock following the obvious series of cracks that split the face 70m to the L of the Gervasutti Couloir. 250m, 6hr

270   WEST PILLAR
V/VI   C Mollier and G Payot, 23 July 1961. Winter: D Galante, R Bessa
61   and D Vota, 4–6 Jan 1975
20

A classic little rock climb that has fixed anchor points allowing a rappel descent from the top of the pillar. Sustained and strenuous dièdre and crack climbing on very good rock. 300m, 6hr

271   NORTH WEST FACE
D+   P and P Gabarrou, July 1978

61

A steep mixed face where a good covering of well frozen snow will greatly facilitate progress. 300m, 7hr

272   NORTH COULOIR
D/D+   P Decorps and G Perroux, Dec 1979

62

Slightly steeper than the N Face, this provides a possible alternative when the former is overcrowded. 60°, 350m, 4–5hr. See also Photo 61

273   NORTH FACE

AD+/D−   F Gonella and A Berthod, 23 Aug 1886. Winter: M Mai, G Miglio
[61]   and E Russo, 3 Feb 1957

An established classic which provides a good introduction to the
steeper alpine ice faces. By keeping on the R side of the slope it is
possible to obtain good rock belays for most of the route. The
average angle is 52° but the first few pitches are steeper. It is usual
to turn the summit block on the L to join the normal route but it
can be climbed direct (30m, IV). 350m, 4hr. See also Photo 62

274   NORTH-EAST RIDGE DIRECT

D/D+   J Bernezat and C Colomb, 17 June 1962. Winter: G Machetto and G
[62]   Motti, 20–21 Jan 1968

*A delightful little route with 10 pitches of fine free climbing on good rock
followed by a pinnacled ridge and interesting mixed terrain. See also
Photo 61*

Reach the base of the NE Ridge from the Torino Hut in 1hr. On the
L flank climb easy snow ledges for 40m to the base of a small pillar
(II) and reach its top by snowy chimneys on the L side (III and IV).
Climb the large dièdre above, at first on the R wall, to a platform
35m (V and V+). Climb cracks on the R for a pitch (V) followed by
a short wall (V) and a chimney to reach steep but easy slabs leading
to a large ledge. A short wall (V) leads to easier ground. Follow the
ridge for 90m (III) then traverse L on snow for 30m before slanting
up R for 2 pitches to the crest. Continue up the ridge, turning the
first gendarme on the L and the next two on the R (III) for 150m to
the summit. 350m, 5–6hr from the hut.

Tête de la Brenva 3504m

A Hess and H Martiny with L Mussillon, 24 Aug 1902

A rock tower to the SE of the Tour Ronde.

275   SOUTH-WEST FACE

V   P Ghiglione and A Ottoz, 24 July 1948

*Reputedly a fine rock climb which has not gained popularity, perhaps
due to the lengthy approach and indirect line.*

Reach the foot of the face in 1½hr from the Brenva Bivouac. The
centre of the face is split by a long narrow couloir. Climb smooth
rocks on the L and slant up R to reach the couloir 150m above the
rimaye (IV). Climb chimneys on the R of the couloir to a small gap

(V). Keep traversing R past another gap to a smooth chimney leading to a third gap with a little gendarme (IV and V). Reach and climb a diagonal crack on the R (V) then slant L up slabs and chimneys to the summit. 500m, 6hr from the hut.

Brèche de la Brenva 3135m

First traverse: E Bradby, J Wicks and C Wilson, 25 July 1904

A fairly easy col that affords a convenient passage between the Entrèves and Brenva glaciers.

276 **ENTREVES SIDE**
PD

From the Pavillon Station go up the path for ½hr then make a rising traverse to the base of the Entrèves glacier. Climb this and the couloir coming down from the Brèche (3hr). The couloir itself can be subject to heavy stonefall and a much safer though more difficult method of approach is to climb the rock on the R via 2 dièdres (IV and V).

277 **FROM TORINO HUT**
PD+

In good snow conditions this is the quickest and most convenient route.

From the hut cross the Cols de Flambeaux (3407m) and Orientale de Toule (3411m). Descend the Toule glacier to a notch in the NW ridge of the Tour d'Entrèves (c3070m). The lower (SE) of the 2 gaps is the best crossing point with a steep couloir leading down to the Entrèves glacier. Rise slightly across the glacier to the couloir and Brèche. 2hr

278 **FROM BRENVA BIVOUAC**
PD

Quite straightforward, taking the L side of the small glacier leading up to the Brèche. The final couloir is short and easy. 2½hr

Père Eternel 3224m

This fantastic pinnacle about 60m high on its long side can be conveniently combined with an ascent of the N Ridge of the Aig de la Brenva. Neither appear to see many ascents.

279 **NORTH-WEST RIDGE**
V/V+ L Grivel, A and O Ottoz and A Pennard, 7 Aug 1927

63

Short and delicate.

From the Brèche de la Brenva climb up the ridge and reach the col on the far side of the Père, via the E flank. On the W side slant up a ledge easily to the NW Ridge. Climb a delicate wall (V), a fixed ladder (!) and a second wall to an overhang (V). Move R then continue up to a second overhang which is avoided on the L (V+). Continue straight up the ridge to the top. 1–2hr

In descent make 1 long rappel to the easy ascending ledge.

Aiguille de la Brenva 3269m

A Hess with L Croux and C Ollier, 25 Aug 1898

A spectacular fin with a fine E face. The best and most convenient approach is via Route 277 from the Torino Hut, but it can be climbed in a day via a stiff walk from Courmayeur.

280 **SOUTH-EAST RIDGE IN DESCENT**
63 First ascent party: (upper section). In descent: G Mono, A and T Romanego with O Bron and L Proment, 20 Aug 1926

The normal route of ascent and descent from the peak.

From the summit follow the SE Ridge by a system of ledges on the R side down to the gap between the Aig and Tour de la Brenva. Descend the couloir on the E side for 50m then slant down R on steep but easy rock until above a vertical smooth wall. Rappel this and the following dièdre to a shoulder (anchors in place). Descend a ridge on the L for 30m and traverse L into the couloir which can be climbed or rappeled down to the Entrèves glacier. 1–2hr

281　　**NORTH RIDGE**
V/V+　　S Olivetti with O Ottoz and F Thomasset, 31 July 1933

`63`

An exposed climb that is rarely done.

From the Brèche de la Brenva reach the col on the far side of the Père Eternal. Reach the gap between the first and second steps on the ridge by climbing cracked walls on the W side (V). Reach and climb a strenuous slanting crack above (V and V+) then an overhanging groove and wall to the top of the second step (V). Follow the crest with 1 short section of V to the summit. 150m, 2–3hr

282　　**EAST FACE (BOCCALATTE ROUTE)**
V/V+　　N Pietrasanta and G Boccalatte, 12 July 1935

`63`
`21`

A bold climb with continuous difficulties in the upper 200m. In particular there is a sustained pitch of V and V+ on slightly doubtful rock. c450m, 5–7hr

283　　**EAST FACE (REBUFFAT ROUTE)**
V/V+　　J Deudon and B Pierre with G Rebuffat, 18–19 May 1948. Winter: P Gleize and J Keller, March 1975

`63`
`21`

Possibly the finest route on this very steep face with sustained and exposed free climbing in the upper 150m. Descent is often made by rapelling the route. c450m, 5–7hr

Aiguille d'Entrèves 3600m

A minor peaklet E of the Tour Ronde with a steep face of sound red granite.

284　　**WEST FACE**
IV/V　　M and T Busi, M and C Fuselli with F and F Salluard, 17 Aug 1952. Winter: G Ambrosi, P Ferraris and G Machetto, 14 Jan 1967

`61`

The route follows a continuous system of cracks and dièdres directly in the fall line from the summit (5–6 pitches). 200m, 4hr from the Torino Hut.

Descend the NE Ridge easily to the Col de Toule.

135

La Vierge 3244m

A small rocky spire at the end of the promontory running N from the Col des Flambeaux. It is best approached from the Géant glacier to the N, but the W Face can also be reached by following the snowy ridge N from the Col des Flambeaux to the gap just before the summit and descending to the contorted glacier on the W side.

285   **NORTH FACE**
V+/A1   C Mollier and G Payot, 4 Sept 1959

Steep and exposed climbing on excellent rock. At present there are 2 short sections of aid climbing.

In the centre of the face climb up past a small niche to reach a series of vertical cracks (V) leading to a sloping platform. Climb a dièdre on the R (V+) to a good ledge then slant up L to a terrace (V+, A1 at the end). Climb steep cracks above (IV+) then work up L via a series of cracks (V+ and A1) to the summit block. 240m, 5hr

286   **WEST FACE**
V/A1   G Bertone and G Machetto, 2 Aug 1968

`22`

Shorter and easier than the previous route.

In the centre of the face, 20m R of a huge dièdre, climb a crack (V) then slant up L to a good ledge. Climb directly up from the L-hand end, crossing a spur, and traverse L to a terrace. On the R climb walls and overhangs (A1) finishing directly on the summit via a dièdre (V). 200m, 4hr

Col du Géant 3365m

First traverse: J Cachet and A Tournier, 27 June 1787

One of the most famous glacier passes in the Alps linking Chamonix and Courmayeur by crossing the range at its midpoint. It is reached easily by téléphérique from both Chamonix and La Palud. (See Route H19 for the approach to the Torino Hut).

Aiguilles Marbrées

Minor peaks (3535m N Summit; 3483m S Summit) on the frontier ridge quickly reached from the Torino Hut. There are two nice little free climbs on good rock – useful for a short day.

1 **NORTH-WEST RIDGE OF NORTH SUMMIT**
IV+ G Brignolo, G Castelli and A Marchiard, 29 March 1966

64

This reaches the top of the second buttress on the ridge by climbing directly up a spur on the W side beginning in a 10m high dièdre (IV+). Afterwards continue up the L flank and follow the crest of the ridge itself (IV) to the N summit. 1 pitch of V. 270m, 3½hr

Descent: Either down a large snowy couloir on the SW flank beginning a little to the S of the summit, or the easy E Ridge towards the Col du Rochefort (3389m).

2 **WEST SPUR OF NORTH SUMMIT**
V+ H Boisier and J Chaffat, 8 Sept 1979

64

A direct line up the yellow pillar to the R of the central couloir with the only pitch of V+ near the top. 8 pitches, 3hr

Dent de Jetoula 3306m

A Hess and F Santi with C Ollier, 9 Sept 1898

A complex rocky peak S of the Aigs Marbéres. The granite is generally good and clears quickly after bad weather.

3 **SOUTH RIDGE DIRECT**
V/V+ L Chiornio and G Salomone with G Panei, 20 Aug 1948

A long, varied though rarely climbed free rock route (mainly IV to V+).

Unfortunately many of the difficulties can be avoided but the direct finish contains a delicate and sparsely protected pitch of VI.650m

From the Pavillon Station (2174m) follow the path towards the Torino Hut until it begins to steepen then make an ascending traverse across the moraine to reach the foot of the S Ridge at c2650m (2hr). Start up R on easy ground to reach the bottom of the first step which lies to the L of a large rocky couloir. Follow the crest of the ridge directly over a succession of towers (several rappels) which in the main could be avoided on the E flank. 650m, 7hr to the summit.

Descent: Either continue to the gap before the Tour de Jetoula (3342m) then scramble down to the E to reach the SE Ridge overlooking the Rochefort basin. Descend this until an obvious couloir leads down R (II) to grassy slopes at the base of the S Ridge (PD, 2hr), or continue over the summit of the Tour and take the W flank of the subsequent ridge to the Col du Géant (PD, 1½–2hr)

4   **WEST FACE**
IV/V H Boissier and J Choffat, 1981

This climbs directly to the summit from the base of the Mt Fréty glacier. 600m, 5½hr

Dent du Géant 4013m

B, D and J Maquignaz, 28 July 1882 to SW summit (4009m)

One of the most famous and spectacular peaks in the range, deserving its overwhelming popularity. The attractive summit, formed by 2 rocky points 25m apart, is an excellent lightning conductor!

5   **SOUTH-WEST FACE (NORMAL ROUTE)**
AD   First ascent party

65

An exposed ascent on excellent rock which has been spoilt by the presence of enormous fixed ropes for most of its length. A very early start is unnecessary as the face will still be in shadow but avoid being late on busy days when descending parties will add to the overall confusion. See also Photo 64

From the Torino Hut cross the glacier below the Aigs Marbréesthen pass R of Pt 3516m to the base of the shoulder supporting the Dent. Climb a snowy couloir, or the rocks on the L side, to a col with a sharp gendarme (3665m) on the L. Turn R and follow an easy ridge until it merges into the face above. Continue more or less in the same line via vague couloirs and little rock steps (frequent stonefall in dry conditions). As angle eases near the top and a large smooth gendarme is seen, reach its base. It can be turned on either side but early in the day contouring round its E side is probably best. The snowy crest beyond leads to a large rock called the Salle à Manger (2½hr).

Traverse round the snow bowl to a terrace at the lowest point of the Dent. Start further L and climb a large detached flake and the slab above (5–6m, III). Traverse horizontally L for 10m on excellent holds to a couloir. Climb it for 30m to a platform on the L. Follow ropes up the exposed Burgener Slabs to the SW Summit (7 pitches from the Salle à Manger; IV and V without the ropes). Descend a chimney to the gap beyond and climb directly up the wall in front (III) to the NE Summit (2–3hr). 180m, 4½–5½hr from the hut.

6 NORTH-WEST FACE
TD

S Benedetti and R Luigi, 1981

66

An icy rock climb. 360m

7 NORTH RIDGE AND NORTH-WEST FACE
D–

T Maischberger, H Pfannl and F Zimmer, 20 July 1900. Winter: R Pellin and C Zappelli, 16 Jan 1964

66

Although infrequently climbed, this is a superb route on good, if often icy, rock and avoids major difficulties on the ridge by short excursions onto the NW Face.

Follow Route 5 towards the Salle à Manger (2½hr) but continue under the S Face until it is possible to descend steeply alongside the N Ridge, at first on an ice slope and then down rock steps, to reach the foot of a large rocky couloir on the E flank. There are 2 distinct shoulders low down on the N Ridge. Climb the rocky couloir, traverse R to a secondary couloir and after ascending this traverse R again to reach the upper shoulder (1¾hr).

It is possible to reach the lower shoulder by an ascent of the snow slope on the NW side of the peak and the obvious ice couloir. From here a short descent and traverse on the E flank can be made to gain the couloir mentioned above. Although more aesthetic it is much longer (c360m) and is very seldom used.

On the NW Face follow a ledge to its R-hand end and climb a 30m crack. Return to the ridge at a small gap. Climb the crest for 10m. Traverse R on a ledge then regain the ridge 10m above. Traverse R again then climb cracks for 30m to a patch of ice. Take the R-hand of 2 parallel cracks slanting L up the walls above and reach the ridge on the R of a large red block. Continue up the crest for 12m then up a vague crack passing over the top of a yellow block. Follow a large ledge horizontally R for 30m to reach 2 parallel couloirs coming down from the gap between the summits. Take the L one for 10m then move into the R and so reach the top. c200m, 2–3hr

8   **NORTH RIDGE DIRECT**
D   E Rey and F Salluard, 20 July 1959

This is a great climb on excellent rock which takes a very direct line on the crest of the ridge.

From the upper shoulder climb just L of the crest for 25m (III) then take a steep crack (30m, V and A1). Continue on the crest for 5 more pitches (IV and IV+) to the summit. 200m, 3hr

9   **NORTH-EAST FACE DIRECT START**
TD   R Ducournau and R Mizrahi, July 1975

66

Reached from the Périades glacier this route takes steep ice on the L side of the lower N Ridge followed by a huge dièdre on the E flank (6 pitches, IV and V with 1 of VI and A1 good rock) to gain the lower shoulder. 550m, 12hr. See also Photo 67

10   **NORTH COULOIR**
TD   P Gabarrou and B Muller, June 1979

66

The steep (65°–70°) icy gully to the L of the previous route. 550m 11hr

11   **SOUTH-EAST PILLAR**
VI/A1/2   A Ottoz and S Viotto, 30 Aug 1950. Winter: P Armando and A
65   Gogna, 27 Dec 1966
23

The prominent pillar which defines the R edge of the S Face with more than 60% artificial climbing at present. Sustained at the grade. 130m, 6hr. See also Photo 66

141

12   **SOUTH FACE**

V/A1   H Bergasser and R Leist, 28 July 1935. Winter: M May and U

65   Prato, 14 March 1956

23

An historic route in which pegs were first used systematically for artificial techniques in the Western Alps. A popular classic. Though climbed less often in recent years, it should now go completely free. The climb suffers a little from having poorish rock on the long L and R traverses in the central section, but all the difficult pitches are on excellent rock. 150m, 4hr

13   **SOUTH DIEDRE**

V+/A2   A Bonino and F Girodo, 18–19 July 1970

65   This essentially takes the line of the huge dièdre system L of Route

23   12. Escape is possible at ⅓ height onto the normal route. Very sustained and strenuous artificial climbing on excellent rock. c150m, 12hr

Clochers de la Noire

14   **POINT 3386m NORTH-NORTH-EAST PILLAR**

TD   B Domenech, S Jouty, P Louis and R Wainer, 16–17 July 1971

67

This is easily and quickly approached from the Requin Hut (1½hr) or a comfortable bivouac on the R bank of the Périades glacier (½hr). Apart from 2 loose pitches, it is essentially sustained free climbing on good rock following a fairly direct line on the L side of the triangular buttress.

The route follows the spur immediately R of the narrow icy couloir which splits the L side of the triangular buttress. At first the spur is steep and smooth (IV to V+ with 2 short sections of A1/A2). Above it becomes a serrated ridge and gives pitches of IV and V to the summit. 550m, 17hr

Descent: Easily but with considerable objective danger down the E snow and ice slopes. It is safer to continue easily along the ridge to the Col Sup de la Noire (3622m) and descend the Géant glacier.

Aiguille de Rochefort 4001m

J Eccles with M and A Payot, 14 Aug 1873

A splendid mountain that provides a classic and extremely popular traverse along narrow curving ridges. The NW Face has 2 ice/mixed routes that are generally menaced by large serac barriers.

15
AD
`67`

WEST RIDGE
From E to W: E Fontaine with J Ravanel and J Simms, 17 July 1900

The normal route and often traversed prior to an ascent of the Dent du Géant, which can easily be included on the return journey. The ridge is an elegant, exposed and corniced snow crest and is extremely popular.

From the Torino Hut follow Route 5 to the Salle à Manger and continue along the ridge either crossing the foresummit (3933m) or turning it on the L. At the last rocks, slant up R to reach a narrow couloir leading to the summit. 4–5hr from the hut.

16
PD+
`66`

NORTH-NORTH-EAST SLOPE
In descent: first ascent party

This is almost always used in descent, effecting a classic traverse of the mountain. The Mont Mallet Glacier is rather crevassed and sports a huge rimaye that must generally be crossed by rappel.

From the summit, descend the N ridge to a plateau and cross slopes below the summit of Mt Mallet to reach snow-covered rocks on the NE face. These lie to the L (N) of a slope containing large serac barriers. In good conditions it is possible to find a way down through these seracs but generally it is best to descend the snow covered rocks for 250m to the glacier. Follow this, keeping close to the L side, joining Route H31 in the vicinity of the Périades bivouac. 4hr to the Leschaux Hut.

Mont Mallet 3989m

L Stephen, G Loppé, F Wallroth with M Anderegg, Cachet and A Tournier, 4 Sept 1871

Situated at the end of a spur running N from the main frontier ridge and easily combined with an ascent of the Aig de Rochefort.

17   **SOUTH RIDGE FROM AIGUILLE DE ROCHEFORT**
PD   First ascent party

66

From the summit of the Aig de Rochefort descend the N Ridge to a plateau and follow a snowy crest to the foot of the ridge. Turn the lower rocks on the R and climb directly towards the summit. Near the top a very steep wall, 4m high, leads to a rectangular terrace from where the summit is easily reached. 1hr. See also Photo 67

18   **NORTH RIDGE**
AD   P Perret with F Simond and E Cupelin, 31 July 1882

66

The classic route from the Mer de Glace which can be combined with a traverse of the Rochefort Ridge to finish at the Col du Géant. Varied and interesting mixed climbing. Serious. See also Photo 67

There are two ways to approach the N Ridge. The first is perhaps the best, safest and most popular whilst also affording superb views of the Jorasses.

     a) From the Périades Bivouac, continue up the R side of the Mt Mallet glacier to reach the base of a broad snow slope leading up to the shoulder on the N Ridge. Cross the rimaye at c3550m and climb the 50° slope to the shoulder (3769m). From time to time this slope can form a serac barrier. In this case reach the ridge much lower down towards the Col du Mont Mallet and follow it, turning any obstacles, to the shoulder (2hr).

     b) Reach the upper and very crevassed Périades glacier either directly from the Requin Hut (3hr) or preferably from Montenvers via the R bank of the Tacul glacier and a bivouac on the moraine (3hr from Montenvers) forming the R bank of the lower Périades glacier (4½hr). On the L-hand side a big slanting snow slope descends W from the shoulder. Cross the rimaye (c3300m) at the base of a narrow slope, adjacent to and slightly L of the main slope. Climb the L edge, following a line of rocky islands alongside a vague rib (500m, 45°–50°) to the shoulder (3hr).

     Continue up the ridge at first on snow, then rock, where it is best to keep on the L side as far as a little step on the ridge before it steepens. Climb a steep chimney and follow the sharp ridge to the summit (1hr).

19
TD
67

WEST SPUR
B Domenech and S Jouty, 4 July 1971

Although the safest route on this side of the mountain and quite a good mixed climb, it is not without some objective danger and has failed to become popular. 1 pitch of VI. 600m, 12hr

Les Périades

The bristling pinnacled ridge over 1½km long, running from the Col du Mont Mallet (S) to the Col du Tacul (N). The highest point is Pt Cupelin (3549m) near the former col. There are numerous short and fairly hard climbs on generally good rock which will appeal to lovers of solitude.

Brèche Superieure des Périades 3432m

20
PD
67

WEST SIDE
R and V Puiseux with G Couttet, 28 July 1925

Situated just S of the Périades Bivouac Hut. This provides an excellent means of access to the Mont Mallet glacier from the Requin Hut or vice versa.

From the Périades glacier reach the foot of the snowy couloir which slants up L to the Brèche. Climb it, or the rocks on the L, to the top. 300m, 40–45°

Pointe Simond 3493m

21
IV/V
67

STYLITE PILLAR
B Domenech and E Hanoteau, 23 June 1974

A very fine rock climb that takes a direct line up the pillar in the centre of the W Face and deserves greater popularity.

Start 30m to the R of the lowest point of the pillar. Climb a short wall (2 moves of A1) then reach the crest and follow it directly (IV with 1 pitch of V). The last 150m to the summit is relatively easy. 550m, 5hr
    Descent: See Route 23

22	**WEST FACE ICE COULOIR**
TD–	D Marchand and G Perroux, 6 June 1980

67

A narrow couloir between the Pts Simond and des Périades. 1 pitch of 80°. 400m, 4½hr.

Pointe des Périades 3503m

23	**WEST FACE**
V/V+	D Marchand, B Miard and G Perroux, 5 Oct 1980

67

Good free climbing up a series of cracks and chimneys just R of the centre of the face. A comfortable bivouac can be made under the Clocher du Tacul (3118m). Sustained for the first 200m then easier.

Descent: Easier routes down the rocky W flanks of both this and Pte Simond are somewhat loose and exposed to stonefall. Although longer it is recommended to return via the Brèche Sup des Périades.

From the summit climb down the E flank in a series of chimneys and follow ledges around to the S Ridge. Scramble down this, turning Pt Simond on the W flank and reach the Brèche before Pt Nina (3455m) where a short snow slope leads down to the Mt Mallet glacier (1hr). Either descend this to the Leschaux Hut or reach the Brèche Sup des Périades and reverse Route 20 to the Périades glacier.

Aiguille du Tacul 3444m

First known ascent: the Couttet Brothers, 1842

This magnificent viewpoint contains a fine variety of routes and is best approached directly from Montenvers via a bivouac at the delectable 'Lac du Tacul', a moraine-dammed lake bed at the foot of the NW Ridge (2179m. Although the lake is long since dried up, snowmelt is still available until mid-season).

For routes on the W side it is better to continue along the moraine on the L of the Tacul glacier until a large grassy spur leads up to snow slopes below the W face just above Pt 2674m. A bivouac is possible at the highest point on this moraine.

24 **SOUTH-EAST RIDGE (NORMAL ROUTE)**
PD– F Burnaby and E Cupelin, Summer 1882

A straightforward and delightful excursion.

Follow the E branch of the Périades glacier to the couloir below the Col du Tacul. After crossing the rimaye strike up L and climb the couloir, or the loose rock on the L side, to reach the NW gap. Climb up the SE Ridge, passing between two slabs that lie to the R of a leaning tower, and reach the summit. 2hr

The Col du Tacul can also be reached directly from the Leschaux Hut via the Capucin glacier and a steep snowy couloir. Although interesting, this can only be recommended in cold conditions with good snow cover – the rock on the flanks is atrocious. 3½hr, AD

25 **WEST-SOUTH-WEST RIDGE**
PD *A nice variant leading directly to the summit*

67

Just before the base of the couloir on the W side of the Col du Tacul slant up L onto the WSW ridge. Reach the summit via the upper slopes of the hanging glacier on the NW side finishing directly up a series of chimneys. 2½hr

26 **WEST PILLAR**
V/V+ M Manfait and B Germain, 10–11 Aug 1977

67
22

The initial 450m red tower finishing on the shoulder (3220m) gives superb, sustained and exposed climbing on excellent granite. Mainly free but with some A1/A2.

Start almost directly below the summit of the red tower in a prominent system of ramps and cracks that lead up to a small snow patch ⅓ of the way up the face. 650m, 12hr

27 **NORTH-WEST COULOIR**
AD+ P Leon, E Ollivier, D Ploix with B Germain, 4 July 1976

67
22

This is a pleasant and rather popular snow and ice climb leading to the upper section of the WSW ridge. 650m, 3hr

28 **NORTH FACE**
D+ M Berthemin with P Gabarrou, 29 Aug 1978

68

A complex face bounded on the R by the long and tedious NNW ridge (poor rock). On the L side of the face a 200m pillar of good granite leads to a long ridge of broken rock. This should be climbed early in the season

147

when ample snow cover gives particularly fine mixed ground in a superb situation.

From the base of the pillar, reached in 1½hr from the Leschaux Hut, slant up R for 3 pitches (IV to V with a short section of A1) to reach a huge dièdre. Climb this (50m, IV and V) and reach the summit of the pillar in 2 easier pitches. The shattered rock crest is followed to its end. Slant up R for a few pitches to reach the hanging glacier which is followed directly to the summit. 850m, 10hr

Aiguille du Tacul: North-East Ridge

The lower section of this 900m ridge is a wide, steep and compact rock buttress. The upper narrower section presents snowy mixed ground.

29   **ORIGINAL ROUTE**
AD   E Frendo and R Grière, 7 Aug 1938

This avoids the lower buttress.

From the Leschaux Hut reach the Capucin glacier and gain the ridge below Pt 3132m by following a line of easy chimneys and couloirs on the E flank (pitches of III). Follow the crest to the summit. 4–5hr

The lower rock buttress has been climbed by 2 difficult routes. Excellent granite.

30   **AFANASSIEF-CORDIER ROUTE**
TD–   J Afanassief and P Cordier, 10 July 1974

68

On the NNW flank start just R of the spur which descends to the lowest point. Climb directly for 150–200m (pitches of IV+) to reach the obvious Lward slanting dièdre. Follow this to the ridge (V and V+, 200m). Continue more easily on snowy terrain to Pt 3132m and follow Route 29 to the summit. 9hr

31   **GARNIER-LACQUEMENT ROUTE**
TD–   P Garnier and P Lacquement, July 1977

68

Climb directly up a 200m dièdre on the N Face (V and V+ on compact rock) and continue on snowy rocks to the ridge. 9hr

Tours des Leschaux

Situated below the N Face of the Aig du Tacul these 5 towers give a number of short rock climbs and one long and delightful traverse on excellent rock. One of the better excursions combines an ascent of the lower tower with the upper spur of the Donjon.

Donjon 2764m

32   **NORTH SPUR**
V/V+/A1   M Truchon, P Blanjoie, L Lagrange with B Germain, 10 July 1978

On the corner between the N and NW Faces of the lower tower is a line of steep dièdres. Follow these throughout (V, V+ and A1) finishing under a large chockstone jammed across an easy dièdre of rotten rock. Descend to the gap (it is possible to escape L here onto the snow slopes). Climb up the next gendarme (the Guardian) passing through a notch between 2 pointed towers and descend to the gap before the Donjon. Climb the face above in 4 pitches via cracked slabs (10m of A1 then IV). 400m, 8–10hr

Descent: Rappel to the gap beyond then descend the E flank in 2 rappels to the snow slopes below.

Dôme de Rochefort 4015m

J Eccles with A and M Payot, 12 Aug 1881

This is the highest point on the Rochefort Ridge but is far less frequented than the Aig de Rochefort.

33   **SOUTH-WEST RIDGE**
PD+   K Blodig and M Horten, 9 Aug 1903

The normal route follows the main frontier ridge in a splendid situation.

From the summit of the Aig de Rochefort descend N to the plateau and follow the snowy ridge NE, turning a rock pinnacle (Le Doigt de Rochefort 3928m) on the L, to the shattered summit rocks. 1–1½hr

34　　**NORTH-WEST FACE**
AD　　First ascent party

72

A nice little mixed route.

From the Périades Bivouac go up the R side of the Mt Mallet glacier and reach the foot of the face. Climb the ice slope to the R of the summit fall-line, moving L in the upper reaches to finish direct on mixed ground. 350m, 2½hr

35　　**NORTH FACE**
D+　　J Cleymann and G Perroux, 20 June 1981

72

The ice gully to the L of the summit fall line with a crux pitch of 75°. 350m, 4hr

36　　**NORTH-EAST RIDGE**
PD/AD　First descent: M Santi and V Sigismondi, 13 or 14 Aug 1909. In
72　　ascent J and R Leininger and P Madeuf, 4 Aug 1937

Described in descent to the Col des Grandes Jorasses. This forms an integral part of one of the most classic traverses in the range – from the Col du Géant to the summit of the Grandes Jorasses.
　　In ascent it provides an exposed rock climb taken mainly on the L side of the steep step. Excellent granite. (V−, 4hr)

From the Dôme reach the Calotte de Rochefort by an easy connecting ridge of broken rocks and snow. Continue along the crest to the step above the Col des Grandes Jorasses. At present this crest is an exposed and very narrow rocky ridge which can be quite time-consuming. Make 3–4 long rappels down the step to the col (2–3hr). 3½–4½hr from the Dôme.

37　　**SOUTH FACE**
TD　　L Pasi and A Piccioni, 16–18 Sept 1971

75

A huge rockwall with a complicated glacier approach. Rarely, if ever, repeated.

Start at the lowest point of the face and climb directly upwards (III and IV) passing to the L of a conspicuous red tower to reach the centre of the grey, compact upper buttress. Climb this by a series of dièdres (V, V+ and some artificial sections). 750m, 20hr

Calotte de Rochefort 3981m

This is most easily reached from the Dôme de Rochefort in 1½hr.
The N and NW faces reached via the Mt Mallet glacier have 4 fine
ice/mixed routes which would certainly have become quite popular
were they not in such a remote location.

38   **NORTH-WEST FACE**

TD   B Grison and G Perroux, 1983

67

Technical ice climbing in the lower section with a thinly iced crux at
80–85°. The last pitch is over rock (IV+). 350m. See also Photo 72

39   **NORTH-WEST RIDGE**

AD+   P Chevalier and M Sauvage, 11 Aug 1928

72

Climbs the NW Ridge and face above finishing directly over the
Calotte. Mixed. 400m, 3½hr

40   **NORTH FACE DIRECT**

AD+/D–   J Asselin, P Gabarrou, A Long and P Silvy, 14 April 1984

72

A broad couloir leads onto the NW ridge at half-height. Near the
top of this couloir slant L up a ramp/couloir line lying beneath a
rock barrier, until it is possible to break through the barrier towards
its upper L-hand end. Finish direct to the summit. 400m, 4–5hr

41   **NORTH COULOIR**

D/D+   A Heckmair and G Kroner, 6 July 1931

72

The steep and narrow couloir on the L of the previous route. 350m,
4–5hr

Descent: Either follow Route 36 to the Col des Grandes Jorasses, or
follow the frontier ridge over the Dôme towards the Doigt de
Rochefort until it is possible to descend steep slopes to the Mt
Mallet glacier.

Col des Grandes Jorasses 3825m

A difficult pass that is gained from one side or the other in order to
reach the W Ridge of the Grandes Jorasses. The Canzio Bivouac
Hut is situated at the E end of the Col. See Huts Section.

First ascent of Pt Whymper (4184m W Peak): E Whymper with M Croz, C Almer and F Biner, 24 June 1865. Pt Walker (4208m E Peak): H Walker with M Anderegg, J Jaun and J Grange, 30 June 1868

A majestic mountain affording every type of climbing. The frontier crest is nearly 1km long and the great N Face has many routes on its spurs and in the dividing couloirs. Most of these are unfortunately composed of poor quality rock and are seriously exposed to stonefall. The S Face sports a number of rock climbs, many again on poor granite.

42   **SOUTH-WEST SIDE (NORMAL ROUTE) VIA POINTE**
AD–   **WHYMPER**
69   First ascent party

The most popular means of ascent and descent. Only slightly longer than the direct ascent to Pt Walker but much safer, especially in descent. Serious

From the Grandes Jorasses Hut go N up rocky slopes to the Planpincieux glacier and ascend this alongside a rocky rib to the Rocher de Reposoir (1½hr). Follow this rocky ridge to its top and cross the snow slope, often icy, to the R (avalanche danger in poor conditions) to reach the Rocher Whymper, a long rocky ridge descending from Pt Whymper (1½hr). Gain the crest and follow it on easy broken rocks, with a few pitches of III, to Pt Whymper and reach the summit of Pt Walker by the snowy frontier ridge. 6–7hr from the hut. Allow 5hr for the descent.

43   **DIRECT TO POINTE WALKER**
AD–   First ascent party of Pt Walker
69

Although the shortest and quickest route to the summit, good conditions are essential. It can only be used as a descent when the snow is hard. Serious

On reaching the Rocher Whymper follow the crest for about 100m, then traverse R to the snow plateau at a point where it is fairly flat. Cross it to the E (this is exposed to serac fall and snow slides) then go directly up a steep mixed snow/rock slope to the summit ridge a little to the W of Pt Walker. 5–6hr from the hut, 4hr in descent.

44 VIA POINTE CROZ

AD–

69

E Hasenclever, W Klemn, F Konig and R Weitsenbuck, 24 Aug 1909

Although longer than the preceding routes, this is by far the safest as it avoids the traverse across the snow slope R of the Rocher de Reposoir if it is avalanche-prone. Serious

On reaching the top of the Rocher de Reposoir climb straight up the edge of the snow slope above and continue on easy snow-covered rocks to the W Ridge a little below Pt Croz. Follow the W Ridge over Pts Croz and Whymper to the summit. 7–8hr from the hut.

45 POINTE MARGUERITE SOUTH FACE

TD+

69

G Alippi, A Pinciroli, L Stuffer and C Troyer, 8–9 Aug 1972

Hard climbing on generally very sound rock with pitches of VI but threatened by stonefall in the lower section.

Start just to the R of a rock triangle, directly below the summit, and climb up for 2 pitches towards a black roof. This is avoided on the R by a short section of A1. Climb up less steep ground to reach the huge dièdre in the upper section of the face. Climb this (sustained V+ and VI) to the summit. 600m, 16hr

46 WEST RIDGE

D

69

H Jones and G Young with J Knubel, 14 Aug 1911. Winter: A and A Ollier, 26 Jan 1964 (after a traverse of the Rochefort Ridge the previous day)

This classic ridge gives a committing traverse in a remote situation. It begins on sound granite, offers interesting mixed climbing in its middle section and finishes with a long easy snow crest. It is an excellent continuation of the Rochefort Ridge traverse after a night spent in the Canzio Bivouac on the Col des Grandes Jorasses. Serious

The bottom of the ridge takes the form of a triangular rock wall containing a conspicuous couloir leading to the R-hand ridge. Climb rocks on the L of this couloir for 20m then slant L on a ramp/crack line for 30m to reach a snowy terrace on the N face. The ground is now less steep but icy. Slant L in cracks for 25m, turn an overhanging block on the R and climb directly to the summit of Pt Young (3966m) on the ridge above (25m, 1½–2hr. Fairly continuous IV from the col). Go down the N side to a small shoulder above a gap. On the R, descend rocks alongside the S-facing couloir coming down from the gap (III) and after 30m

153

traverse across the couloir and round the buttress that follows (IV) to another couloir. Climb this for 20m then take rocks on the R side to reach the gap between the 2 summits of Pt Marguerite (4065m, 2hr). A very sharp and airy rocky ridge leads to Pt Hélène (4045m). Cross this and the 2 gendarmes that follow to reach Pt Croz (4110m). The ridge becomes fairly broad and snowy. Follow it to Pt Whymper turning any obstacles on the R, then descend a sharp snow crest to the gentle slopes that lead up to Pt Walker (3–4hr). 300m, 7–8hr from the hut.

Grandes Jorasses: North Face

This enormous wall, one of the six classic great N faces in the Alps, cannot fail to inspire alpinists. Over 20 routes have been established. Those to the R of the Croz Spur give, with one exception, difficult ice/mixed climbing in the lower half – severely exposed to stonefall – whilst the upper reaches give technical climbing on poor icy rock. Whilst extremely dangerous in summer, they are logical winter lines. In general, routes on this face rarely come into perfect condition and on those occasions the famous lines can attract large numbers.

47
TD
70

POINTE YOUNG NORTH SPUR

First climbed from the Mont Mallet glacier by H Furmanik, A Heinrich and K Zozitowiecki, 29–30 July 1968. The top buttress is a safe and worthwhile climb in its own right and is easily approached from the upper slopes of Route H31 to the Canzio Bivouac, just before the rimaye: E Cavaleri and A Mellano, 13–14 August 1958 (350m, D)

Difficult mixed climbing in the lower half is followed by some fine climbing on the good granite of the upper buttress.

Reach the foot of the vague spur on the R side of the face in 3hr from the Leschaux Hut. Climb it or the ice slopes to the L (stonefall). Where it becomes very steep just below the level of the upper Mt Mallet glacier, move R into a couloir and climb it to the crest. This point, about 50m below 2 small gendarmes, can be reached from the glacier on the R by crossing a steep narrow couloir.
　　　Follow the crest of the spur avoiding the gendarmes and a grey tower that follows on the R (III and IV). Climb a small tower by a chimney and a slabby buttress (IV+) with a small roof that is avoided on the R (V). Climb a short wall on the crest (4m, A1) and, by a dièdre on the L side of the final buttress (IV), reach easy rocks leading to the summit. 800m, 12–14hr

48   CROZ SPUR

TD+/ED1 M Meier and R Peters, 28–29 June 1935. Winter: J Marmier and G Nominé, 10–13 Feb 1971

71

This was the first route to be climbed on the N Face. Although an established classic, it is far less frequented than the Walker Spur, being a more serious undertaking with considerable stonefall risk. When well-iced such as in autumn or spring, it becomes a brilliant mixed route. A winter ascent of the N Face of the Jorasses gives one of the greatest adventures in the Alps and then the Croz is perhaps the most logical route to follow. The grade given applies to good conditions. Often harder. See also Photo 70

From the Leschaux Hut go up the glacier to the foot of the face (2½hr) and either a) cross the rimaye on the R side of the Central Couloir, go up the slope and climb the couloir that leads to the gap behind the first tower, or b) probably safer but more difficult: traverse below the first tower and climb a couloir on its R (NW) flank (60°) to the gap.

Climb the ridge above for 40m then traverse L to the couloir and go up it directly to the gap behind the second tower (2–3hr, stonefall danger throughout and should be climbed as early as possible).

Climb the crest of the spur for 120m (easy, then IV). Traverse R across the central snowfield (50°) to reach a couloir/dièdre at the top (2hr). Climb rocks to the R of the dièdre (IV) and rejoin it after 25m. Continue up the back for a further 25m to a platform, then traverse L and go straight up steep slabs for 2 or 3 pitches (V) to reach the 55° upper snowfield (2½hr. The section between the snowfields is exposed to stonefall).

Climb the snowfield and slant up R beneath the upper rocks to a couloir/chimney which leads back L on broken rock to a well-defined gap in the ridge about 150m below Pt Croz. Continue up the crest for 60m turning the first step on the R.

Either go round the base of a secondary ridge on the R to reach an open couloir. Follow this to a small col then traverse R (6m, IV+) and climb slabs and flakes. From the top of the flakes make a 15m rappel into a small couloir and follow it to the ridge R of Pt Croz. 1000m, 13–16hr from the hut.

Direct finish – much harder: Climb the dièdre/couloir between the secondary ridge and the main spur on the L. Exit L after 30m on an exposed ledge then climb up 30m to the base of the final wall. Climb this by a dièdre (sustained, V+) to the summit (4–6hr).

155

49   **CROZ SPUR DIRECT**

ED2   H Keine and K Werner, Aug 1974

70

This variation is sheltered from stonefall but the middle 400m section of the spur gives difficult climbing on poor rock. See also Photo 71

From the gap behind the second tower, climb the crest to a terrace below the steep section (IV to V+, often icy). Take a short dièdre on the R (IV) then climb a wall with an overhang (V and A1) followed by a system of dièdres (V), finishing on the upper snow field by a very difficult aid pitch. Climb the steep wall above the snowfield for 5 pitches (VI and A1) to reach a small tower below the crest of the spur. Continue up cracks and grooves for another 4 pitches, joining the direct finish, to the summit (IV to V+).

50   **DIRECTE DE L'AMITIE TO POINTE WHYMPER**

ED3/4   L Audobert, M Feuillarde, M Galy and Y Seigneur, 19–27 Jan 1974

71

This route which combines hard mixed climbing with very steep rock is one of the most difficult undertakings in the Alps. The lower section is seriously exposed to stonefall but once properly established on the upper wall, there are few objective dangers. The rock section, 650m of excellent red granite, is comparable to the E face of the Grand Capucin and has not yet been climbed without a fair degree of aid. See also Photo 70

Climb the icefield for 8 pitches following a succession of rognons (45°–50°), then slant L up a ramp line for 8 pitches (IV, V and A1) to a snow cone beneath the very steep rock wall directly below Pt Whymper. Climb almost vertically to the top via a series of cracks, dièdres and overhangs (generally V and A1 with one section of A2/3. There is a very large roof in this section that would be very problematical to reverse if a retreat was necessary from above). 1100m, allow at least 3 days for a summer ascent.

The next 2 climbs are in the Central Couloir. Very cold and icy conditions are required for them to be in condition and objectively safe.

51   **JAPANESE ROUTE**

ED3   Y Kanda, Y Kato, H Miyazaki, T Nakano and K Saito, 19–29

71   March 1972

This follows the main deeper R-hand couloir throughout. The rock is bad and the climbing seriously exposed to stonefall. There is no recorded second ascent. See also Photo 70

Climb the central ice slope (300m, 55°) then follow the main couloir (70° ice, V and A2) to reach the upper snowfield (50°–55°). The line continues, giving a series of steep mixed pitches and rock at V and A1 in chimneys and couloirs, to the summit ridge. 1200m

52 BRITISH ROUTE
ED3   N Colton and A MacIntyre, 6–7 Aug 1976

71

Although still exposed to stonefall, this is a little more sheltered than the Japanese Route and leads to the summit of Pt Walker. It has more technical ice climbing and it has been repeated a number of times in both summer and winter. See also Photo 70

Climb the L side of the initial icefield and take the thin couloir L of the Japanese Route for 5 very steep ice pitches (Scottish 5). Cross the small second icefield and take another couloir on the L that broadens out into the third icefield (Scottish 5). Rotten rock up the flanks of the Walker Spur (IV to V) leads to the top (15–20hr). An alternative finish more commonly followed in winter is to join the top section of the Japanese Couloir (Scottish 4/5 mixed). 1200m

53 WALKER SPUR
ED1   R Cassin, L Esposito and U Tizzoni, 4–6 Aug 1938. Winter: W
Bonatti and C Zappelli, 24–30 Jan 1963

71

A magnificent classic and generally accepted to be one of the best routes in the Alps. Though never extreme, the climbing, on open faces and in cracks, is continuously interesting and the rock for the most part is good. The lower section is exposed to stonefall and best climbed very early in the morning having started from the Leschaux Hut. A fast party should complete the route in a day but a bivouac will still be necessary on the descent. Despite the passage of time, this is still one of the most sought after rock/mixed climbs in Europe and a lasting tribute to its creator. See also Photo 70

Reach the foot of the spur in 2½hr from the Leschaux Hut. Climb the snow/ice slope to the R of the spur for 2 pitches, traversing L above the level of the small col to reach broken ground. This point can also be reached via a loose gully on the L side of the spur (IV) but this is not recommended. Climb up the steep loose ground then the L side of the ice slope which cuts the lower part of the spur, and when underneath the steep walls above, climb up L on snow or ice for 2 pitches until a steep 20m slab (V) leads upwards to a stance.
    Traverse broken ground to the R followed by a smooth ledge.

Return back L up steep slabs to a ledge below 2 vertical grooves in a wall on the R. Climb the L-hand groove, the Rebuffat Crack, for 15m, step into the R-hand groove and climb it to a good ledge (V and VI, or A1). Descend slightly to the R then slant up Rwards for 3 or 4 pitches on bands of ice and rock until it is possible to climb straight up for 70m to the foot of the second step.

On the R flank of this pillar climb the 75m Dièdre in 3 pitches, the first of 25m (IV+) to a stance below an overhang, then 20m (V) and 30m (V). Climb up L for 50m on snowy rock to a wall with chimneys on either side. Take the one on the R (IV+) and after 10–12m traverse R across a ledge for 15m to a slab. Cross this (V) to a point where a short diagonal rappel (fixed rope usually in place) can be made to reach a small ledge. Traverse R again and climb over a small black overhang (V) then continue Rwards to a platform.

The large step above is called the Tour Grise and is climbed on its R flank. Go up a short crack for 10m to some overhangs. Traverse L for 12m (V+) and slant up to the R in a crack system for 2 pitches (V/VI−)to reach a small depression below an overhang. Climb it (V) and continue up to a snowy ledge system that leads off R towards the Central Couloir. Climb directly up the steep wall above (V) then slant back L to the crest of the spur above the Tour Grise (IV+). Climb the ridge, generally on the R side, for about 6 pitches (IV and III, some poor rock). Continue up a mixed zone leading to a triangular snow patch. Either climb straight up to the obvious chimney/couloir above or climb the snow patch on the L to the top and traverse 20m R to reach the couloir about 30m above its base. This is the Red Chimney and is climbed on shattered and often icy rock for 2 pitches (V/V+, many pegs) until it is possible to slant up R in a chimney (IV) to reach an excellent flat stance on top of a pulpit (bivouac) and below the smooth walls of the Tour Rousse.

Climb a short wall (IV) to a horizontal ledge and follow this R until at its end one can climb a short groove (wet or icy, can often be the hardest pitch on the climb) to reach an easy couloir. Follow this on broken rocks and snow to a small shoulder on the ridge coming down from the summit. 3 pitches lead to the cornice. 1200m, 16–20hr from the hut.

More direct routes have been followed on the crest of the spur:The Direttissima by H Bouvard and P Gabarrou over 5 days in 1986 (ED3/4, VIII− and A1/A2) and L again is 'Rolling Stone', a 1000m 35pitch ED3. 50°–80° ice and VI/A3 (rotten rock). First ascent: J Kutil, T Prochazka, L Slechta and J Svejda, 24–29 July 1979. Winter: E Grammont and B Grison, 13–17 Feb 1984

54   **POINTE WALKER – NORTH-EAST FACE**
ED3   G Bertone, M Claret and R Desmaison, 10–17 Jan 1973

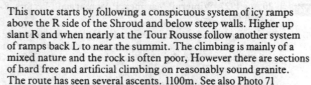

This route starts by following a conspicuous system of icy ramps above the R side of the Shroud and below steep walls. Higher up slant R and when nearly at the Tour Rousse follow another system of ramps back L to near the summit. The climbing is mainly of a mixed nature and the rock is often poor, However there are sections of hard free and artificial climbing on reasonably sound granite. The route has seen several ascents. 1100m. See also Photo 71

55   **THE SHROUD**
TD+   R Desmaison and R Flematty, 13–26 Jan 1968. Direct start first climbed by L Berardini and R Paragot during an early attempt (1963).First complete ascent: P Braithwaite and P Moores, 23 July 1975

This beautiful hanging icefield to the L of the Walker Spur was the last of the great ice faces to be climbed in the range. Nowadays it has become classic but needs very cold and icy conditions to render it safe from stonefall. The route reaches the Hirondelles Ridge at half-height and although it is considered more aesthetic to continue over the summit, many parties descend the ridge from here. See also Photo 70

The original route climbs steep ice grooves on the L flank of the Walker but the direct start is the one most commonly followed nowadays.

The R-hand couloir is 250m, 75°–80°, Scottish 4. Slant L (60°–65°) to reach the L edge of the Shroud and follow it (50°–55°) climbing the broken rocks above at their narrowest point (7–10hr). 750m, 12–15hr from hut to summit.

The steeper L-hand gully was climbed by R Graham and A Hyslop in 1980 and the obvious direct finish up the depression leading to the summit of Pt Walker by H Sachetat and J Séguier 14–15 Jan 1983, who found very difficult and dangerous climbing on poor rock.

56   **MACINTYRE ROUTE**
TD   A MacIntyre, T Rhodes and W Todd, June 1976. Winter: L Kryje and B Mrozek, Feb 1982

This climbs the ice slope in the great corner situated just L of the Shroud. It is a safe route being fairly sheltered from stonefall. A heavy snow covering is desirable or else the top section will give very hard mixed climbing and a steep narrow icegully. Scottish 4, 600m. See also Photo 71

57 NORTH-EAST (HIRONDELLES) RIDGE

D/D+

74

G Gaia, S Matteoda, F Ravelli, G Rivetti with A Rey and A Chenoz, 10 Aug 1927. Winter: P Martinez, P Monzat and J Pectors, 8–9 March 1977

An established classic that is not sustained but does have one quite difficult section. Its remote situation has ensured that this route is still infrequently ascended. Icy sections can be slow to clear. Serious. See also Photos 70 and 71

From the Col des Hirondelles (Route 73) cross snow slopes to the foot of a triangular facet. This forms the L flank of the lower part of the ridge with a summit just before a V brèche. Climb straight up broken rock and snow for about 100m, a little R of centre of the triangle. Slant up L and climb a deep chimney with a slightly overhanging start (15m, IV) to the ridge. Continue up the ridge to the V brèche (III and IV). Traverse L to reach the first of two steep parallel cracks, initially choked with flakes, and climb it to a platform on the L (The Fissure Rey, 20m, V/V+). Climb the dièdre above to a second platform (III+).

The best variation from here is the Gobbi Crack. Move R to a crack in the back of a dièdre and climb it by bridging for its entire length (100m, IV+) to a platform on the ridge. If this is iced then from the second platform climb up a steep and verglassed pitch exiting L to a small shoulder (IV/IV+). Move into a long couloir coming down from the ridge and follow it to the crest (III). Continue up the ridge which broadens, then becomes more mixed and broken and finally joins the Tronchey Ridge. Keep on the R flank of the final ridge to the summit of Pt Walker. c750m, 6–8hr

This imposing face of excellent compact granite now has four routes, the most recent climbing the well-defined pillar on the L of the Original Route (P Cavagnetto and E Rosso, 7–8 Aug 1988 (750m, ED2/3, VII and A2).

58   **ORIGINAL ROUTE**

ED2   G Gagliardone and G Gervasutti, 16–17 Aug 1942. Winter: J
Marmier and C Rudolf, 7–9 March 1977

A committing and serious route which is probably Gervasutti's greatest creation. The original line followed the Y-shaped couloir in the lower part of the face but this is raked by heavy stonefall that begins at dawn. A circuitous and probably easier variant start, as described below is considerably safer. The main difficulties are concentrated in the 350m wall above, where several variations are possible. There are small bivouac sites all the way up the route, though a very fast party could possibly complete the ascent in 1 day.

From the Gervasutti Hut reach the Col des Hirondelles via Route 73 and traverse steep slopes to the L, keeping close under the face, to reach a tiny icefield about 100m L of the Y couloir (4hr). Climb the icefield then bear up L for 2 tricky wet pitches (V) to reach the base of an overhanging wall. Slant up R for 3 pitches on broken ground to the large snowy terrace at the top of the Y couloir. The route now follows a series of cracks and corners to the R of the prominent dièdre on the L side of the wall. Traverse L along the ledge (stonefall) until a short pitch leads to the base of a R facing corner with a big square fluke overhang 10m above. Climb this (35m, V+) to a long ledge on the L. From the L end of the ledge make a difficult move (VI) into a corner and climb it (40m, V+) and the L ward slanting dièdre that follows (30m, V+). Reach another dièdre on the R and belay about 10m below a wide overhanging crack. Climb diagonally L across a bulging wall (VI) to a ridge on the L and follow it to a large sloping ledge (V). Climb R across a wet slab (V) then down across a further slab (V) to a prow. Immediately above an obvious pillar is attached to the overhanging headwall. Climb up to the pillar and then take the crack on the R side to the top (35m, V+). A thin crack (A2) slants through the headwall with a difficult exit onto a smooth slab (VI). Slant up R for 2 pitches (V+ then V, wet) to a large terrace. Climb up R to reach a small gap on the broken ridge which is followed more easily (III and IV) for 3 pitches to the Tronchey Ridge. Follow this on very loose rock (III) to the summit. 750m, 18–22hr from the hut.

59 **EAST FACE DIRECT**

ED2/3 C and F Delisi, 13–15 Aug 1983

74

In the centre of the face is a great dièdre capped by roofs. Slabs above lead to the overhanging headwall. The main difficulties are concentrated in 10 pitches (V+ and VI; A3). 750m

60 **RIGHT-HAND ROUTE**

TD J Boivin and F Diaferia, 31 Aug 1981

74

The obvious line of weakness on the R-hand side of the face. 750m, 10hr

61 **SOUTH-EAST (TRONCHEY) RIDGE**

TD– T Gilberti and E Croux, 22–23 Aug 1936. The direct ascent of the

75 third tower, described below, was completed by J Gourdain and L Terray, 31 July–1 Aug 1949. Winter: L Cozzon, L Henry, R Salluard and C Zappelli, 9–10 Jan 1973

This long and remote rock ridge is the only way of reaching the summit of the Grandes Jorasses without setting foot on a glacier. Although considered a superb undertaking, it is very rarely done. See also Photo 74

From the Jacchia Bivouac follow the ridge over the Aig de Tronchey to a small brèche. Continue up the ridge turning a red gendarme on the L and returning to the ridge by a steep chimney (IV). Follow the L side of the ridge (pitches of III) until about 50m below the first tower, then traverse L round a smooth pillar to a couloir leading up to the gap between the first and second towers. Climb the couloir then rocks on its L side (III) to the ridge. Follow this until it becomes very hard. Traverse across a snowy couloir L of the ridge and climb up to a spur coming down from the third tower. Climb the crest of this spur for a pitch (IV) then continue up to the L until a series of broken ledges lead back R to the gap below the third tower.

From the foot of the tower traverse R easily for 20m then climb straight up poor rock for 50m (IV) to a sloping terrace. From its L end make a difficult tension traverse to a smooth wall and climb it for 15m (IV then V+/VI). Now traverse R (V) to an overhanging dièdre and slant up R for 12m across a vertical wall to a small ledge. A short pitch (V) followed by easy rock leads to the ridge. Continue up this on very loose rock to the summit (II and III). 950m, 10–12hr

The third tower can be avoided by traversing below it on the E face and returning to the ridge up a series of icy walls and couloirs (II and III). This reduces the overall grading of the climb to D.

62   **TRONCHEY RIDGE INTEGRAL**
TD   G Bosio, L Ferrero, U Manera and F Ribetti, 10 July 1982

74

The complete traverse of all three towers, following more or less the crest throughout, gives high quality free climbing in a wonderful situation. Only one or two pegs remain in place. See also Photo 75

Follow the previous route until under the penultimate rocky gully below the first tower. Climb the gully to the ridge and follow it over the first tower passing the summit on the L side (III and IV). On the R cross a fine dièdre and reach the short horizontal crest below the second tower (IV and V). Climb up to the overhangs of the second tower (IV and IV+) then work up L to a ledge(V). Continue straight up for 20m (IV+) and where the wall begins to overhang follow a slanting crack on the L under a big roof (V). Go down to the L, climb a dièdre-slab and cross L again to a sloping shelf (V) that is in the middle of the wall between the crest of the tower on the R and the snowy couloir (leading up to the gap between the second and third towers) on the L. Climb up for 15m then slant R to the crest (V+). Climb a vertical wall (V) and continue easily to the base of the third tower.

A few m to the R of the crest climb up 20m then slant up R in a good crack to below some overhangs of broken rock (V−). Climb a grey slab then work L under roofs until it is possible to go over them and up a series of cracks to the second overhang (V+). Traverse L across a smooth slab (V) then go up a fine wall, working L to finish under a prominent roof (V+). Climb this (A2 and V) and continue up shallow dièdres to a ramp that slants up R to easy ground (IV+). Reach the top of the third tower and follow the crest easily to the summit of the Grandes Jorasses. c950m, 16hr

Grandes Jorasses: South Flank

63   **SOUTH FACE**
ED2   G Grassi, R Luzi and M Rossi, 19 June 1985

75

This was first climbed directly in the summer of 1972 and gave a non-homogenous climb on wet rock (VI and A1) with severe stonefall danger. Under very cold and snowy conditions a line slightly to the L gave a magnificent climb up a series of icy gullies containing several steep sections of Scottish 5. Due to its aspect it is rarely in condition and is best attempted in spring. The approach from the Tronchey Valley takes 5hr. 1200m, 12hr

64 **SUPERCOULOIR**

ED2 G Comino and G Grassi, 20 Aug 1978. Winter: P Gabarrou and F Marsigny, 27 Feb 1985

75

This deep narrow couloir to the R of the central pillar is very rarely in condition. It gives a succession of 4 vertical to overhanging sections of ice up to 30m high. 250m, 10hr

65 **SOUTH PILLAR**

TD P Ghiglione and A Ottoz, 29 Sept 1948

69

This distinct pillar of excellent compact granite gives a fine rock climb with good belays. The number of ascents has been limited by the long approach and a very remote situation.

Descend 200m from the Grandes Jorasses Hut to reach the glacier. Follow the steep and crevassed upper slopes of the E branch to a rocky spur that constitutes the L side of a large snowfield below the W flanks of the Pra Sec ridge. At the top of this spur traverse L and descend slightly for about 120m to reach the base of the pillar below the first tower (5hr).

Start about 6m L of the spur and climb slabs, dièdres and chimneys to an area of broken rock (IV to V+). Go up to the foot of the second step which lies about 220mm above the start of the climb. Climb a ridge, on the L of a huge smooth wall, to a ledge at the top of a narrow icy couloir which flanks the W side of the pillar. Traverse R across the couloir and climb directly up the crest (IV to VI) to the summit of the pillar. Surmount the serac barrier above and continue to the summit of Pt Walker. 550m, 15hr from the hut.

Tour des Jorasses 3813m

This satellite peak of the Grandes Jorasses gives some superb rock routes on its magnificent S face of solid granite. One route in particular has gained considerable popularity. From the summit it is possible to descend the NE ridge towards Pt Walker as far as the gap before a secondary E summit. Make 3 rappels to the Upper

Grandes Jorasses glacier and follow Route 48 down to the hut. However Route 67 has a well-equipped rappel descent from the top of the dièdre.

Although it is possible to reach the face directly from the Grandes Jorasses Hut (1½–2hr, see Route 65) the glacier is very crevassed and it is better to approach from Route H20 when about 1hr below the hut.

66 **SOUTH RIDGE INTEGRAL**
TD   A Nebiolo and F Piana, 3–4 Aug 1976

75
24

This route has very good climbing which is quite sustained in the lower section. It follows the crest of the ridge closely starting at the lowest point. Serious difficulties near the crest are avoided from time to time by logical deviations onto the SW face. V+ and A1. 1000m, 20hr

67 **SOUTH DIEDRE**
TD+   G Calcagno, L Cerruti and G Machetto, 5–6 Aug 1970

75
24

This modern classic is considered to be one of the finest rock climbs in the range. The climbing of the huge L wall of the top dièdre is particularly superb. The original route contained a section of sustained aid climbing but this was avoided on the third ascent and the climb has been done completely free. The bottom of the face is exposed to stonefall so an early start is needed. A fast party should be able to complete the round trip, over the summit, from the hut in one day but accepted practice nowadays is to rappel back down the route at the end of the major difficulties which lie in the first 400m. VI/VI+. 700m, 6–8hr

68 **SOUTH-EAST FACE 1988 ROUTE**
VII+   D Ankar, M Piola and P Strappazzon, 12 & 13 Aug 1988. Winter: F
75   Arneodo, P Brignolo and E Costa, 29 Jan 1989

The slabs and overhangs to the R of the dièdre were climbed in 14 magnificent and sustained pitches which are protected by 57 in situ bolts. Rappel Route 67. 450m of difficulty: unavoidable VII+

69 **SOUTH-EAST FACE**
ED1   M Bena, J Sochor, J Sveida and K Zivny, 2–4 Aug 1977

75
24

This follows a line of dièdres on the R side of the huge compact walls to join the South Dièdre at the end of the difficulties. 400m of V and VI– with 1 section of A3. 700m

Routes further to the R are threatened, in their lower sections, by ice and stonefall from the vicinity of the hanging glacier.

Aiguilles de Pra Sec 3549m, 3490m and 3438m

Not marked on IGN. The E faces of the S and Central points, reached in 3hr from the Tronchey Chalets via the Pra Sec glacier offer some steep free climbs that quickly come into condition after bad weather. The rock is very sound but occasionally a bit lichenous.

70   **SOUTH POINT (BRITISH ROUTE)**

D+   P Crew, L Dickinson and B Molyneux, Aug 1969

75
26

The first route to be climbed on the E Face follows a diagonal line of chimneys and deep cracks to a small shoulder in the middle of the face directly below the summit. A deep chimney followed by a series of cracks on the R (1 pitch of VI) leads to the gap between the S and Central points. 600m, 7hr

71   **SOUTH POINT (ITALIAN ROUTE)**

D+   G Grassi and A Nebiolo, 10 Aug 1971

75
26

This follows the diagonal break to its R-hand extremity and is basically a series of major variations on the British Route. However the climbing is finer and more homogenous. IV and IV+ with 2 pitches of V. 600m, 7hr

72   **CENTRAL POINT**

TD−   F Bessone, U Manera, A Nebiolo and E Pessiva, 2–3 Sept 1978

75
26

After climbing the crest L of a prominent dièdre, this route follows a ramp line to a detached pillar in the middle of the face. An almost direct line up a series of slabs and dièdres, interspersed with sections of easier ground, leads to the R-hand ridge a little below the summit. Mainly IV and V with some V+ and A1. 600m, c15hr

Descent: Follow the SSW Ridge easily. In the middle section 3 pointed gendarmes are turned on the R. Near the base slant down L to a snow patch and descend alongside the S ridge to grassy slopes. 4hr to the Tronchey Chalets. PD

Col des Hirondelles 3480m

First traverse: T Kennedy, J Marshall, G Loppé and L Stephen
with J Fischer, U Almer and H Devouassoud, 14 July 1873

Between the Grandes Jorasses and Pts des Hirondelles. The name is
positioned too far N on IGN. Rarely used as a pass, it is usually
reached from the Italian side over complicated glacier terrain. The
French side is a very unpleasant rotten rock rib and is generally
used as a means of descent to the Leschaux glacier. The couloir to
the R of this rock rib has been climbed directly to the Col but is
seriously exposed to stone and ice fall (D).

73
PD
`73`

ITALIAN SIDE
First ascent party

From the Gervasutti Hut cross the glacier to the S then turn W and
work up the middle skirting close to the foot of the SE ridge of the S
Peak of Pts des Hirondelles. Ascend a snowy cwm and steep slope
to the Col or preferably work L along a system of rocks below the S
flank of the Col and reach the top by a short steep ice slope. 3hr

74
`70`

FRENCH SIDE DESCENT
From the Col walk down to the NW and locate the top of the long
rocky rib leading to the Leschaux glacier. Descend this by
continuous rappelling. 400m, Fixed anchors, 1½hr

Pointes des Hirondelles 3524m

These two summits, about 100m apart, offer 2 pleasant routes that
can be combined to make a fine little traverse.

75
PD–
`73`

SOUTH SUMMIT SOUTH-EAST RIDGE
F Ravelli, G Rivetti and E Croux, 25 June 1924

Follow the ridge throughout. c150m, about 1½hr in either direction.

76
AD
`73`

NORTH SUMMIT EAST RIDGE
G Machetto, C Pivano, F Ratto, B Re, F Riva, B Taiana, R Zabetta
and N Zappa, 15 July 1962

Reach the foot of the ridge in 1½–2hr from the Gervasutti Hut. Go
up steep snow slopes on the R of the first buttress and reach the gap
beyond, at the foot of the main ridge, by steep broken rock. Follow
the ridge, mixed then rocky steps near the top (III and IV) to the
summit. c500m, 4hr

Pointes des Frébouze 3530m

This set of spikey towers on the rocky ridge S of the Petites Jorasses has several routes on the French side that have seldom been repeated. There is no easy way off the summits and it is probably better and certainly more convenient to rappel the route of ascent.

77 **CENTRAL PEAK WEST FACE**
TD–/TD M Vaucher and R Wohlschlag, 1–2 July 1957

77 This climb follows a line of dièdres that split the lower third of the face (8 pitches, IV to V+). An easy couloir/chimney line (200m, some IV) leads to the upper 200m wall. Climb this via cracks and overhanging walls (V and A1) to reach easy ground 60m below the summit. Good rock. 550m, 18hr. See also Photo 76

78 **WEST RIDGE**
TD–/TD L George and J Isbérie, 14 Aug 1949

76 This fairly sustained route follows more or less the crest of the ridge throughout, climbing mainly in dièdres and one or two easy couloir systems. The harder pitches give open face climbing on steep granite slabs. Mainly IV and V with a few A1 moves. 600m, 10hr. See also Photo 77

79 **NORTH-WEST FACE**
TD J Charlet, R Ghilini and G Peynaulet, June 1979

76 On the L side of the face, a steep and difficult ice runnel leads to the conspicuous ice field. Climb this and the 80m rock wall above (good granite) to the summit. Cold and icy conditions are needed to render this climb in condition. 500m

Petites Jorasses 3650m

A Guyard with H Devouassoud and A Cupelin, 23 Sept 1876

Although an undistinguished summit, the faces on this complex peak give some magnificent rock climbs.

80 **EAST-NORTH-EAST SLOPE**
AD– *Although little used, this route offers the shortest means to the summit. At present it is probably safer from objective dangers than the NE Ridge and in good snow conditions is the quickest means of descent.*

73

From the Gervasutti Hut, follow the glacier NNW into the upper basin under the Aig de Leschaux. Cross the rimaye and work L up a steep snow slope. Climb up a subsidiary snow ridge on the L followed by broken rocks to the R and reach the snow crest of the S Ridge leading to the summit. 3½hr from the hut, 2½hr in descent.

81	**NORTH-EAST RIDGE**
PD+	First ascent party

73

At present this route gives prolonged exposure to ice avalanches as it traverses open slopes between serac barriers on the S flank of the Aig de Leschaux to reach the Col des Petites Jorasses. The safest, though roundabout, alternative is to reach the col via a traverse of the Aig de Leschaux. The NE ridge itself is climbed on the L flank via a series of ledges. 5–6hr from the Gervasutti Hut.

82	**EAST FACE**
TD+	W Bonatti and P Mazeaud, 10–11 July 1962

73
25

A very fine climb on excellent compact granite. A fast party travelling light should easily complete the route in a day. There have been very few ascents to date and although the bottom section has required a fair amount of aid, it is feasible that the route could be climbed completely free. 450m, 10–12hr

83	**SOUTH RIDGE**
D–	A Castelli and M Rivero, 18 Aug 1935. Winter: E Gremmo and M
	Rava, 8–9 March 1969

73

A fine classic climb on excellent rock in an impressive setting. This is very much an uncrowded corner of the range and although the ridge comes into condition quickly after bad weather it is still infrequently climbed.

Reach the bottom of the ridge in ¾hr from the hut. Climb the snow slope on the L of the ridge for 60m then slant R up a snow tongue to reach a terrace on the E side. A direct start (V with a few aid moves) reaches this point from the base of the ridge via cracks and dièdres.
   Climb the crest for 10m to a platform (IV+) then continue to a pointed block on the ridge (IV+). Descend on the L flank and climb a red dièdre capped by a roof (IV). Move R just below the roof to the ridge and go up to a terrace (V). A few easier pitches up the crest lead to a steep wall climbed by a rising hand traverse from L to R (IV). More short easier pitches follow, often taken on the L flank (III), until a short vertical step is climbed by a strenuous crack (IV+). Continue up the snow ridge to the summit. 400m, 5–6hr from the hut.

This magnificent face of excellent compact granite offers several high-quality climbs.

84 LA BEAUTE DU MONDE

ED2

77
28

C Dalphin, M Piola and P Steiner, 12–14 Aug 1981

A direct route up the R side of the W face gives a mixture of aid and difficult free climbing. The central section is very steep and sustained, comparable to the S face of the Fou with difficult free pitches of open face climbing. At present there is little gear in place and the climb will require a bivouac. Unavoidable pitches of VI+. 700m. See also Photo 76

85 ORIGINAL ROUTE

TD

76
28

M Bron, A Contamine and P Labrunie, 20–21 Aug 1955. Winter: J Grimm and T Gross, 15–18 March 1973

This is well known as one of the great classic rock routes in the Alps. The climbing is more delicate than strenuous and is often very exposed. It is possible to rappel in a direct line back down the W face from the top of the route (in situ anchors at 50m intervals) but the traditional descent goes down the Italian side to the Gervasutti Hut. See also Photo 77

From the Leschaux Hut walk up the L side of the Leschaux glacier and climb up snow slopes to reach the start of the route, at the base of the conspicuous dièdre splitting the lower wall, in 2hr. 700m to the summit, 8–12hr

86 CZECH ROUTE

TD

77
28

I Koller and J Stejskal, 4–6 Aug 1976

A sustained free climb that runs directly up the L side of the face to join the Original Route at the chimney above the snow patch. 700m. See also Photo 76

DESCENT

From the small notch on the SW Ridge at the finish of the Contamine (Route 85), rappel to a ledge on the S side. Descend a series of ledges going first L then back R and make another long rappel to more ledges. Go down these to the R and rappel steep walls to the upper snow slopes. Descend these to the rimaye which is usually crossed by rappel and go down the Frébouze glacier to the Gervasutti Hut. 3–4hr

87   NORTH-WEST PILLAR

TD/TD+   F Nagao and Y Yamazaki, 18–19 Aug 1981

76

After the initial rock step and hanging glacier, the NW pillar takes
the form of a pear-shaped buttress. The route takes a huge crack
line in the centre then after 2 pitches deviates R to the crest which it
follows directly up a series of cracks to the summit. The climb is
not sustained but is completely free with 25 pitches from IV to VII.
850m, 12–14hr

88   NORTH COULOIR

TD   P Gabarrou and A Long, 19 May 1980

76

Cold and snowy conditions are essential for this very steep ice gully.

A steep ice slope leads up to the L edge of the hanging glacier.
Climb up to its highest point on the R and follow the steep gully just
L of the NW pillar to the E summit. The central section gives 100m
of delicate mixed climbing. c600m, 12hr

89   POINT 3607m NORTH-WEST COULOIR

TD+/ED1   R Baumont and G Smith, 26 June 1978

76

This exceptionally steep ice runnel has 300m of sustained climbing
including 2 overhanging ice bulges. The route was descended by
rappel after the first ascent in 3½hr. 500m, 7hr

90   POINT 3576m NORTH-WEST COULOIR

TD   E Lambert, G Perroux and B Sanchez, May 1981

76

Another steep couloir between the previous route and the Col des
Petites Jorasses. 430m

91   COL DES PETITES JORASSES NORTH-WEST COULOIR

TD–   P Gabarrou and P Michod, 1 July 1979. Winter: P Gabarrou, V
76   Gala and D Marquis, 18 March 1986

When in condition this gives a superb 70° ice climb and allows the
Leschaux to be climbed entirely on ice from this side. Bolt belays
have been established at every stance to facilitate a rappel descent.
400m

171

Aiguille de Leschaux 3759m

T Kennedy and J Marshall with J Fischer and J Grange, 14 July 1872

An attractive peak in an uncrowded corner of the range. The rock is often suspect and many of the climbs can feel quite serious.

92
PD

73

NORMAL ROUTE FROM ITALIAN SIDE
First ascent party by the direct route

The S side of the mountain presents a hanging snow slope which gives the quickest route to the summit in good conditions. Unfortunately it is prone to avalanche and should generally be avoided in descent. It is described below as an alternative to a more circuitous but much safer ascent via Pt 3654m.

From the Gervasutti Hut go up the glacier to the NNE and reach a low saddle on the SSE Ridge of Pt 3654m. Climb more or less on the crest to the top then turn L (W) and continue along the ridge over Pt 3662m. Follow the snow crest (large cornices on the N side) to the summit rocks of the Aig (3½–4hr). It is possible, if conditions are good, to follow the glacier slopes to the E of the ridge coming down from Pt 3654m. 500m

    Variant: Go up the glacier to the NNW keeping close to the rock walls of Pt 3654m, then ascend the steep snow slope below Pte 3662m. Near the top scramble onto rocks on the L forming a barrier below the upper slopes of the Leschaux. Climb these and the steep snow slope above directly to the E Ridge. 3hr, PD serious.

93
D

77

WEST FACE AND SOUTH-WEST RIDGE
C Bonington, J Brown, R Ford and T Patey, 18 July 1964

Although not sustained, this is probably the best route of its standard on the French side but is rarely climbed. The rock is excellent and the route can be descended by rappeling the difficulties.

The SW Ridge does not end at the Col des Petites Jorasses but curves down on the French side towards the base of the NW couloir descending from the col. From the Leschaux Hut follow Route 119 to below the face (2½hr), climb a short chimney through the rock barrier and slant R across the snow to reach the buttress on the R. Cross the buttress easily and work up its R flank (this point can also be gained from the snow slopes to the R). Near the foot of a large couloir, slanting L up the face, traverse R on a series of ledges for

100m to gain the SW Ridge. Climb the ridge for 150m in steep cracks (III and IV) to a shoulder. Climb a chimney to a steep dièdre 40m high. After 10m in the dièdre a tension traverse L allows an escape to be made onto easier ground (V). Climb a steep buttress (IV+) and follow a couloir/chimney to a notch in the SW Ridge, 100m above the Col des Petites Jorasses. Climb the R flank of this ridge, turning any obstacles, to the summit. 700m, 7hr

94   WEST FACE DIRECT

TD+/ED1 P Gabarrou and J Poncet, July 1986

77

A difficult free climb taking a beautiful crackline in the steep upper wall. Stonefall can be a problem on the lower snowfield, but an early start should eliminate this.

Start as for Route 93 but continue directly up the lower snowfield to the rock. Climb it for several pitches starting L of the couloir which comes down from an open depression (often a snow patch) in the centre of the face (200m V, then III and IV). Climb up the L side of the depression (a line of weakness hereabouts leads off L towards the upper NW ridge) to the steep upper wall.
      An obvious huge crack R of the summit fall-line gives the line. At one point it is necessary to slant up L, returning to the crack higher up by a pendulum (V to VII). In the upper section the crux pitch gives moves of VII/VII+. The crack finally reaches the ridge above at a notch. When 40m below this point slant up L to the summit. 700m, 10–12hr

95   NORTH-WEST RIDGE

D   F Gaia, F Ravelli and G Rivetti with A and A Chenoz, 31 July 1927.
        Winter: B Musi and G Signo, 16 Jan 1989

77

An interesting route of classic status that has rarely been ascended in modern times. The climbing is not at all sustained and it is possible to descend this route with 1 rappel down the difficult pitch.

From the Col de l'Eboulement, reached from either the Triolet or Leschaux Huts, climb the N ridge of L'Aiguillon as far as a shoulder. Traverse the L wall overlooking the Triolet glacier to reach the SE ridge and descend this to the Col de Leschaux (½hr). When approaching from the Triolet Hut one can climb the couloir directly to the Col de Leschaux (3½hr, AD).
      Move onto the L side of the first step and climb a couloir between the main ridge and a secondary ridge to the L. From the

top slant L on broken rock or mixed ground to the gap before the second step. Follow the crest to a slab which constitutes the crux of the climb. Bypass the first overhang on the R, the barrier above on the L, and reach the top of the slab (40m, IV and V). Follow the ridge to the top of the second step and reach the base of the third by a sharp and spikey crest. On the R side, slant up slabs and chimneys (III) to the L of a big couloir and reach the summit. 350m, 4hr and 21 pitches from the Col de Leschaux.

Aiguille de Leschaux: North-East Face

The upper half of this 800m face is a steep rock wall with a prominent dièdre system descending from the gap between the second and final steps on the NW ridge. The rock is poorer than elsewhere in the range though not too outrageous. The initial NE slope is exposed to stonefall and must be completed before dawn.

96 **IDIOT WIND**

ED2 C Dale and J Silvester, 2 Aug 1984

78

A hard free climb on the wall of the second tower.

Climb the initial ice slope to gain a small icefield R of the line of the Cassin Route. Climb the corner above the top of the icefield and slant up L along an easy ledge line until c50m R of the Cassin Route. Climb an orange dièdre for 2 pitches then traverse R to the prominent line of dièdres in the upper wall. Finish up the NW ridge. 9 difficult pitches mainly VI/VI+ with the crux of VII+ over a blocky overhang near the top. 800m, 8hr

97 **ORIGINAL (CASSIN) ROUTE**

TD+ R Cassin and U Tizzoni, 14–15 Aug 1939. Winter: F Anghileri, P

78 Maccarinelli and S Panzeri, 1–3 March 1976

This is probably the least known of Cassin's major routes and has only had a handful of ascents. The main difficulties are concentrated on the 250m headwall.

From the Triolet Hut, follow the path onto the moraine and cross the upper plateau of the Triolet glacier to the foot of the face (2hr). Climb the ice slope for about 400m (45°) then loose mixed ground towards the large dièdre coming down from the col between the second and final steps. Start rock climbing in a dièdre (IV+) which leads to a thin crack slanting up to the L of a small roof. Climb the crack (20m, V+) to a terrace and continue up easy ground to the main dièdre. Climb a chimney (IV+) to a small shoulder and trend R above a vertical wall (V and A1) to reach a narrow ledge. Descend a little to the L and climb a short wall (A1 and V) before moving L towards a groove with overhangs at the base (IV). Climb the impending wall on the R (A1) to gain the groove. Climb it (V+) and the short crack above (IV) to a ledge. Pull up between two blocks and climb a steep dièdre to a large terrace (V−). Climb up and across a vertical wall on the R (A1 and V+) to reach an icy gully. Climb this and the dièdre above for 2 pitches (V and V+) and reach the NW ridge by an easy chimney. Follow Route 95 to the top. 800m, 12–14hr from the hut.

98   DIRECT ROUTE
ED1   A Gogna and M Rava, 22–23 Aug 1972

78

This takes the line of a shallow couloir-dièdre slanting L for 250m across the upper face to an exit on the E ridge just below the summit. First ascended with a fair amount of aid but when dry has now been climbed almost completely free. Recommended.

Reach the terrace above the 20m thin slanting crack on the Cassin Route then work up L over mixed ground to enter the dièdre-couloir. Climb up the back for a pitch, then near the L ridge and finally on the ridge itself to reach a narrow shoulder (120m, VI). Climb a steep crack on the L (15m, V) back to the ridge, followed by a slab on the L (A2?) to reach a terrace in the main couloir-dièdre. Go up this with an excursion onto the L wall at one point to reach the base of a 15m chimney (VI). Climb this to a terrace (V) and continue up the couloir for 2 pitches (V+ then IV) where easy ground leads up R to the summit. 800m, 15hr from the hut.

99   NORTH COULOIR
TD+   J Barry and D Nicholls, Aug 1979

78

The short steep ice couloir leading up to the E ridge from the top L corner of the icefield gives technical climbing that is very exposed to stone and ice fall. Scottish 5, 700m, 12hr

Petit Mont Gruetta 3226m

R Todhunter with J Knubel, 1 Aug 1913

A fairly easily accessible little peak on the long SSE ridge of Mt Gruetta.

100 **SOUTH-SOUTH-EAST RIDGE**
AD– M Bordone and E Calcagno, 17 Aug 1925

79

A pleasant rock route, mainly II/III with 1 harder pitch.

Follow Route H24 as far as a point on the IGN map marked Bivouac Frébouze (no longer there) then slant up scree slopes to a noticeable depression in the SSE ridge (3hr). Climb the ridge for 400m towards an enormous green slab and avoid it by traversing diagonally R across a very steep wall. Cross a couloir and reach a secondary ridge which is followed on the L side for 100m. The angle now eases and shortly the main ridge is rejoined on the L. Continue up this to the summit. 700m, 4–5hr

Descent: 3 methods have been adopted over the years though the first described has recently become the most popular. Allow 4–5hr for each.

 a) Go down the SSE ridge for 20m then make 3 successive rappels on the L flank and regain the ridge above a shoulder. Continue down the ridge directly making several impressive rappels over steep buttresses (slings in place).

 b) Follow the SE ridge down to its base then traverse horizontally R to cross the depression in the SSE ridge.

 c) Descend the N ridge for c50m to a notch. A snowy couloir leads down for 300m to the Frébouze glacier which can be traversed then descended to the Gervasutti Hut path.

Petit Mont Gruetta: South-West Face

A marvellous slabby wall of excellent granite. A good bivouac is possible on the moraine below the face, ¼hr above the site of the old Frébouze Hut.

101 **GRASSI-MENEGHIN ROUTE**
TD– G Grassi and I Meneghin, 21 July 1983

79

This is considered to be the finest route on the face. It gives more homogenous and possibly even finer climbing than the 1976 Route and is rapidly evolving into a modern classic. The line generally follows a prominent spur towards the R side of the face.

Start at a big white dièdre on the R of some huge smooth slabs. Climb the dièdre until it becomes smooth and difficult (IV) then work up L towards a grassy ledge. Climb some smooth slabs L of a Rwards sloping ledge (V+) and go up a ramp on the R to the top of the initial dièdre. Slant up L to a leaning crack next to some vertical walls (III/IV). Climb this crack and the smooth runnel above (V and V+) to large ledges. Climb a Rwards sloping ramp (V) then slabs on the R of a dièdre, returning L to reach its top (V). Slant L up a crack and climb a dièdre with a flake (V+) from where walls and slabs lead up R to easy ledges (III/IV). Follow these R for a pitch then slant up R to the crest of the spur (IV). Climb the crest quite easily to a barrier of overhangs. Traverse R and climb back L on a ramp (IV). Climb a second ramp and reach a huge flake on the R. Above, surmount a wall and a deep dièdre to reach the crest of the spur (V). Climb just R of the crest, then on it (IV) to an overhang. Avoid this on the L (IV), rejoin the spur and climb the second overhanging step directly (V−). Continue more easily to the top of the spur, which is quite distinctive and lies on the SSE ridge. 400m, 7hr

102	**BRITISH ROUTE**
TD	P Cresswell and T Penning, 1 Aug 1988

79

This takes the slabs and overlaps starting about 40m to the R of the huge dièdre used by Route 103 and gives very good free climbing especially in the steeper lower section.

Climb the good-looking crackline for 45m (VI+) then move R and climb a groove for 25m (VI+) to a ledge. Climb the groove on the L for 25m (V+) to another ledge then move down R to a stepped groove. Climb it for 30m (VI+) finishing on the R. Go up to a break then move R to a crack. Climb it for a few m before moving R to a ramp which can be followed to a grassy ledge and pedestal stance (35m, VI+). Climb up for 40m, crossing an overhang on the L (VI+) to reach a slanting band and follow it diagonally L for 110m (mainly VI with 10m of VII−) to a ledge below grassy grooves close to the 1976 Route. Climb the grassy grooves moving slightly R for 2 pitches (V) then follow an obvious slanting line of weakness R for 3 pitches (IV/IV+) to a distinctive spike on the crest of the SSE ridge. c400m, 8hr

103   **BARTHASSAT-EMERY ROUTE**
TD   M Barthassat and J Emery, 5–6 Aug 1976

79

An exposed and entirely free climb comparable in quality and difficulty to the W face of the Petites Jorasses. This is the established classic on the face.

Follow Route H24 towards the Gervasutti Hut and when it reaches the E branch of the Frébouze glacier go up a triangular snow slope on the R to the base of a huge dièdre directly below a red tower in the upper section of the wall (3hr). Climb slabs on the L of a wet crack (VI) and reach the dièdre. Climb it for 2 pitches (IV to V+) and traverse L below a roof to gain a good ledge (V). Continue up the dièdre and reach an overhanging area of rock on the R (III then V). At first traverse horizontally R on compact slabs (V+) then slant up R on a ramp system to a small terrace (IV+). Continue traversing for 12m (V+) then climb straight up past another small terrace (IV+) turning an overhanging area on the R (V+). Continue straight up for 30m (V) until an easy pitch leads to the base of a large depression in the face (III). Climb a dièdre that slants up to the L in an area of grey rock (V). It turns into a ramp and leads to a large grassy ledge protected by a roof. Climb up L for 40m in a strenuous diagonal crack (VI). Leave it and climb up R to a dièdre (V+) situated directly above the roof. Climb the dièdre for 40m (V+) then go up L for 2 pitches (III) to the foot of the red tower. Slant up the wall behind this in a series of couloir-chimneys (V/V+) then climb directly up a chimney system slanting gently to the R for 3 pitches (IV then III) to gain the NW ridge 50m or so below the summit. c500m and 20 pitches, 8–10hr

104   **TOCCATA E FUGA**
TD+   T Gallo, G Ghigo and C Giorda, 11 Aug 1985

79

A direct route to the red tower. c500m

105 ·   **ORIGINAL ROUTE**
D–   B Ferrario and A Oggioni with W Bonatti, 19 June 1959

79

Almost directly below the summit a large couloir splits the face. The route initially climbs rock to the R of this couloir starting from the lowest point of the face, then crosses it and climbs a prominent couloir-dièdre system returning R to the couloir near the top of the face. III and IV with 1 pitch of V. 600m, 4–5hr

Mont Gruetta 3684m

L Dècle with H Devouassoud and E Cupelin, 15 Aug 1876

Although this peak has a wide variety of excellent climbs both old and modern, they have as yet seen only a handful of ascents.

106 WEST RIDGE
PD   First ascent party

79

The normal route to this remote summit. A pleasant and quite straightforward climb.

From the Gervasutti Hut follow Route 92 to Pt 3654m. Continue easily up the rocky ridge to the summit. 3½–4hr

107 SOUTH-SOUTH-EAST RIDGE INTEGRAL
D+   A Cicogna, L Dubosc and N Mussa, 5–6 July 1942

79

A very long climb on excellent rock which has rarely been repeated. See also Photo 80

After climbing the SSE ridge of the Petit Mont Gruetta, continue along the ridge climbing the R side of a large buttress and crossing a succession of gendarmes near to the crest (mainly III but 2 pitches of V). c1100m, 12hr

108 SOUTH-EAST RIDGE
TD+   E Carlini, I de Lazzer and A de Monte, 17–18 Sept 1942

80

On the L side of the E face and starting over 100m above the glacier is an elegant ridge. Unfortunately the rock in the upper half is loose and somewhat dangerous though never harder than IV. The ridge is approached on good granite by slanting L up cracked slabs and walls from a point 50m to the R of the wet couloir. The lower part of the ridge as far as a conspicuous gendarme gives hard free climbing with some short sections of artificial. 600m, 10hr

109 PILASTRO DEL SORRISO
TD   L Ferrero and U Manera, 18–19 Aug 1982

80

A very fine free climb, with one or two points of aid, on the front face of the large rounded pillar descending from the lower half of the SE ridge. Recommended by the first ascent party. In a dry year glacier recession could make the start of the climb problematical.

To the R of the start of the SE ridge (reached in 2½hr from the

Gianni Comino Bivouac Hut) a line of cracks rise up to the R to the base of an overhanging dièdre. Climb these to a grassy ledge (V+). Reach the base of a large overhang and surmount it on the R (V+) to reach an easy ramp that slants up L to some blocks. Work up R and climb a wide crack (V+). Climb the slab above to a small pillar with a block leaning against the base (V then IV). Climb the dièdre above to reach an overhanging crack and struggle up this to an easy gully (V+). Cross a slab on the R (V+) and continue traversing to reach the huge ledge system well visible from below.

The Pilastro rises from the R edge of these ledges. Climb up to the R of a small pillar and follow superb grey slabs to the base of a vertical crack (V+, delicate). Follow the crack to a roof then traverse R to a ledge (V+ with several aid moves). Climb a slab and a 30m dièdre (IV and V) then continue up for another 40m at first on the L (IV) then through some overhangs (V) to a slab. Climb it and the dièdre above to the crest of the pillar (IV+). Above lies a smooth slab. Climb it and continue on easier ground just to the L of the crest for 4 pitches to the top of the pillar where it joins the SE ridge (V then III and IV). 250–300m, 6–8hr

It is now possible to climb the upper half of the SE ridge on rotten rock to the summit of the Gruetta in a few more hours: c550m

Descent: The first ascent party rappeled the SE ridge to the vicinity of the conspicuous gendarme then down the E face to the ledge system and finally down the line of ascent. Allow 3hr

110 LE KARMA
TD+ G and R Vogler, 7 July 1982

80

This climb follows the conspicuous system of dièdres for 200m to their junction with the SE ridge (6 pitches on excellent granite, V to VI+). Above, nice slabs (IV) lead up to a point where the ridge deteriorates into loose couloirs and cracks. 550m, 8hr

111 EAST FACE ORIGINAL ROUTE
TD+ U Manera and C Sant'Unione, 13 Aug 1974

80

This excellent climb on the R side of the face is essentially free and sustained for the first 300m. The granite appears to be of very good quality throughout but stances are small. The length and difficulty of approach have ensured that subsequent ascents have been reserved only for the most adventurous. See also Photo 82

From the Gianni Comino Bivouac Hut reach the R side of the Gruetta glacier and go up it (very crevassed and contorted) to reach the foot of the face (3hr). Start in the centre of the face where there is a break in the line of overclimb a wall (V+). Take a wide crack on the R (IV/IV+) for 40m then a slanting dièdre (30m, IV) to a ramp and follow this Rwards for 30m (III) to a narrow chimney. Climb the chimney for 75m (IV to V+) towards some huge overhangs, then slant down R for 10m before climbing straight up some slabs for 50m (V) to a block. Climb a short wall above (V) then slant up L for 2 pitches (III and IV) before traversing easily L for a pitch to some slabs. Climb the easy slabs and a small spur of red granite to the final buttress. 3 pitches up this (III and IV) lead to the summit. 550m, 10hr

Mont Gruetta: West-South-West Face

This rock wall above the E branch of the Frébouze glacier can be approached in 2½hr from the Gervasutti Hut.

112   **POINT 3554m SOUTH-WEST SPUR**
D+   T Bartels, R Goedeke and A Nehring, 14 July 1975

79

The rock on this spur is very good and the climbing thought to be reminiscent of the Mer de Glace face of the Grépon.

Start in the couloir to the R of the spur and after a couple of wettish pitches cross a snow patch. Climb up towards a tower (V−) then slant L below it onto the spur which is followed more or less on the crest with small deviations onto the L side (mainly IV with 2 pitches of V) to Pt 3554m. 450m, 6hr

Either continue up the final section of the SSE ridge (IV/V) to the summit of Pt Gruetta or make 4 rappels down the couloir to the N of the spur and slant down R to the glacier.

113   **SOUTH-WEST PILLAR**
TD   A Nebiolo and F Piaña, 11 July 1977

79

This is a sustained free climb on good rock taking the prominent pillar to the S of Route 112. If continued over the summit of Mt Gruetta it becomes a serious and lengthy excursion.

To the R of the base of the pillar slant up R for 80m then traverse L 60m (II and III) to the obvious dièdre system. Climb it, passing some black overhangs on the R (V) then move L on a slab (V+) and climb 2 successive dièdres (IV+) to the foot of a huge dièdre. Climb up the R wall for 3 pitches (IV, V+, V) to a col of rubble then overcome the red buttress above by a ledgeline on the R (IV+, 30m) coming back L above on mixed ground to reach the SSE ridge. 450m, 8–10hr
     Either continue up the SSE ridge (IV/V) or descend down the vague couloir to the N of the pillar on bad rock; several rappels.

Mont Gruetta: North Face

A superb-looking slabby wall, easily approached from the Triolet Hut in 1½hr, which unfortunately has large areas of friable rock in the upper reaches. Most of the face is seriously exposed to stonefall in dry conditions.

114   **BOCCALATTE ROUTE**
TD   G Boccalatte, E Castiglioni and T Gilberti, 23 July 1937

81
29

A mixed climb that takes a line up the steep smooth rock wall to the R of the central couloir. It was the original route on the face and is relatively sheltered from stonefall. In less than perfect conditions it becomes quite hard and has still received very few ascents. 750m, 12–14hr

115   **CORACRAZION**
ED3   M Charlton and J Silvester, 4–5 Sept 1986

81
29

The central couloir. Very cold and snowy conditions are needed to climb the ice-covered slabs at the base of the route. Both these and the head wall give very sustained mixed climbing. The first ascent party thought protection was often poor and that several pitches required a bold approach. Scottish 5/6. 750m, 17hr

116   **DIRECT ROUTE**
ED1/2   J Bougerol and A Mroz, 31 July–2 Aug 1971

A serious and difficult route with considerable stonefall danger. It is essentially a rock climb on open slabs and walls with several mixed pitches. It has now been completed with only 2 points of aid. 750m, 14hr

Mont Rouge de Gruetta 3477m

E Bradby, J Wicks, W Wills and C Wilson, 28 July 1910

This rarely visited summit lies just to the NE of Mt Gruetta.

117   **SOUTH-WEST PILLAR**
D+   U Manera and I Meneghin, 4 Aug 1981

The long crest running S from the main summit forms two secondary summits before descending to the gap between Mt Rouge and Mt Vert. From the lower of these summits a very fine pillar descends in a SW direction to the Gruetta glacier. This is a splendid rock climb and highly recommended by the first ascent party. The difficulties are concentrated in the lower two thirds of the climb. See also Photo 80

From the Gianni Comino Bivouac Hut reach the base of the pillar in c2hr and climb up to the R in small gullies and shattered rock. Reach the crest by a long traverse to the L (IV) and climb up it by vague cracks and dièdres (V and V+) to a line of overhangs. Climb a short ramp on the L then traverse back R to reach a dièdre more or less on the crest (IV and V). Climb this and the crack that follows (IV+: an excellent pitch) and exit R. Go up slabs to a huge dièdre and climb it (V−). Continue on the L of the crest then the crest itself (IV+) to a monolithic terrace. Climb the steep triangle of rock above by its central crack system (V and V+) to reach a shoulder. The ridge now becomes much easier and is followed, with one or two short sections of IV, to the top. 400m, 5–6hr

Descent: Go down the S ridge a little way until it is possible to work down the SSW flank (several rappels necessary) Or: climb along the SE ridge for some distance towards the main summit of Mt Rouge. At a prominent notch in the ridge, a steep snowy couloir leads easily down to the Gruetta glacier.

183

Mont Vert de Gruetta 2810m

The last point on the long SE ridge of Mt Gruetta.

118 **SOUTH RIDGE**
IV T Bartels and R Goedeke, 3 July 1975

82 *A short but splendid climb on excellent granite that quickly comes into condition. There is one pitch of V−.*

Reach the bottom of the ridge easily from the Gianni Comino BivouacHut and climb the rock to the R of 2 huge L-ward slanting ledges that occur at ⅓ and ⅔ height. Follow the ridge directly all the way to the top. 300m, (3½hr).

Descent: This is lengthy and not that easy and it may well be best to rappel back down the route. However it is possible to continue along the NW ridge to the foot of the huge red buttress of Mt Rouge de Gruetta (2 pitches of IV+) then descend a couloir on the L and snowfields below to reach the glacier (2 rappels in lower section. 4hr)
      From the first notch in the NW ridge one can descend on the Triolet side to the moraines in 3hr (several rappels).

Col de l'Eboulement 3434m

First recorded traverse: E Broome with J Biner and A Cupelin, 4 Aug 1893

The easiest passage between the Leschaux glacier and the Val Ferret.

119 **SOUTH-WEST SIDE**
PD From the Leschaux Hut go up the glacier and take the E branch
77 keeping close to the L side all the way. Reach the base of the rocky buttress (3245m) and climb steep snow slopes on the R to the rock buttress below the col. Start on the L and climb straight up steep but easy rock then slant up R to the col. 4hr. See also Photo 83

120 **EAST SIDE**
PD From the Triolet Hut follow the path to the moraine, reach the flat plateau above the icefall and walk directly towards the Col des Leschaux between the Aiguillon and the Aig de Leschaux. Climb the couloir descending from this col and at half-height break out R across the rocks towards the Col de l'Eboulement and reach it by a steep rocky wall. 3½hr

Aiguille de l'Eboulement 3599m

C Mathews and A Reilly with M Balmat and M Ducroz, 7 July 1866

Situated in an uncrowded corner of the range this rarely climbed summit offers a magnificent panorama especially towards the Jorasses and Rochefort ridges.

121   **NORTH RIDGE**
PD   First ascent party in descent

`83`   *The normal route from France, which also offers the best means of descent if making a traverse of the peak. See also Photo 84*

From the Leschaux Hut ascend steep grass and scree slopes to the moraine on the L side of the Pierre Joseph glacier. In good conditions it is possible to go up the L side of the glacier but generally it is better to continue to the top of the moraine. Ascend a ravine of scree on the L then scramble over a steep barrier of slabs and onto a terrace which slants R to the glacier. Traverse the glacier, passing just above a small rocky rognon at the foot of the SW ridge of the Petite Aiguille de Talèfre, to reach the upper plateau. Above is the SW face of the Aig de Talèfre which is characterised by 2 large couloirs separated by a rock ridge. To the R of these is an ice couloir. Climb this or the rocks on the R and at the top traverse R to the Col de Pierre Joseph (3500m). Go up the easy snow ridge to the summit turning a rocky point on the R. c300m, 4hr from the hut.

122   **NORTH-WEST SIDE AND NORTH RIDGE**
AD   J Moro, J Pruvost and C Roch, 30 July 1931

`83`   A much finer and almost completely independent variation, is to climb directly onto the hanging glacier below the col. Break through the L side of the supporting rock buttress and slant up R to a snow crest in the centre of the glacier. Climb this, avoiding any barriers of ice on the R, to reach the upper part of the N ridge quite close to the summit. 5½hr. See also Photo 84

123   **EAST FACE DIRECT**
TD–   J Ferenski, J Franczuk, T Gibinki and A Mroz, 3 Sept 1969

This has one superb pitch across an overhanging smooth wall (A1 and V/V+) but the rest of the route is loose and unpleasant and can hardly be recommended. 500m, 6–8hr

124 **SOUTH-WEST (GRELOZ) COULOIR**
AD−   Probably C Mathews and A Reilly with M Ducroz and M Balmat, 7
83   July 1866

*This fine little snow and ice route offers the quickest way to the summit in
good conditions and probably provides the best route on the mountain.*

Follow Route 119 towards the Col de l'Eboulement and climb the
long snowy couloir starting L of the rocky buttress 3245m. It
steepens to 50° at the top and the summit is reached easily on the R.
400m, 4½hr

125 **POINT 3133m SOUTH-SOUTH-WEST FACE**
V−   G Buscaini and S Metzeltin, 24 July 1978
83

*This Pt lies on the long rock SW ridge of the Aig de l'Eboulement. The
SSW face gives an interesting route on good rock but unfortunately not
homogeneous in difficulty. Mainly II with 1 pitch of IV and 1 of V−.*

From the Leschaux Hut follow Route 119 to the rocky island
2820m. Traverse L to reach the lowest and most westerly point of
the rocks above. Climb up the ridge on the R and follow this with a
traverse R at half-height to avoid the steep walls of Pt2976m. 300m,
4½hr

From the top of Pt 3133m either traverse R across the bowl
and continue up the SW ridge on good rock to the summit of the
Aig; or descend the couloir on the R with 1 rappel at the base.

Aiguille de Pierre Joseph 3361m

This is the last main summit on the long W ridge of the Aig de Talèfre. All the lower section of this ridge is characterised on the SW flank by spurs and ridges of good solid granite. Routes can be reached easily from the Leschaux Hut in 20min, clear quickly after bad weather and are becoming quite popular. Traditional descents, byeasy scrambling down the rocky flank, are described, though many routes are rappeled on reaching the top.

126 **SOUTH-WEST FACE CENTRAL SPUR**
IV+ P Angueloff, P Bodeaux, D Mille with J Beaugey, 16 July 1978

85

Reach the crest of the central spur by climbing 3 pitches up the couloir on the L. Follow the crest more or less to the foot of the huge overhanging buttress at half-height, either in dièdres or on slabs to the R (III and IV, good stances and belays). Traverse L into the couloir and climb up it to the R of a big gendarme. Keep working R in a chimney system to reach the ridge and follow it to the summit (IV+) which is most easily reached from the Couvercle side. 600m, 8hr

The quickest descent is to take the short NW ridge down to the moraines of the Talèfre glacier at 2904m and follow these back round via the Pierre à Bérenger.

127 **POINT 2940m SOUTH-SOUTH-WEST FACE**
VII+ J Engelmann and D Mattei with C Ansey and A Comte, 25 July 1966

85
30

This razor sheared buttress of deep red granite gives an excellent 7 pitch rock climb to the summit of the forepeak. It is best reached by descending the Leschaux glacier and climbing up the Pierre à Bérenger moraine. The route has been climbed completely free but aid can be used in the central section to reduce much of the difficulty. c350m to the summit, 6hr

Descent: From the summit take a long diagonal line down grassy ledges and terraces on the Leschaux side to a brèche immediately below the summit of Pt 2842m. Rappel 20m on the N side and follow easy-angled slabs to the Talèfre moraine where the Pierre à Bérenger track is joined.

128 **POINT 2842m SOUTH-WEST FACE – LE NORD EN FACE**
VI/VI+ O Guenay and T Hahne, 8 Aug 1986

85
27

A rather unsustained climb on the smooth walls to the R of the Engelmann-Comte and well visible from the Leschaux Hut. Despite this, the climbing is good with 2 strenuous pitches and unavoidable moves of VI/VI+. A few blade pegs are necessary for protection.

Start at a cairn below a blocky pillar leading up to the steep walls. This 9-pitch climb can be completed in 2–3hr and descended in 5 rappels. 200m

129 **POINT 2842m SOUTH-WEST FACE**
IV+ J Engelmann with A Comte, 26 Aug 1965

85
27

An outstanding little rock climb on the cornerstone of the Leschaux and Talèfre Glaciers. It has 1 pitch of V+. It can also be approached from the Couvercle Hut in 1hr. 250m, 4hr
    A rappel either from the summit blocks or the brèche to the SE (see Route 127) leads to the Talèfre moraine.

130 **POINT 2842m WEST FACE GRAND DIEDRE**
V/VI B Lambert and J Libegue, 11 July 1985

The prominent dièdre on the W face was climbed directly to the summit to give a fine free climb. 250m. See Photo 85

Pointe Supérieure de Pierre Joseph 3472m

131 **NORTH RIDGE**
PD– J Gibson, G Morse and J Wicks, 29 July 1892

86

The normal route of ascent and best means of descent to the Couvercle Hut. It is usual to continue to the summit of the Aig de Talèfre. See also Photo 84

From the Couvercle Hut, follow the path down to the Talèfre glacier and cross it to the base of the N spur at 3009m (2hr). Cross the rimaye well to the R of this point and slant up L to the rocks of the N ridge. Follow these (II) to the summit. c450m, 4hr from the hut.

132 **NORTH-EAST COULOIR**
AD   J Emery and B Jillot, 5 Aug 1956

84

In good conditions this gives a quick and enjoyable route to the summit. Average angle 50°. c350m, 3hr from the Couvercle hut. See also Photo 86

Petite Aiguille de Talèfre 3605m

Crossed on the normal W ridge route to the Aig de Talèfre, this peak offers some interesting mixed climbing on its N face.

133 **NORTH-EAST COULOIR**
TD−   S Badier and P Bourges, 24 Sept 1978

84

This starts just to the R of Route 134 where 3 pitches on ice followed by 3 pitches on steep mixed ground lead to a point where the couloir veers to the R. 3 or 4 more pitches of mixed climbing lead to a rocky amphitheatre and the summit is reached via a steep rock pitch (IV+). Scottish 3/4, 470m, 4hr. See also Photo 86

134 **NORTH FACE**
TD−   H Agresti, A Bouverot, L Chantelat and G Poncet, 5 Sept 1978

84

Reached in 2hr from the Couvercle Hut, this route climbs steep icy rock just L of the crest of the lower section of the N spur (excellent granite). It then slants up R to reach the brèche between 2 prominent gendarmen. The summit buttress is climbed slightly on the R. 470m, 4hr. See also Photo 86

Aiguille de Talèfre 3730m

J Baumann, F Cullinan and G Fitzgerald with E Rey, L Lanier and J Moser, 25 Aug 1879

There are two main summits here with the SW (3726m) top about 60m along the ridge from the higher NE top. A superb face rises above the Talèfre glacier offering a variety of excellent mixed climbs. They are as good as most in the range, yet still uncrowded.

135
PD+

`84`

WEST RIDGE (NORMAL ROUTE)

J Gibson, G Morse and J Wicks, 29 July 1892

The safest and most practical means of ascent and descent from the peak and a lovely introduction to alpine ridges giving varied climbing with splendid views.

From the Couvercle Hut follow Route 131 to the summit of the Pt Sup de Pierre Joseph (4hr). Continue along the corniced ridge to the summit of the Petite Aig de Talèfre (½). Descend a steep chimney on the S side to reach the gap below and follow a sharp snow ridge then snowy rocks to the SW summit. Traverse the L side of the ridge and follow the crest of easy rocks to the NE summit. 6½hr from the hut. Allow 4hr for the descent.

136
D/D+

`84`

VIA NORTH COULOIR OF COL DES AIGUILLES DE TALEFRE

C Dumont and H Fiorioli, 31 July 1930. Winter: L Berthaud and D Brunet, 16 Feb 1983

This is a splendid ice route with no objective danger which is now climbed quite frequently. See also Photo 86

The couloir is reached in 2½hr from the Couvercle Hut and is 450m high, 50°–55° but steepening to 60° at the top (3hr). Continue along the W ridge to the summit. 7hr from the hut.

137
PD+

`83`

SOUTH-WEST FLANK

First ascent party

This climbs the rock buttress between the 2 couloirs mentioned in the description of Route 121. Although possibly the quickest route from the French side to the summit, it is quite dangerous with atrocious rock and an ever-present threat of stonefall.

138
PD

`87`

EAST RIDGE

C Cunningham with E and J Rey, 15 July 1882

Although rarely done, this is a reliable and safe route from the Triolet Hut.

From the hut cross the flat basin of the Triolet glacier viaRoute 120 to the foot of the SE ridge of the Aig Savoie. Go up the R side of the glacier bay between this and the Aig de Talèfre to reach the upper plateau (2hr). Cross the rimaye somewhat to the R of the E ridge and slant up the crest. Follow it to a snowy shoulder. A narrow and delicate snow ridge followed by an ice slope leads to the final rocks. Go up L then back R to reach the NE ridge not far below the summit. 4½hr from the hut.

139   **SOUTH-EAST RIDGE**
PD+   G Gaia, F Ravelli, G Rivetti with A Rey and L Proment, 3 Aug 1926

87

A more interesting route than the E ridge which it joins in the upper section.

Starting from the lowest point on the ridge climb the rock buttress and continue up a long and rounded hump of snow, on the L of a wide open snowy couloir, to the foot of some steep rocks. Climb these on sound granite and work R to a narrow snow slope leading to the shoulder where Route 138 is joined. c850m, 5–6hr from the hut to the summit.

Aiguille de Talèfre: North-West Face

Split by a series of rocky spurs and icy runnels, this superb face is easily reached from the Couvercle Hut in 1½–2hr. Due to its relative steepness, fresh snow is shed fairly quickly and all routes are fairly safe from objective danger and are recommended. Belays are good throughout but are not always obvious.

140   **NORTH-WEST COULOIR**
D+   P and P Gabarrou, 4 June 1978

84

Essentially a 55° ice couloir with one or two shorter and steeper mixed sections. 600m, 5hr. See also Photo 86

141   **DIRECT ROUTE**
TD   R Ponti with P Gabarrou, 23 July 1978. Winter: C Profit, Feb 1982

84

Interesting mixed climbing linking up a system of icy runnels but really only a more direct variant to Route 142. The steeper R branch of the lower gully is taken to the central icefield, where from the top R corner another gully line gives 3 or 4 steep mixed pitches to the summit icefield. Scottish 4. 600m, 6hr. See also Photo 86

142   **DUFOUR ROUTE**
TD   G Dufour, D Fourner, B Richermoz and P Royer, 20 July 1978

84

This follows the icy runnels just L of the Direct Route and

alongside the rocks of the NW spur. Technically it is a slightly easier proposition than the Direct Route and together with the latter gives possibly the finest climbing on the face. 600m, 6hr. See also Photo 86

143 BETHERMIN-GABARROU ROUTE
TD M Bethermin and P Gabarrou, July 1979

84 A mixed climb on the L flank of the NW spur. Pitches of IV and V.650m, 10hr. See also Photo 86

144 CENTRAL COULOIR
TD A Billet, M Davaille and E Trotskiar, 31 July–2 Aug 1957

84 The most obvious and aesthetic line on the face. The average angle is 56° but the last 100m give very steep and tricky mixed climbing which is best attempted in very snowy conditions. 600m, 6–8hr. see also Photo 86

145 EAST COULOIR AND NORTH-EAST RIDGE
D+ M Azéma with A Charlet, 3 June 1945

84 The main difficulties occur at ⅓ height with steep mixed climbing through the narrows. c650m to the summit, 5hr. See also Photo 86

Col Savoie 3491m

First traverse: G and W de Meyendorff and J Morin, 8 Aug 1924

This is not a practical passage between the Talèfre and Triolet glaciers and is rarely gained from either side.

146 NORTH SIDE
D– A steep ice couloir which is very exposed to stonefall. It is also possible to climb the rock buttress to the L, reaching the crest well above the base from the N flank. c240m, 2–3hr

86

147 SOUTH-EAST SIDE
PD Follow Route 138 to the upper plateau and make a long rising traverse R on snow-covered rocks to reach the col. Stonefall danger near the base. 4hr from the Triolet Hut.

87

Aiguille Savoie 3603m

A Brun with J Ravanel and L Tournier, 1904

Although this summit is rarely reached from the French side it is being climbed with increasing frequency from the Italian side via the delightful SE ridge.

148   **NORTH RIDGE**
PD   First ascent party

`86`

The normal route which is generally straightforward but can become delicate if heavily corniced. It is the most practical descent when traversing the mountain.

From the Col de Talèfre (Routes 150 and 152) follow the sharp and exposed crest to the summit. 40min

149   **SOUTH-EAST RIDGE**
AD   P Preuss, 17 Aug 1913

`87`

This long ridge projecting into the Triolet glacier basin gives a safe and interesting climb of classic status on very sound granite. A highly recommended outing in a remote corner of the range.

From the Triolet Hut follow Route 152 towards the Col de Talèfre. Either reach the SE ridge on the L at a point where it sinks into the glacier above its lower projection and Pt3133m (2½hr) or climb the lower projection directly (II, 1hr longer). Follow the crest, at first on its L side (III) then directly, climbing a narrow chimney (IV), for about 1–1½hr until slabs lead up to the foot of a conspicuous yellow gendarme. Turn this on the L and reach a snowy saddle. Climb up the crest of the ridge to the L and reach the foot of the steep final buttress. Climb this directly (80m, IV/IV+) and reach the summit. 400m, 5½hr from the hut.

    It is possible to avoid this upper section by traversing R from the snowy saddle onto the E face, then working up a series of steps with square-cut blocks until a chimney line (III) leads to the summit. 5hr

150   **EAST FACE**
V   P Armando and S Bellini, 4 Aug 1969

`87`

A short rock climb on good granite.

Follow Route 152 and start in a small couloir directly below the summit (3hr). 3 pitches lead to a good ledge (IV and V). Slant up R to a vague spur and follow it to the summit (III and IV). 300m, 7½hr from the hut.

Col de Talèfre 3544m

First traverse: E Whymper with C Almer and F Biner, 3 July 1865

This is the easiest pass between the Triolet and Talèfre glacier basins.

151
PD+
86

WEST (FRENCH) SIDE
A short couloir which is somewhat exposed to stonefall.

From the Couvercle Hut cross the glacier to the Jardin and follow the edge of the moraine on its R side to the uppermost point. Now bear R and cross the glacier towards the col. When near to the base (3218m) of a spur coming down from the W ridge of the Aig Savoie, slant up L below a serac barrier to the upper plateau. Slant up L and climb the couloir (45°, 250m) or the loose rocks on the L side, to the col. 4½hr from the hut.

152
PD
87

EAST (ITALIAN) SIDE
Easy mixed climbing with a slight danger of stonefall.

From the Triolet Hut follow the path to the lateral moraine and continue along this to the flat plateau of the Triolet glacier. Walk up the glacier keeping close to the SE ridge of the Aig Savoie until nearly below the Col du Piolet. On the L is a slabby wall. Cross the rimaye and slant L on easy rock to reach the start of a snow band that leads L above the wall for 200m, finishing at the Col de Talèfre. 4½hr from the hut.

The E branch of the Triolet glacier, under the rocks of Mts Rouges de Triolet, is often less crevassed and can be reached by following the lateral moraine to the very top. Slant L above the rocky island 3210m until below the Col du Piolet.

General Index

Index of Climbs

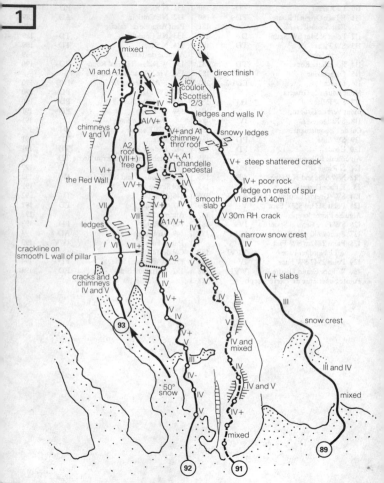

mixed

VI and A1

V−

direct finish

icy
couloir
(Scottish
2/3)

IV

ledges and walls IV

AI/V+

chimneys
V and VI

V+ and A1
chimney
thro' roof

snowy ledges

A2
roof
(VII+)
free

V+ A1
chandelle
pedestal

V+ steep shattered crack

VI+

the Red Wall

V/V+

IV+ poor rock

ledge on crest of spur
VI and A1 40m

VII

V+

smooth
slab

ledges

VIII

A1/V+

V 30m RH crack

IV

narrow snow crest
IV

crackline on
smooth L wall of pillar

I VI

VII+/I

V

IV

A2

IV+ slabs

cracks and
chimneys
IV and V

III

IV

IV

III

V+

IV
IV

V

snow crest

93

V+
V

IV and
mixed

III and IV

III

50°
snow

IV

IV−

IV and V

mixed

V

IV+

89

mixed

92   91

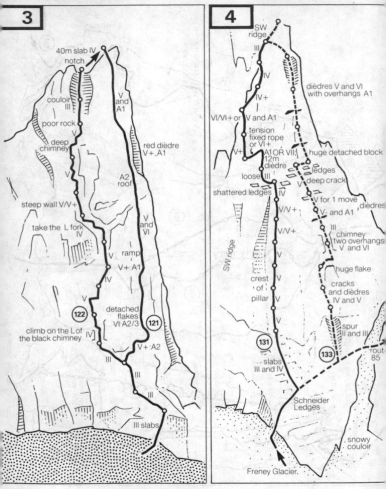

Aiguille Croux SE Face

Pointe Gugliermina

3

40m slab IV
notch
couloir
III
poor rock
V
deep
chimney
V
V
and
A1
red dièdre
V+,A1
A2
roof
steep wall V/V+
take the L fork
IV
V
and
VI
ramp
V+ A1
IV
detached
flakes
VI A2/3
(122)
(121)
climb on the L of
the black chimney   IV
V+:A2
III
III
III
III slabs

4

SW
ridge
III
IV
IV+
V
VI/VI+ or
V and A1
tension
fixed rope
or VI+
V+
A1 OR VII:
12m
dièdre
loose III
shattered ledges
IV
V/V+
V/V+
crest
of
pillar
V
SW ridge
slabs
III and IV
dièdres V and VI
with overhangs A1
huge detached block
ledges
deep crack
V for 1 move
V· and A1
III
chimney
two overhangs
V and VI
huge flake
cracks
and dièdres
IV and V
spur
II and III
(131)
(133)
rout
85
Schneider
Ledges
snowy
couloir
dièdres

Freney Glacier.

206

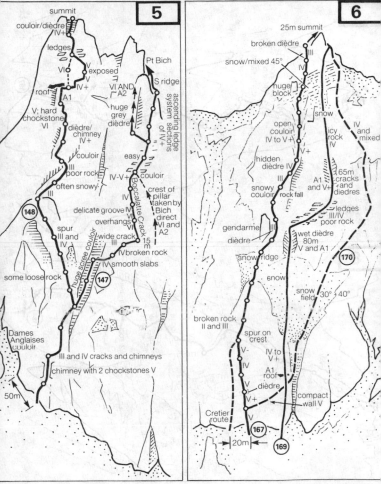

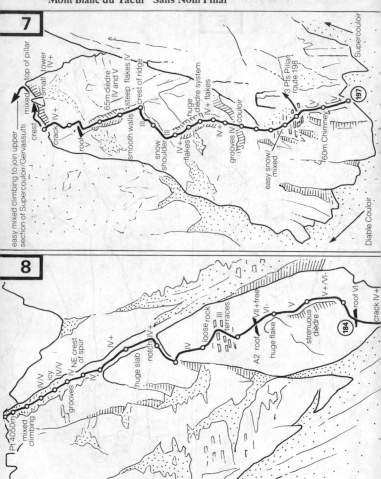

Mont Blanc du Tacul
Three Points Pillar

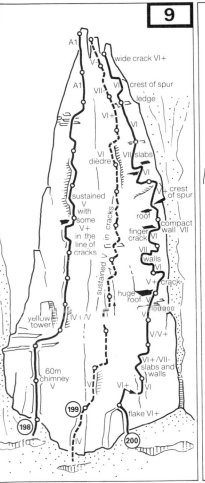

9

- A1
- wide crack VI+
- V
- A1
- VI — crest of spur
- VII
- ledge
- VI+
- VI
- VII slabs
- VI dièdre
- VI
- crest of spur
- V+
- roof
- sustained V with some V+ in the line of cracks
- sustained V in cracks
- compact wall VII
- finger crack VI
- VII walls VI
- V+ crack
- huge roof
- V lodge
- yellow tower
- IV/V
- V/V+
- 60m chimney V
- VI+/VII– slabs and walls
- VI
- VI
- VI+
- VI
- flake VI+
- IV
- 199
- 198
- 200

Mont Blanc du Tacul
Gervassutti Pillar

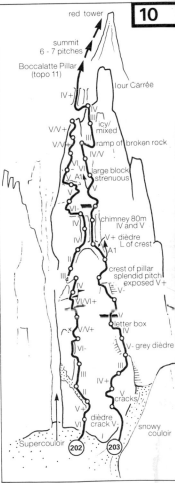

10

- red tower
- summit 6 - 7 pitches
- Boccalatte Pillar (topo 11)
- Tour Carrée
- IV+ III
- III
- icy/mixed
- V/V+
- ramp of broken rock
- V/V+
- IV/V
- VI large block A1 strenuous
- V
- VI–
- chimney 80m IV and V
- IV
- V+ dièdre L of crest
- A1
- II
- crest of pillar splendid pitch exposed V+
- III
- IV
- VI/VI+
- V
- V–
- letter box
- V/V+
- IV
- VI–
- V– grey dièdre
- III
- III
- IV+
- V cracks
- II
- V+
- VI dièdre crack V–
- snowy couloir
- Supercouloir
- 202
- 203

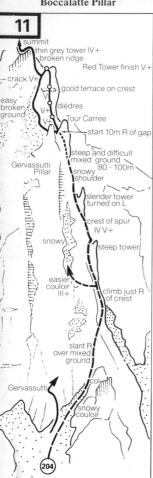

11

summit

thin grey tower IV+

broken ridge

Red Tower finish V+

crack V+

good terrace on crest

easy broken ground

dièdres

V

Tour Carrée

V+

start 10m R of gap

steep and difficult mixed ground 80 - 100m

Gervassutti Pillar

snowy shoulder

slender tower turned on L

crest of spur IV V+

snowy

steep tower

easier couloir III+

climb just R of crest

slant R over mixed ground

Gervassutti

col

snowy couloir

(204)

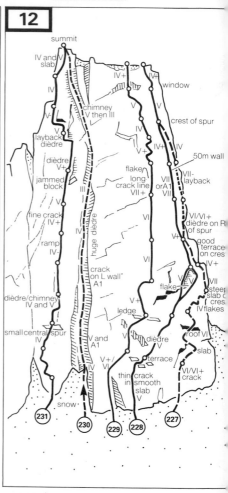

12

summit

IV and V slab

IV+

IV

IV+

V-

V

V+

window

V

IV

chimney V then III

crest of spur

V

V

IV

V+

IV+

IV

layback dièdre

dièdre V+

jammed block

III

flake

50m wall

long crack line

VII or A1

VII- layback

VII+

VII

fine crack IV+

IV

huge dièdre

VI

VI/VI+ dièdre on R of spur

ramp IV-

good terrace on crest

VI

V

IV+

crack on L wall A1

VII

flake

steep slab on crest

dièdre/chimney IV and V

V

EV

IV flakes

ledge

small central spur IV

V and A1

V+

roof VI

V+/ VI

V

dièdre V

slab

terrace

snow

V+/ IV

thin crack in smooth slab

VI/VI+ crack

(231)

(230)

(229)

(228)

(227)

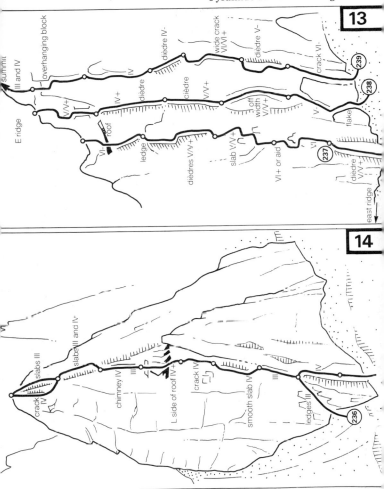

13

Summit

E ridge

III and IV

overhanging block

IV

diédre IV-

wide crack VI/VI+

diédre V-

crack VI-

239

238

V/V+

diédre IV+

diédre V/V+

off width V/V+

V

flake

VI- roof

ledge

diédres V/V+

slab V/V+

VI+ or aid

237

diédre V/V+

east ridge

14

crack IV

slabs III

slabs III and IV-

chimney IV

III

L side of roof IV+

crack IV

smooth slab IV

III

IV

ledges III

236

NE side

SE side

junction with
Salluard route

IV+

IV+

IV+

V

strenuous chimneys and
cracks V+ some A1

ledge on crest

couloir IV

cracks V

roof V+

30m easy

242

summit   III and IV

IV+

ledges   dièdre V

steep   VII   IV N side icy
crack

IV   chimney
crack
IV   V+
and
V   Red
Dièdre
VII   top

ledge   V+   III

aid   dièdre
IV+   hole

VI+   terrace   IV

IV   deep
dièdre

IV and V−   247   VI+

ramp   V
IV
and
V   V/VI−

grey   248   dièdre
dièdre
VI   IV and V   IV+ cracks
V/VI   and
deep   V   terrace
chimney   slab
VII   VI   short wall V

IV   IV and V
V/A1   twin   chimney
6m dièdre   cracks
IV+   VI   big terrace

chim   slab VII   dièdre
V+   IV   V+

huge   crack V   243
dièdre
crack   VI   V   VI

crack   VI−   VI−   IV
VI+/VII−   ledge
246   hard   IV+
layback VII
245   244

212

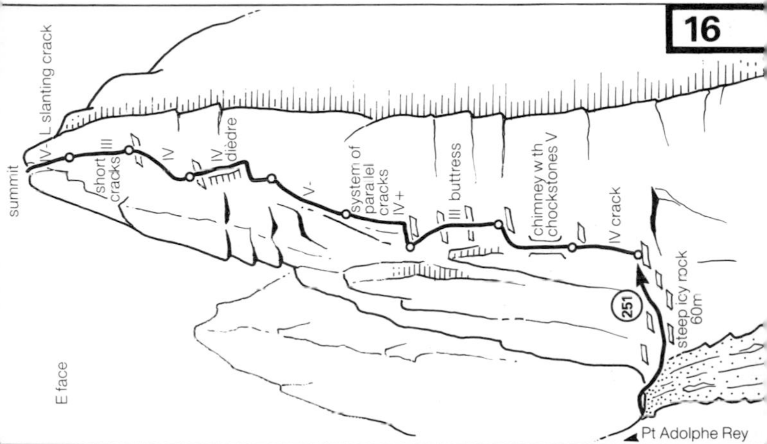
summit
IV- L slanting crack
III
short cracks
IV
IV dièdre
V-
system of parallel cracks IV+
III buttress
chimney with chockstones V
IV crack
251
steep icy rock 60m
E face
Pt Adolphe Rey

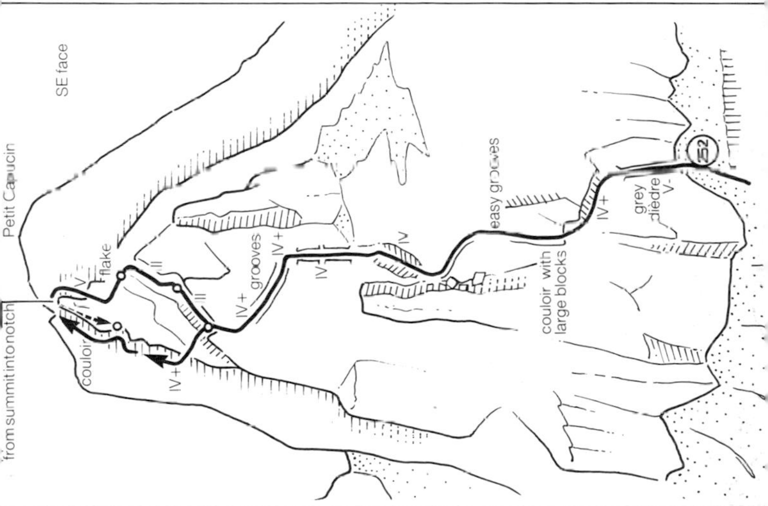
Petit Capucin
SE face
from summit into notch
couloir
IV+
V
flake
II
II
IV+ grooves
IV+
IV
IV
easy grooves
couloir with large blocks
IV+
grey dièdre V-
252

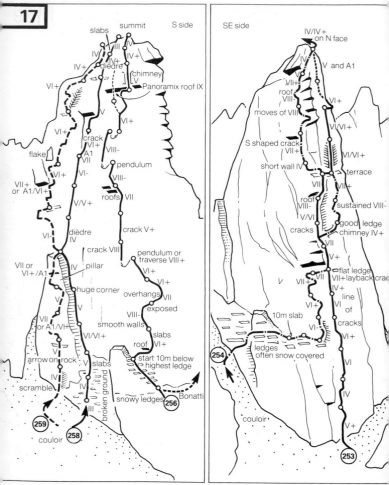

S side

SE side

slabs — summit

IV/IV+ on N face

IV/III — IV
IV+ — IV+
diédre
V — IV+
VI+ — chimney
V
Panoramix roof IX

V and A1
VII+
roof
VIII- — VI+
moves of VIII
VI/VI+
S shaped crack
VII+ — VI/VI+
short wall IV
VII — terrace
VII+
roof
VIII- — sustained VIII-
V/VI
good ledge
cracks — chimney IV+
VII
V+
flat ledge
VII — VII+ layback cra
V — VII+
line
VI — of
VI- — cracks
VI+

VI+
N
VI+
crack
VI+
A1
VII
flake — pendulum
VI+ — VIII-
VII+
or A1/VI+ — VI-
V/V+ — roofs VII

diédre
IV — crack V+

VII or
VI+/A1 — IV — crack VIII
pillar — pendulum or
traverse VIII+
VI+
huge corner
V — VI+
V — overhangs VII
exposed
VII — VIII-
or A1/VI+ — smooth walls
VI/VI+ — slabs
arrow on rock — roof VI+
V — slabs — start 10m below
IV — highest ledge
scramble
IV
III — broken ground
snowy ledges — Bonatti

10m slab

ledges
often snow covered
254
V

VI-
VI+
VI
IV
couloir
V+
253

258
259
couloir
256

214

18

19

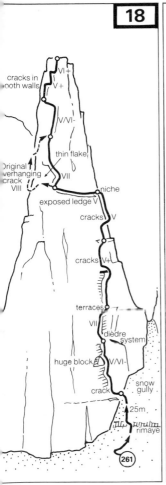

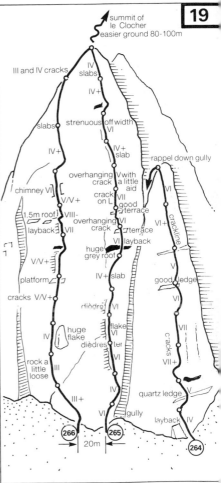

Chandelle (18)

- cracks in smooth walls
- VI+
- V+
- V/VI−
- thin flake
- Original overhanging crack VIII
- VII
- niche
- exposed ledge V
- cracks V
- V
- cracks V+
- terraces
- VII
- diedre system
- huge block V/VI−
- crack
- snow gully
- 25m
- rimaye
- 261

Clocher (19)

- summit of le Clocher
- easier ground 80-100m
- III and IV cracks
- IV slabs
- IV+
- slabs
- strenuous off width VI
- IV+
- IV+ slab
- rappel down gully
- overhanging crack
- V with a little aid
- crack on L VII
- VI
- chimney VI
- V/V+
- good terrace
- 1.5m roof
- VIII−
- overhanging crack VI
- layback VII
- terrace
- VI+ crackline
- huge grey roof
- VI layback
- V/V+
- IV+ slab
- platform
- cracks V/V+
- diedre VI
- V
- good ledge
- VI
- IV
- huge flake
- flake VI
- diedres later
- VII
- rock a little loose III
- VI
- cracks VII+
- III+
- IV
- quartz ledge
- V
- VI gully
- layback IV
- 266
- 265
- 264
- 20m

215

Tour Ronde

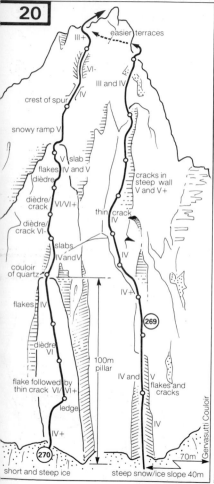

20

III+

easier terraces

VI-

III and IV

crest of spur

IV

snowy ramp V

V slab

flakes IV and V

dièdre

dièdre/crack VI/VI+

dièdre/crack VI-

slabs IV and V

couloir of quartz

flakes IV

dièdre VI

flake followed by thin crack VI/VI+

ledge

IV+

270

short and steep ice

cracks in steep wall V and V+

thin crack IV

IV

IV+

269

IV and V

V flakes and cracks

IV

100m pillar

70m

steep snow/ice slope 40m

Gervasutti Couloir

Aiguille de la Brenva

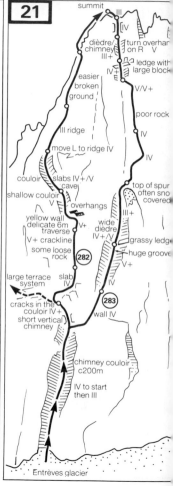

21

summit

III

IV

dièdre/chimney III+

turn overhang on R V

ledge with large block

easier broken ground

V/V+

poor rock

III ridge

IV

move L to ridge IV

IV

couloir slabs IV+/V cave

shallow couloir

top of spur often snow covered

overhangs

III+

yellow wall delicate 6m traverse

V+

wide dièdre IV/V+

V+ crackline some loose rock

282

grassy ledge

huge groove

V+

large terrace system

slab IV

283

cracks in the couloir IV+ short vertical chimney

wall IV

chimney couloir c200m

IV to start then III

Entrèves glacier

216

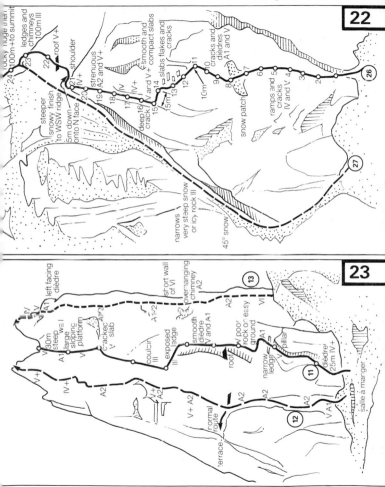

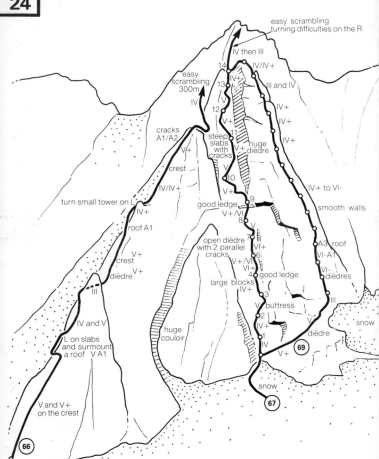

easy scrambling
turning difficulties on the R

IV then III

easy
scrambling
300m
IV

14 IV/IV+
IV+ III and IV
13 V
V IV+
12 V+
V+ IV+
cracks
A1/A2
V+ 11 IV+
steep huge
slabs dièdre
crest with
cracks
IV/IV+ V
10
turn small tower on L V+ IV+ to VI-
IV+ 9
good ledge smooth walls
roof A1 V+/VI
8 V
V+ A3 roof
crest V+ open dièdre 7 VI-A1
dièdre V+ with 2 parallel VI+
cracks 6 VI-
III V+/VI dièdres
IV and V VI+
L on slabs large blocks 4 good ledge
and surmount IV+ III
a roof V A1 3
V buttress
2 V
IV+ dièdre
1
IV 69
V+

V and V+ snow
on the crest 67

66

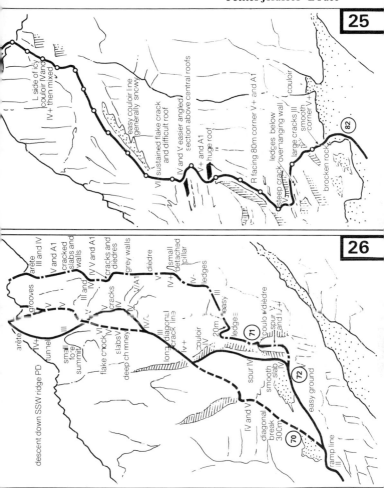

25

L side of icy
couloir IVand
IV + then mixed

easy couloir line
generally snowy

sustained flake crack
and difficult roof

IV and V easier angled
section above central roofs

V+ and A1
huge roof

R facing 80m corner V+ and A1

couloir

ledges below

deep crack overhanging wall

large cracks III
smooth
corner V+

brocken rock

82

26

arête
III and IV
V and A1

cracked
slabs and
walls

IV V and A1
cracks and
diedres

grey walls

diedre
IV +

small
detached
pillar

IV-
ledges

arête
grooves
V

III and
V cracks
IV

easy

III
20m

ledge

coulo'e diedre
spur IV and V+

71

arête
III
IV+
funnel

small
fore
summit

flake crock VI
slabs V
deep ch'mne'e

IV/-

long
diagonal
crack line
IV+

couloir
IV

spur IV

smooth
slab

72

descent down SSW ridge PD

IV and V
diagonal
break
300m

easy ground

ramp
line
II

70

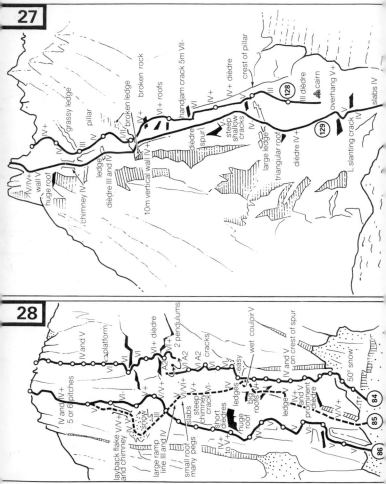

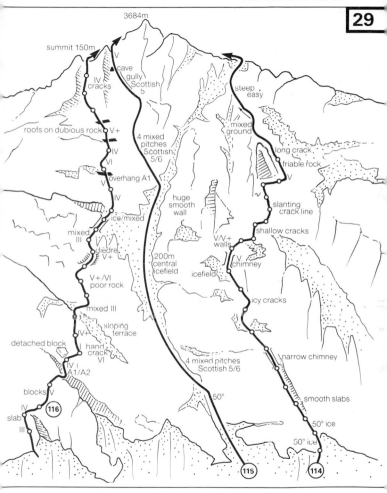

3684m

summit 150m

V

IV
cracks

cave
gully
Scottish
5

roofs on dubious rock   V+

IV
VI

overhang A1

IV

ice/mixed

mixed
III

diédre
V+

V+/VI
poor rock

mixed III

IV+

sloping
terrace

detached block

hand
crack
VI

IV
A1/A2

blocks IV

(116)

IV

slab

III

4 mixed
pitches
Scottish
5/6

huge
smooth
wall

200m
central
icefield

icefield

steep
easy

mixed
ground

long crack

friable rock

V

slanting
crack line

shallow cracks

V/V+
walls

V
chimney

icy cracks

narrow chimney

4 mixed pitches
Scottish 5/6

smooth slabs

50° ice

50° ice

50°

(115)

(114)

221

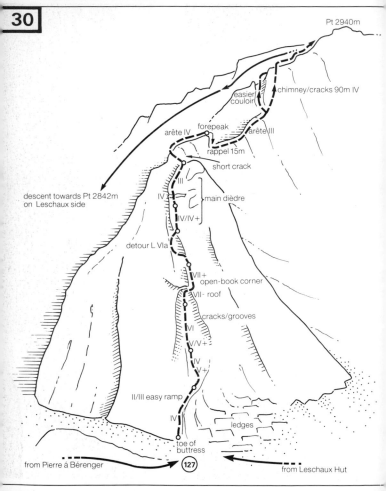

Pt 2940m

chimney/cracks 90m IV

easier couloir

arête IV

forepeak

arête III

rappel 15m

short crack

III

IV

main dièdre

IV/IV+

descent towards Pt 2842m on Leschaux side

detour L VIa

VII+ open-book corner

VII- roof

cracks/grooves

VI

V/V+

IV

V+

II/III easy ramp

IV

ledges

toe of buttress

from Pierre à Bérenger

127

from Leschaux Hut

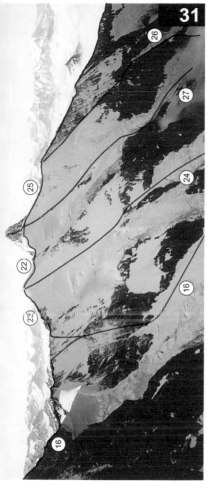

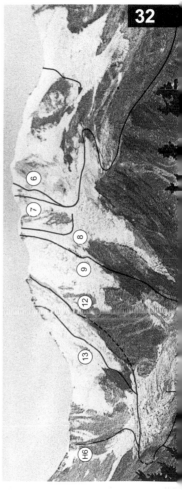

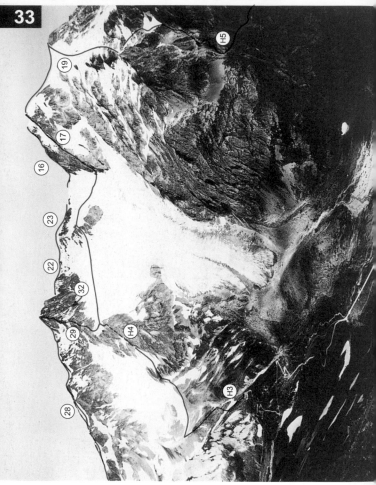

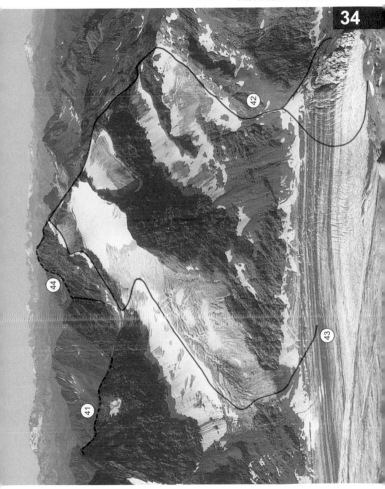

36

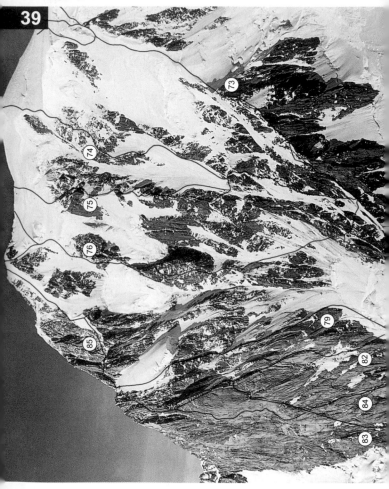

41

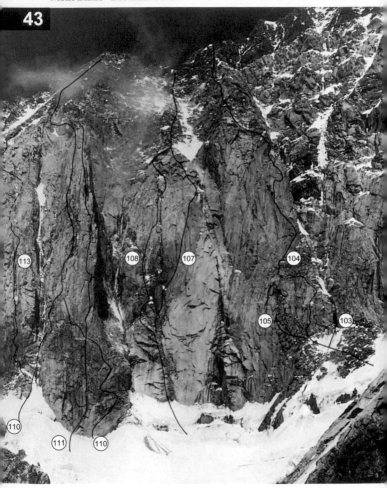

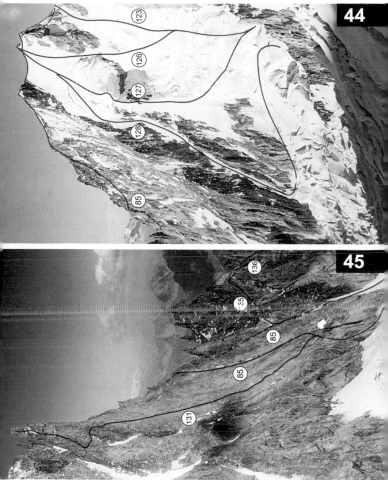

Mont Maudit SE Face

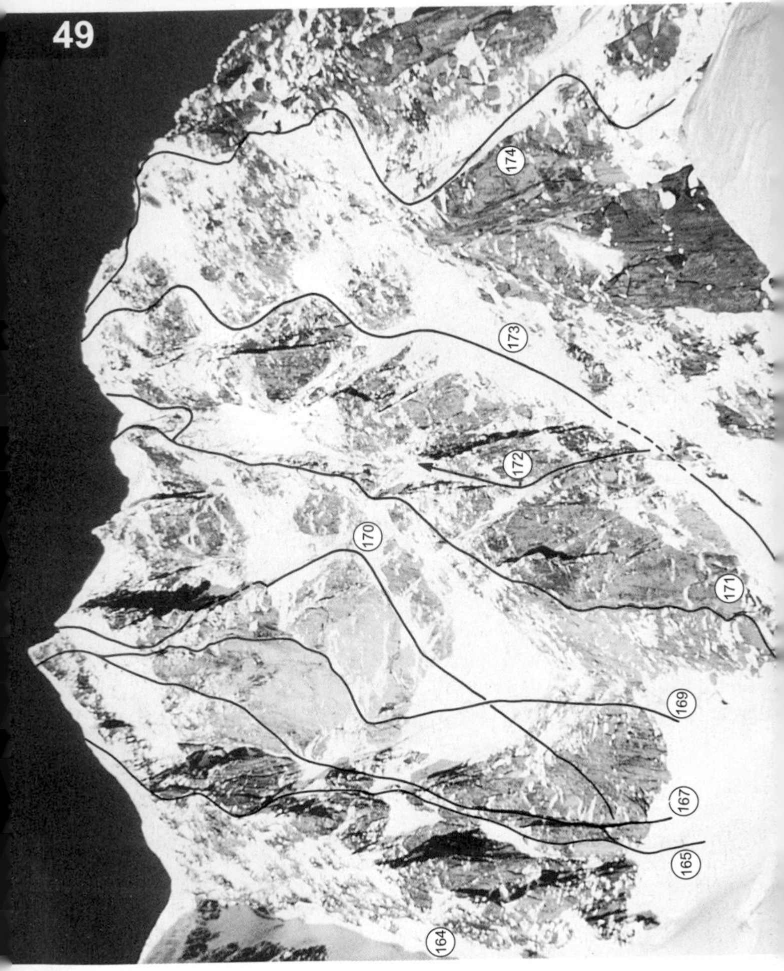

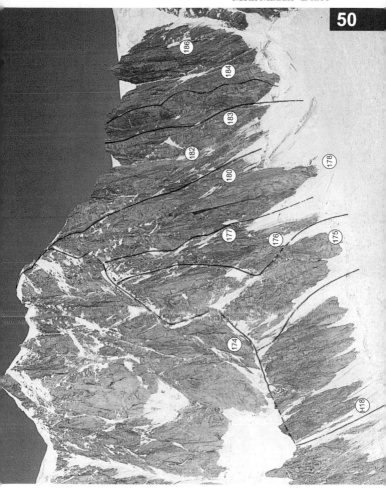

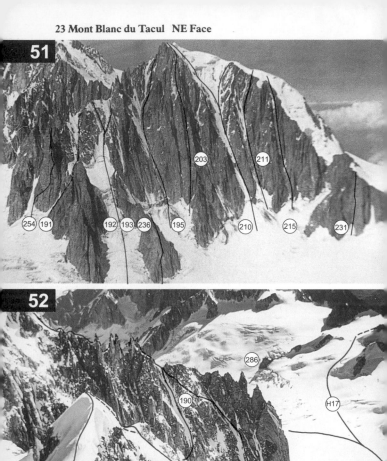

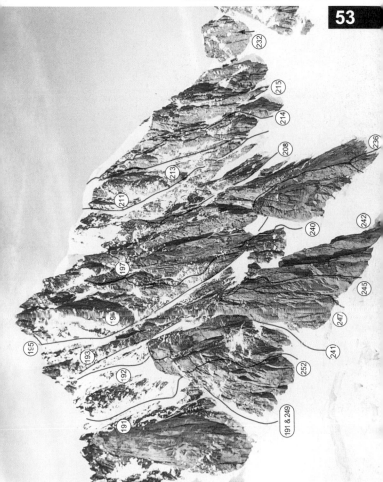

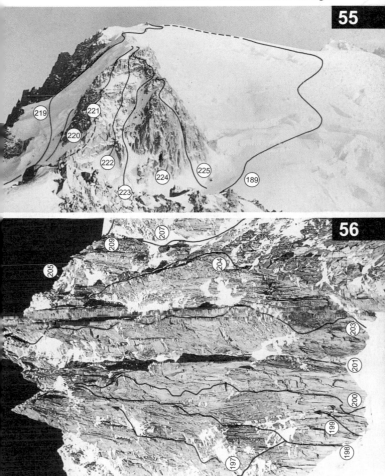

57

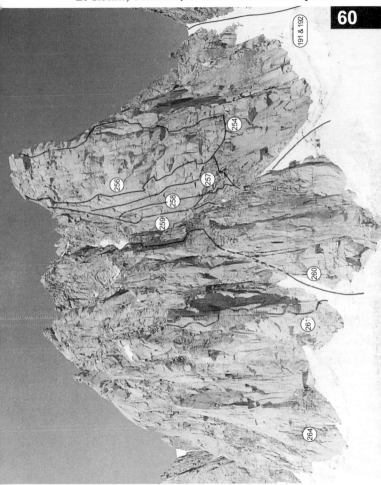

Dent du Géant S Face

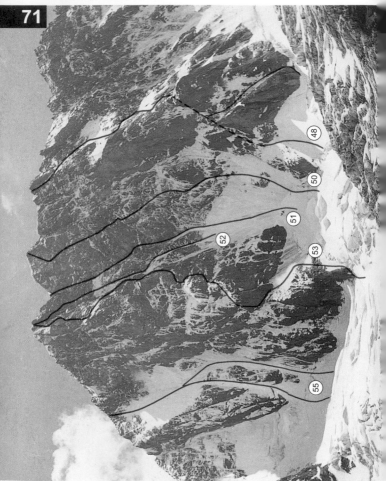

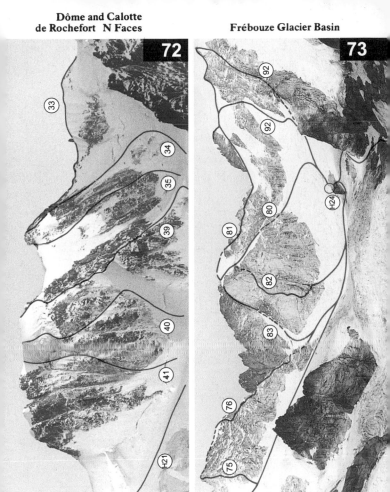

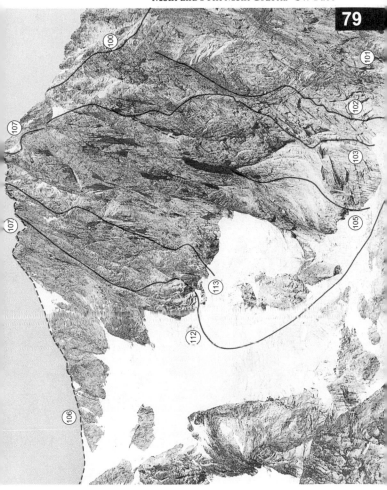

Aiguille de Talèfre
NW Face

Aiguille de Pierre Joseph
SW Face

84

85

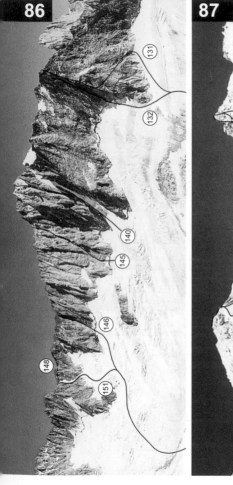

86

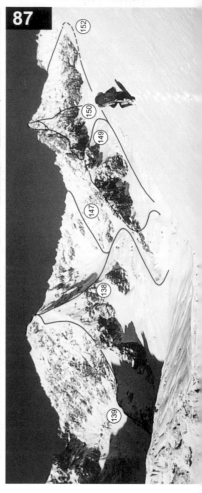

87

Addendum

Various changes to the existing routes in Volume 1 have been noted in this reprint, pending a complete re-write in the next edition. Alterations in route description have been kept to a minimum and generally concentrate on the more popular classics. Due to recent climatic changes it is now, more than ever, essential to note that approaches involving travel over snow slopes and glaciers are changing dramatically from one year to the next. Climbers are urged to assess the current conditions and employ common sense.

Since the guide was written there have been numerous and generally well-equipped rock climbs of very high quality established on the Aiguille Croux, the satellite peaks of Mont Blanc du Tacul, the Petites Jorasses, Aiguille Savoie and Monts Rouge de Triolet, as well as modern ice climbs on the Tour Ronde-Trident Ridge and Petites Jorasses. Some of these will undoubtedly replace existing routes in the next edition of selected climbs.

First Winter Ascents (FWA) have only been added in the list below when the route has been noted for other reasons. Arabic numerals refer to French grades which will be standard in the next edition.

General Information

Page 11:   Add Michel Piola to acknowledgements

Page 17:   New guides of relevance to this volume include Gino Buscaini's 'Monte Bianco Vol I' (CAI), Francois Damilano and Godefroy Perroux's 'Neige, Glace et Mixte' and Michel Piola's 'Le Topo du Massif du Mont Blanc Vol II' (Editions Equinoxe). There is now a new English edition to 'The 100 Finest Routes'. Information on all new routes can generally be obtained from the Office de la Haute Montagne (OHM).
Digitally displayed weather forecast etc. at Tourist Office in Place de l'Eglise. Full five-day weather forecast and comprehensive snow/avalanche bulletin on the board in the OHM.

Page 19:   More accurate grading table in later AC Guides eg. Bernina and Bregaglia.

Huts

H1   Warden 1st April - 30th September. Tel: 50 54 62 51.
H2   Tel: 79 07 32 55.
H3   Room for 80. Warden 15 July - 15 September. 0165-84 37 43.
H7   Room for 60.
H8   Total room for 120.
H10   Cosmiques Hut new in 1991. Private. Room for 120.

	Reservations obligatory, Tel: 50 54 46 16. Very expensive! Currently an overnight camp still appears to be tolerated (just!) in this region.
H13	Room for 104. Tel: 0165-80 95 53.
H17	At the time of writing this is being dismantled.
H19	New hut; room for 215. Old hut; room for 50, Tel: 0165-84 54 84.
H20	Tel: 0165-89170.
H21	Generally, water available from frozen lake.
H26	Tel: 0165-89544.
H29	Will be linked to Charpoua and Leschaux by newly constructed Balcon de la Mer de Glace.

Routes

Col de la Bérangère to Col du Géant

34	1,000m.
35	Wide couloir between Petit Mont Blanc and Aig de l'Aigle. FA: W Bonatti and G Catellino 26th June 1960: 1000m: AD+: 3-4 hrs.
36	B Domenech, P Domenech-Leyland, G Martellotti and R Weiner 14 July 1978: D: 40° – 50°: 6-8 hr. This is the narrower left hand of the two couloirs on the NE Face. R hand couloir: S de Benedetti and I Negro, 1983: AD+.
51	TD – . and 50°. FWA in 1986 .
52	TD – .
64	PD+/AD – .
69	At least TD: 80°.
70	TD+ and 90°.
71	TD – .
84	All free at ED5/6 and 7c. FWA 1992.
85	Summit of Aiguille Blanche to Eccles Huts (and vice versa) is AD.
89	Direct Finish is IV/V and A2.
91	All free at 7a+.
95	All free at 5/5+. Monolithic gendarme climbed direct in 1995 by chimney on front face at ED1: 6b.
96	The few parties repeating this route have found it much harder than the stated grade. FWA 1993.
105	Climbs to the left of the red dièdre attempted in 1965, starting from close to the base of the Hypergoulotte (serious stonefall possible). Five routes on this pillar.
106	ED3/4 and 90°.
110	All free at 5+/6a. A logical two-pitch direct start to avoid the stone-swept couloir exists on pedestal at base (5+/6a).
111	All free at 7a+.

112	At least ED3 with difficult mixed climbing.
114	Probably D. Ascent to Col Eccles is 45°– 50° (or rocks on edge when dry).
115	D+/TD – for length only. Climbed twice in winter.
117	AD+ and IV+.
130	TD+ (VI – and a little A1). Cuts through Gervasutti traverse.
131	All free at 6b.
132	ED2 and 6b.
144/ 148	Glacier changes in recent years have made access very difficult after early season.
152	Climbs vague pillar left of 151 to finish on SW ridge (one pitch V+ and A1).
160	Include R Cassarotto on first ascent. Steep, sustained and probably ED1.
166	TD. A cleaner line than the original but often swept by stone fall. It is possible to start c80m to the R, directly below the crest of the spur. Climb three steep pitches (VI and some aid) to easier ground. Higher, pitches of IV to V+ on excellent rock will be encountered.
168	Christened Dom (ED2).
163	Second ascent and FWA in 1990s.
178	Climbed free at 7a+ in 1994. Additional modern routes now allow a rappel descent from the top of the pillar.
179	FA: P Gabarrou and B Muller.
180	Sustained at TD.
186	V/V+ maximum.
189	PD.
190	Ascent to Pointe Carmen is V.
192	Lower section wrongly marked on photo 51. Route starts in same glacier bay as 195 and slants up L to cross spur.
194	Re equipped to allow a rappel descent (bolts) from the end of the difficulties. Very popular. Direct Finish through mixed ground up to the L at same grade.
197	G Comino etc.
199/ 200	Topos misleading. These routes lie very close together.
200	Tobaggan gives best rappel descent.
201	Free ascent of initial goulotte is Scottish 7 (tech.).
203	On the topo the route does not cross the right flank after pitch 15. Above this is an A1 pitch (6a/b free), then chimneys leading to ramps (III). These ramps end at a distinct brèche and above this is the 20m crack. From junction with route 204 it is more like 8-9 pitches to the top of the Grey Tower. The latter can be avoided by a short rappel into an easy gully on the right.
204	Very few parties follow the direct route on the crest of the middle pillar.

206	An approach via a rising traverse from the right to reach pitch 2 avoids rimaye and sérac problems. Crux of route is 6a+. Good quality climbing: 950m.
215/ 216	Extremely popular winter objectives with well-equipped rappel descents.
227	6c+: 6b obl.
228	6b: 5+ obl.
229	All free at 6a.
230	Not particularly good or popular.
231	Some moves of 6a in cracks.
237	6a on pitch 2.
239	6a on pitch 3. Now more popular modern routes on this face.
240	V and A1. Rarely climbed.
242	Rarely climbed in favour of modern routes to the left.
247	VI/A0 in initial 6m dièdre. Still climbed from time to time.
248	Fairly sustained at 6a to 6b with several moves of A1 on pitches 2, 6 and 7.
251/ 252	Much less frequented in recent years. Several very popular modern routes on Roi de Siam.
255	7a+ with a few moves of A0. Possibly the most demanding route on the face. FWA 1993.
258	Topo is misleading. Above junction with 259, there are three pitches to below the big roof which is avoided on the right at 6b and A0 (crux).
260	Now possible to rappel directly down face using bolted anchors on one of the modern routes.
270	Line is further right in the top section to that marked on photo 61.

Col du Géant to Col de Talèfre

5	Crux would be VI without fixed ropes.
12	All free at around 6c.
18	Rimaye has become quite problematical.
26	15 pitches. All free at 6b. Some rockfall damage in lower section.
36	In ascent there are two very hard pitches, at the start (V/V+), which are often icy.
46	Route finding on ascent to Pointe Young is difficult with no clear line (IV or above everywhere). Traverse around Pte Young on loose ramp. Make a 20m rappel down S face then an improbable hand traverse around smooth buttress to icy couloir which is climbed to Pte Marguerite. D+.
48	ED1 and nowadays best attempted out of season.
52	Bold climbing at Scottish 6 (tech.).
59	Christened Groucho Marx (ED3: 6b and A3).

67	6-pitch direct start reaches dièdre from R (6c+ cracks) and gives best rappel descent in lower section of route.
68	Christened Etoiles Filantes (ED3: 6c+; 6c obl).
82	All free at 7a. Best finish is to slant up left below the headwall and climb the R facing dièdre (6b) to reach the upper part of the South Ridge.
84	Climbed free at 7c.
85	In topo it is the long steep chimney and not the small roof which is VI/VI+. The roof itself is much easier. Most parties now rappel the face via the anchors of Anouk, a very popular modern classic at ED1 (6b+).
86	Well worthwhile and all free at 5+.
90	Line marked on Photo 76 is Duverney/Gabarrou (1988: TD+. R fork Gabarrou/Vimal, 1992: TD+). 1981 Route follows the couloir visible to the R of Route 91.
109	Allow 3hr for approach from hut. Aid pitch avoided by two-pitch free variation to the L at 6a. Upper part of SE Ridge is long and very loose. Parties descend from the top of the pillar via the bolted rappel anchors of the 1993 La Roue de la Fortune.
110	Line marked on photo 80 is Via della Conca Grigna (Manera/Meneghin, Ribetta, 1982: TD+ 5/6a and A2). Le Karma follows the shorter corner to the L (and L of pillar climbed by 109) and ends at a gap below the first tower on the SE Ridge (TD+: 6a+).
141	Recommended. Finer than Swiss Route on Les Courtes.

MEMBERSHIP

The Alpine Club is a UK based mountaineering club catering specifically for those who climb in the Alps and the Greater Ranges of the world. Throughout its existence the Alpine Club has included in its membership most of the leading British climbers of each generation, and now has members in more than 30 countries. We have members of all ages and abilities, and most active alpine climbers are qualified to join.

Benefits of membership include:

- concessionary rates in most alpine huts

- discounts on all Alpine Club guidebooks

- Alpine Journal free to members

- discounts on climbing equipment

- free use of the Alpine Club Library

- regular lectures by prominent mountaineers

- climbing meets in the UK, the Alps and the Greater Ranges

- BMC affiliation

If you climb regularly in the Alps or the Greater Ranges, why not join us?

Details of membership are available from the Assistant Secretary, Alpine Club, 55-56 Charlotte Road, London EC2A 3QT
0171-613 0755